From the Ground Up:

A History of the State University of New York at STONY BROOK

by Joel T. Rosenthal

Published by:
116 PRESS
116 Jones Avenue, Port Jefferson, NY 11777

Joel T. Rosenthal:
From the Ground Up: A History of the State University of Stony Brook
© *2004 by Joel T. Rosenthal*

All Rights Reserved. No part of this book may be used or reproduced in any matter whatsoever without written permission.

Printed in the United States of America on Acid Free Paper.

ISBN: 0-9754855-0-4

Photographs of SUNY Stony Brook courtesy of the University Archives, SUNY Stony Brook.

For Jack Meiland
Who always said that education counted.

Table of Contents

Preface vii
1. Introduction: OK, Let's Get Started 1
2. The Political Economy of SUNY: The Birth of the Baby 31
3. Building the Campus: Home Away from Home 55
4. Building the Academy, Part I: Filling the Faculty Offices .. 89
5. Building the Academy, Part II:
    What Else Do Professors Do? 121
6. The Academic Administration:
    Leadership from the Top 151
7. Student Life and the Student Community 183
8. Town and Gown 215
    Appendix: Coser versus Moore 239
    Illustrations 245
    Index 259

Abbreviations

A & S	College of Arts and Sciences
AAUP	American Associations of University Professors
AVP	Academic Vice President
BA	Bachelor of Arts Degree
BS	Bachelor of Science Degree
CEAS	College of Engineering and Applied Science
CED	(School of) Continuing Education
	(Later renamed: SPD– School of Professional Development)
DoD	Department of Defense (of the US Government)
EVP	Executive Vice President
HSC	Health Sciences Center
MA	Master of Arts Degree
NEH	National Endowment for the Humanities
NSF	National Science Foundation
PhD	Doctor of Philosophy
SAC	Student Activities Center
SUNY	State University of New York
TA	Teaching Assistant
VPSA	Vice President for Student Affairs
UUP	United University Professions

Preface

To acknowledge everyone who has helped me organize my thoughts – let alone everyone who has contributed to the building of Stony Brook and to my perception of that task and process— is obviously an obligation of monumental proportions. It is too big a job, too long a roll call of names. Furthermore, it would come much too close to being my autobiography since 1964. No one in her or his right mind would want to read very much of that. Accordingly, I cannot seriously or properly even begin to empty the well of the debts of memory and experience, of reflection and conversation, of interaction and disagreement, that I have incurred in a Stony Brook career that now runs pretty close to four decades.

Many of those I could mention are no longer at Stony Brook; some are no longer among the living. Still others would probably rather not have me do their thinking for them, or even see their name among my sources of inspiration. At the same time, I leave myself open to charges of ingratitude and neglect; both charges have merit. No offense intended; one volume, and one with a fairly personal agenda or style, and opening with a moderately short preface, can hardly do justice to everyone (or everything).

This history of SUNY Stony Brook is very far from being an official one. It has neither been commissioned by the University nor submitted for a seal of approval. I have neither sought nor gained access to confidential or personal materials, whatever that might entail for a public institution in a state with fairly rigorous sunshine laws. Nor have I based this volume on interviews, at least not beyond some casual questions and a lot of unstructured reminiscences. I have tried to thank those I have pumped for details: it is certainly easier than having to "look it up" for issues that are well within the wide boundaries of social memory. I discovered, when I told colleagues that I was going to work on this project, that everyone seems to have her or his version of the history of Stony Brook – all waiting to be told, to be written, to be preserved for the records. Since I could not merge other peoples' tales into a single volume of reasonable dimensions I simply focused on telling it my way. We could well have a Rashoman version of the University's history; the same event as seen by a student, a faculty member, an administrator, someone from the community, etc. But not here, not this time around.

My sources for this volume are an open book, in the most literal sense: university catalogues, some of the reams of official publications, presidents' annual reports, departmental brochures, student publications, memos and ephemera I squirreled away over the years, and more of this sort of stuff. I have relied on memory a good deal; I suspect errors of fact are lurking below, eager to expose the fallacies of that particular data bank. I have brought in quite a few personal reflections and some touches of autobiography where they seemed useful in terms of fleshing out some general comments – or when I could not stay as laid back as I had hoped to be. I often express myself and tell the tale in a vernacular of critical appraisal and enlightened hindsight. I hope I have not done so without some eye on the important goal of historiographical fairness. The history of Stony Brook, as I present it, is not offered as a narrative, but rather as the exposition of a process. Furthermore, it was a process carried out in the public arena, each step taken under the public gaze and choreographed to the tune of public debate and discourse. Thus decisions and opinions hatched and/or implemented at the Stony Brook level, as well as those reflecting the force and momentum of larger powers and socio-political developments, are all to be taken into account. Sides were taken, at the time, and it seems reasonable that in telling the story of Stony Brook sides can/should still be taken.

Though Stony Brook's history is a short one as measured against those of the 19th century land grant universities, let alone those of the great private colleges (and universities) that trace their origins to the 17th and 18th centuries, it has already attracted considerable interest. Sidney Gelber, virtually on the ground from the beginnings at Oyster Bay, brought his experience and erudition to this task, and he has now told his version of the story with a wealth of background and a restraint that are beyond my reach: *Politics and Public Higher Education in New York State: Stony Brook – A*

Case History (2001). Even more recently, Kristen J. Nyitray and Ann M. Becker have published *Stony Brook, State University of New York* (2002). In addition to these volumes, interviews with various old timers and founding fathers were taped by Karl Hartzell, who himself presided over the University in its first years at the Stony Brook campus site. Howard Oakes – no longer here to make sardonic comments about my version of the story – was the long-serving VP for the Health Sciences, and he put together an insightful and well-written history of the Health Sciences Center (and I thank Jane Yahil for loaning me her copy). In the 1970s President John Toll asked several of my colleagues in the History Department to turn their hand to a history of the University; I believe material was collected but never written up. President John Marburger in turn asked several of his assistants to collect materials for the University's 25th anniversary in 1982. This led to a lobby display in the Fine Arts Center, unfortunately dismantled and then cannibalized for its pictures. In recent years the Library's Department of Special Collections has been active in mounting pictures in various Library corridors, depicting scenes from both early and more recent days. And Peter Kahn of the Physics Department is at work on a history of his own department, and his "In Appreciation: Remembering Max Dresden (1918-1997)", *Physics in Perspective* (5/2003, pp. 206-33) is but the first item in this enterprise. So I hardly venture into a virgin wilderness, though I like to think I bring a perspective that has not been presented.

    Some of my debts are specific: I asked questions and people were invariably helpful and interested. Thanks to Sandy Weedon and Kathy Dan of Athletics, to Sara Lipton of History (about the Art Department), to John Lutterbie of Theatre Arts, to Alan DeVries of Residential Life about the dorms, to Emily Thomas and Eileen Dellaposta of Institutional Studies for access to various kinds of hard data, to Mitzi Collver, Kristen Nyitray and Ann Becker of Special Collections in the Melville Library, to Shiram Amran who helped me at the start of this work, to Frank Erk for information about unionization and the old days in general, to Ann Brody of Conferences and Special Events for specific information and for general support and interest, to Barbara Weinstein (now of the University of Maryland) for information on the Dube affair, and to Peter Kahn of Physics who probably knows more about my material than I do. Barbara and Paul Grannis continued to express interest in my progress, slow though it has been, and Gary Marker helped me line up undergraduate students who dug up data and guided my ideas about how much or little to present, and in what fashion. Kirsten Nyitray and F. Jason Torre both worked far beyond any call of duty to help me with the illustrative material that appears below. Ken Wishnia has shared some of the hard-learned lessons of self-publishing, for which I am grateful. Without the help of Valerie Schwarz this probably would have sunk below the horizon.

Some debts rest, not on specific advice or information, but rather on collegial involvement over the many years that were needed for the making of my version of the Stony Brook experience. And in this regard the troubles of the 1960s and early 1970s – even more than those of more recent years - will always loom large in the memories of those of us who were helping to build the university, to launch our own careers, and to debate about the place and role of the academy in a troubled world. Karl and Sue Bottigheimer (who both read this manuscript in an unfinished stage), Gene Lebovics, Mike Zweig, Judy Wishnia, and Sandy Petrey could all write tales comparable to mine. Ted Goldfarb of Chemistry and I talked, over the years, about the need for a "people's history" of Stony Brook, before it all got laundered into conformity and normality, though Ted died without seeing this product of our joint idea. Bob and Lee Weinberg and Ken Abrams played major roles in my own coming of age. And beyond those I cite by name, I owe a debt of gratitude to the personnel– faculty and staff – of the History Department. Over the years they have been supportive and sympathetic beyond expectations or deserts, and they have often expressed a confidence in and endorsement of my views and achievements that may be considerably exaggerated but personally comforting. And, of course, the students. Casey Stengel supposedly said, after his Yankees won still another championship, something to the effect of "I couldn't have done it without the players." For "players," read "students." Over the years thousands of them have registered for my courses: they could expect to read *Beowulf,* hear about the Battle of Stalingrad, and figure out that he's a soft touch for an Incomplete. But they also create the conditions for a dialogue with the instructor, whether they say very much in class or not. I like to think that the State of New York, at least in its SUNY Stony Brook incarnation, has given them a decent return for their money. And beyond such exchanges and reciprocities, I offer this book in case they are concerned with how and why their University has come to be the one they know and, presumably, love so well.

A final and wholly personal note. My wife Naomi first saw the Stony Brook campus on a hot Sunday in July, 1964, as we drove past what campus there was, visible from State Highway 25A because the intervening trees had been bulldozed in the interests of quick construction. As the stark and garish buildings came into sight she almost cried, and she almost made me turn back to Chicago. She got over the first impulse and we lacked money for a return trip, even with gas at 25 cents a gallon. Today she is still reluctant to admit it, but she has more than learned to cope with life in the outer reaches of the metropolitan area. She, and my children, are prone to remind me that there is no such thing as a story you haven't heard before. This book merely serves as further confirmation of what they have been saying for many years.

CHAPTER ONE
OK, Let's Get Started

This book is meant to accomplish a variety of goals. One is to offer a rather loose and quixotic narrative of the relatively short history of the State University of New York at Stony Brook. The second is to offer a sort of running explication or exposition of what a university is and how it works– with Stony Brook furnishing the data, or serving as the case study. The third is a sort of personal memoir; my own take on the more personal aspects of the first and second goals.

Why am I writing what has turned out to be a full-sized volume? And for whom? The answer to the "why" is that the story of the founding and growth of SUNY Stony Brook - a story of a mere three or four decades - presents an intriguing case study of public life and education in the second half of the 20th century.[1] As such it is a tale well worth telling. It carries more than its share of the particular as well as the idiosyncratic, and at the same time it illuminates many of the general themes that run through American social and political history between the great depression of the 1930s and the end of the 20th century.

For whom? By the early 21st century, when this volume has finally left my word processor, Stony Brook has (or will have, if we prefer) produced tens of thousands of alumni, along with thousands of current and former employees and almost 20,000 current students. Everyone in this vast audience – past or present— either has been or still is part of an on-going story or process. They might, on occasion, wonder how it all came to be - or so an historian likes to think. It is easy to say that we are all part of history, as well as that we help make it. This is a cliche that an academic historian does (his) best to avoid, or at least to use with great caution. And yet in this case - because the process has been such a recent one and because the fruits of these individual and collective labors

1

are still fresh before us - it seems permissible to talk (and to think) in this way. From the interaction between large impersonal forces and those we can tie into on a personal and individualized basis we can trace the tale of how one branch of the State University of New York arose, took shape, and went about its business. More specifically or precisely, were I to aim at a modal reader of my version of Stony Brook's history, I would say that I am aiming at an alum, perhaps from the 1970s or 1980s, male or female – one who now looks back with interest and curiosity about the institution that might now be dunning him or her for a badly need contribution that can also serve as an income tax deduction.

Why turn to my version of the story? First off, be fully aware, from the very start, that this is going to be a personal history, not an "official" one in the sense of being commissioned or endorsed by the University. It is not based on interviews with the living or the dead, nor on an exhaustive review of executive memos, dredged from the dusty archives. It is, in a sense, a tale of me-and-Stony Brook. Though I do not want the volume to tilt too heavily toward autobiography, this is certainly my version of what it has all been about; personal, partisan, judgemental, and – for better or for worse— deeply involved. In a sense Stony Brook and I grew up together, to use an awful phrase, and my views of the University are too deeply colored by the roles I played and the opinions I formed and expressed over the years to worry, at this late date, about being objective or disinterested. If that had been my game plan, I should have kept my mouth shut in 1964. I did not do so then and I am hardly likely to do so now.

I came to Stony Brook in 1964, a young historian of medieval Europe - about which, more below. It is a pretty obvious fact of life that medieval historians rarely write about themselves, and they have even less occasion to write about events in which they have been personally involved, people they have known. Therefore this book is a new departure for me, despite many years of writing about Europe between the 7th and the 15th century. As I said, my own experiences will shape my assessments. They will frame the structure of the narrative and the analytical framework within which the narrative is cast. Through the saga of Stony

Brook's history I have rarely been a neutral or a silent figure and this is not a neutral book. During much of my career I have been involved in campus activities (mostly various roles in faculty governance and politics) and I have often held, and articulated, a strong view of events and policies– and more often than not in a fashion contrary to the wishes and policies of the University's administration.

However, my own story is but a small part of the whole story I aim to convey. I try to tell my tale with fairness and sympathy for those who made and carried out policies with which I often disagreed. Four decades of teaching have made it second nature for me to assign grades; so I assess policies, people, choices made, roads taken and untaken, buildings built and unbuilt. But I want to emphasize that I have not been moved to write in order to "get even" or to settle scores. Stony Brook has treated me well, and I hope my criticisms do not stem from personal slights or animus. Analysis and explication, rather than narrative history, are my goal; I do not want to just set out "what happened," any more here than in the classroom. But I should not ride the crest of too many illusions; I know my students in class would often be happy with a straight story, instead of primary sources and analytical comments. Why should any who read this book be all that different– especially as they may well have been my former students.

So be warned. For "just the facts," stop now; the telephone book or *Who's Who in Baseball* is a better bet. On the other hand, I work from the premise that people and institutions have "history;" they are agents in change, not simply objects or inert bodies that are acted upon. They change and interact, over time, and what we can see, in looking back, is the process as well as the current point at which we now stand. The past, like the present, is a mix of the personal and the impersonal, of policies and agendas, of interactions and reciprocities – and all with traceable roots and antecedents. Some of the relationships that govern our lives are harmonious and mutually supportive; others are based on conflicting perspectives and on fundamental oppositions rooted in the cultural and social as well as personal baggage we carry. Historians convey to their students that the course of historical development and change is not inevitable. The past became the present (and the future) through choices, contingencies, and process.

In offering an historical guide to the SUNY Stony Brook, I am also presenting a case study in the history of public higher education. This is of some interest to those who worry about the larger contours of our society. In its aggregate sense the story of public higher education covers several million people at any given time, and it involves billions of dollars from the public revenues of the 50 states (plus our territories) and the federal government (plus those additional billions that come from other sources, mostly for sponsored research). Higher education is very big business and it is also expensive business.

Many colleges and universities, around the world, have been the subject of their own histories. Such volumes mostly focus on institutional foundation and a glorious past. Most of these books have been written by loyal alumni or long-serving faculty, moved in good part by their filio-piety.[2] The customary style of such presentations stems from a worthy desire to honor founding fathers - not many founding mothers out there - and to keep alive their memories and our sense of wonder at how their vision became reality. In many such histories there is a pervasive strain of the "whig interpretation of history" - that is, the tale caries us upwards and onwards, from small beginnings to the glories of the present. We learn of the planning and endowment of the physical campus, of famous and rich alumni, of athletic champions and championships, of honors for faculty (let's count Nobel Prizes and Guggenheim and Macarthur Fellowships), and more of this stuff.

Like the Republic itself, this is primarily an account of progress. We began small but we worked hard and we have prospered - with or without God's help. Some of us have chosen to remain small (and elite): Dartmouth in New Hampshire, Wesleyan in Connecticut, and Wellesley in Massachusetts are all familiar and successful examples of quantity control. In some cases the institution's history is tied to a particular mission: general education and liberal arts, as for The College of the University of Chicago, or the coupling of big science with industrial technology (and profits), as for MIT and Cal Tech, or graduate training, as the specialty for The

Johns Hopkins University.[3] And for the great public universities - Michigan, California at Berkeley, Wisconsin, to name but a few - it was the ability to combine so many of these desiderata with generous support from the state government and the alumni that makes the saga so up-lifting and "American."

The history of SUNY Stony Brook that I am about to unfold is not heavily steeped in pious regard for founding fathers. Their roles are too recent; they are far too human to those who have known and worked with them; they were too obviously caught up in and moved by larger forces to be depicted as standing on the lonely pinnacles reserved - at least in pieties of institutional history - for Ezra Cornell at Cornell or William Rainey Harper at Chicago. Rather, I would like this history to be seen as a "people's history" in the sense that it depicts Stony Brook as the outgrowth of the public will (as represented and given shape by public officials, private interests, and the *res gestae* of those who contributed from the inside). The public university is a branch of the government of the State of New York, and as such it bends before the winds that blow from Albany and elsewhere. Beyond this, I acknowledge the powerful lead of the administrators and functionaries on the spot, and I hope neither to neglect nor to over-estimate the role of faculty and staff, and/or the students - undergraduate, graduate, part-time, full-time, commuters or dorm residents, etc. Moreover, this quick embrace pays little attention, for now, about distinctions of color, race, ethnicity, sex and gender, sexual orientation, class, or culture; some of these factors will have their day later on. And finally but by no means least; the university is a work place - bread on the table and rent or mortgage money for thousands of employees who make neither policy nor headlines but without whom the wheels would soon come to a full stop.

Though autobiography is self-indulgent, the truth is that we are all prone to bursts of self-indulgence. Having said that – the mandatory disclaimer – I will now begin by setting myself into the story of the history of Stony Brook. This should help explain my perspective and lay out my credentials as participant observer and running critic.

When I was approached, in 1963, about applying for a position in the Stony Brook History Department, I was teaching at Roosevelt University in downtown Chicago. Long Island was a geographical phrase, somewhere east of Brooklyn; SUNY an unfamiliar acronym; "Stony Brook" a name befitting Hollywood's versions of suburbia. In the Hollywood depiction of the flight from The City, the commuting father's role might fall to Robert Young, returning each day, promptly and soberly, for a chaste kiss from Loretta Cummings, the devoted stay-at-home mother of 2.45 children. Whether it was despite or because of this image, I came east for an unstructured interview and some spartan entertainment by a History Department of eight or nine men and an acting chair (the regular chair being the acting dean, as an indication of the haphazard structure of those early days). I was offered a position on the spot; I accepted almost at once and arrived, for work and play, midsummer, 1964. This turned out to be a life decision.

Except that Stony Brook was a new campus and that it had moved in 1962 from its first home at Oyster Bay, I knew little of its history. In personal terms I was excited by the prospect of a new school. When I accepted Stony Brook's offer I turned down a job at a venerable midwestern university that seemed rather stuffy in comparison - though I had little grasp of what building a new university really meant. To myself, as to the hundreds of other faculty hired between 1964 and the end of the peak years of growth around 1970, the combination of a pleasant community, of so many young colleagues, and of a dual focus on teaching and research, seemed a good deal. The 1960s were a golden age for young academics - as they also were for the buyers of such talent - and new jobs and cross-country treks were a familiar part of academic culture. We used to say that if we didn't like where we were it would be easy to find another job, and there really was a grain of truth to this sort of bombast.

My facetious tone is not to imply that I had been sold a garden of Eden only to discover a campus at which serpents came with the apples. Rather, my experience - the common experience of innumerable like-minded young(ish) colleagues across the academic scene - is that we became part of the process, of the building and organizing of the life and future in which we were already/simultaneously a part. And, as this happened, we eventually came to realize what was happening; self-consciousness and the desire for a voice, a share in the action, became part of our academic coming of age. In many ways the university seemed to be "our" university. We (as faculty) were involved in decisions about hiring and granting tenure, about courses and degree requirements, about the assessment of scholarship and teaching, and the establishment of rules and procedures - all the components of building an academic community.[4]

I talked above about my reasons for writing and the audience I have in mind. Though I try to tell my tale with little sentimentality or nostalgia for the "good old days," I want to call attention to the fact that the passing of the years has marked a change in the reality of what Stony Brook is – or the reality of what is Stony Brook. In 40 years we have gone from a rough and hectic pioneer life to one approaching suburban normality, adjusting these metaphors to fit the patterns of academic maturation. By the start of this new century, President Kenny has focused much of her interest (and available money) on physical appearance— on a cosmetic image deemed commensurate with the University's much-heralded academic prowess. There has been a vast and expensive re-doing of the central mall; trees, shrubs, signs, sculpture, banners with mottos, news of season ticket plans, and other such touches. There are strawberry festivals and an emphasis on "fun" as integral to student life. Along with talk about a research college – an empty if harmless phrase— there is a move to make Stony Brook more conventional; bigger sports, a stadium, a zeal to heed the dictates of industry in return for funding, and a move toward privatization and corporization. A profitable and exclusive contract with Coca Cola is but a sign of the times, as Stony Brook looks and feels more and more like everyone else.

Therefore it is no longer easy to convey the quantity and the quality of the contrast between this current identity and that of the early days. Ideological conflict amidst on-going physical construction and expansion was the characteristic of the early years. Stony Brook's times of troubles in the late 60s and early 70s were famous, or infamous, and it is quite likely that their dire shadow worked against the "company" image of a low-cost, high-quality research university. Drug busts and police raids, legislative hearings and jailings, take-overs of buildings, a moratorium on classes, and the like. These events are a basic part of the story, for their on-campus significance and for what they reveal about the turmoil of those memorable years. The dramatic confrontations of town and gown, of students and administration, etc, are better understood when set into the context of such factors as state budgets and gubernatorial ambitions, the demographics and geography of student recruiting and retention, of the national climate toward research and funding, and of the bitter divisions within our nation over race and Vietnam.

Stony Brook is but a pebble on the great shore. Larger secular forces carried us and washed over us. Hindsight (or historical analysis) makes clear that by the 1960s we were nearing the last days of a liberal consensus about society that had run from FDR's New Deal through LBJ's domestic agenda. Some mourned this transition; others said the winds of change were long overdue. This message was brought home by the election of Richard Nixon in 1968 (and reaffirmed in spades by his landslide reelection in 1972). Vietnam rang the death knell on what we can look back on as our collective national innocence - the great divide between the end of World War II and tomorrow's bad news. For African Americans the Civil Rights Movement played a further role, but Stony Brook was a very white world in those days and the local scene was more concerned with foreign than domestic policy (in so far as they are separable). In the conservative and hawkish climate of Suffolk County, New York, the War in southeast Asia seemed close at hand – as local men and women went to the armed forces and fought and died— whereas protest marches in Selma, Alabama, and sit-ins in Greensborough, North Carolina, were very far away.

To put the protests and disruptions of the late 1960s and early 1970s into a less parochial context, while working to explain life at Stony Brook in the peak years of physical and demographic growth, we can think of the campus as the local variation on the national theme-cum-dilemma. It was a somber drama, one that swept across much of the western world. Protests over government policies and social injustice soon led to a larger questioning of traditional authority and hierarchy. SUNY Stony Brook, in a sense, became a theater - battle ground is too dramatic and self-important, and it was but one of hundreds of such theaters - in which this drama was being enacted. Our campus crises were neither unique nor hard to explain, and an awareness of being but a cog on a large wheel of dissent must have exacerbated local frictions and factions. The campus experienced much internal division, whether sparked by the arrival of the police, or of military recruiters, or simply by tripling in dorm rooms built for two.

And meanwhile, as they say on the soaps, Stony Brook was working its way to young adulthood. This meant developing a wide range of undergraduate and graduate programs and all the rest that went with being a research university. An impressive panorama of graduate programs was being established from scratch, while a large and ever-growing physical campus was going up and the recruiting and hiring of faculty and staff conducted at a there's-no-tomorrow pace. It seemed to many of the faculty that the remorseless pursuit of the University's long range goals (research and growth), as championed and implemented by President John Toll and those who shared his views and priorities, was blinding the university to the immediate needs of students and to a rare opportunity to create an intellectual and socio-cultural community that was diverse and polymorphic.

Along with many of my friends and like-minded colleagues, I was usually willing to give voice to my dissatisfaction; I did so, as did many others, and frequently, and in all sorts of ways. Many of us saw our role as that of a loyal opposition, speaking out against the administration's policies and actions. We shared the same concerns and aspirations for the University, but with a different view of the strategy and timing that would advance them; we offered a different assessment of the agenda of social and intellectual (and educational) priorities. To us the administration embodied a top-down approach to growth and development, and the fact that the administration was virtually all male and all white hardly helped convey confidence about its mesh with the changing world of the headlines. In those years of radical reexamination of the social structure, an academic administration that focused so exclusively on priorities of growth and expenditure was hardly apt to be sympathetic to a call for participatory democracy, whether from uppity students or vocal faculty.

Because I came to, and have worked at, and am now writing about Stony Brook as a faculty member - and now as an aging and senior one - this book cannot help but reflect a faculty perspective. Faculty concerns loom larger here than they do for students on the ground, and certainly much more than they do for administrators - many of whom hold faculty in contempt as underworked and over-privileged eggheads who "never had to meet a payroll." As my comments are meant to answer the challenge of "whose university is it?" with the response, "it is, or it should be, everybody's university," so the answer to "who runs it" is open for debate and will be one of the subtexts of this book.

I also try to take into account something easily glossed over - the demography and class structure of the university. When Stony Brook was founded it was a school of a white middle-class co-ed student body, mostly taught by a comparable faculty that was overwhelmingly male, and these factors were pretty much taken for granted. The student body came mostly from somewhere west of the campus; Nassau County, Queens, Brooklyn, and even the exotic reaches of Manhattan (and the Bronx). Jewish students were a very large minority, and many came from family backgrounds not so different from those of the faculty who taught them.[5] For all the novelty, there seemed to be a good deal of social and cultural homogeneity.

When the university developed its vast site and went into daily operation, it relied upon hundreds and then thousands of blue collar, working class employees; old and new residents of Suffolk County. The university's employees were a basic if undervalued part of "the family." Many were New York State civil servants; the clerical staff have always been predominantly female, mostly local (and from south of Nesconset Highway, as the socio-economic composition of Suffolk County runs), working for low salaries but attracted by convenience, job security, and personnel benefits. These people - and their numerous (and often male) counterparts in maintenance, the physical plant, and the University Hospital - are part of the backbone of the university, though they are virtually without a voice.

I said above that I did not want to wallow in anecdotes or in a yearning for days gone by. Nor am I going to present a straight account of a lot of data, whatever that would entail. To present my tale as set in wider contexts, and to analyze rather than narrate, I proceed below by way of thematic chapters. Each deals with the development of one aspect of the university: the physical campus, the state of New York's view of Stony Brook, the growth of academic departments and graduate education, the contours and dilemmas of student life and activities, and so forth. There will be duplication and digressions, just as in my classroom lectures. But, after all, confusion, duplication, and repetition are themes inherent in the history of Stony Brook, just as they are to my style of presentation.

One virtue of thematic presentation, with its back tracking, is that it helps convey a feeling for how many things were going on at once - and usually with but haphazard (half-assed?) coordination. The need to "prioritize" resources and agendas, as the university dealt with new and ever-expanding challenges, had to be matched against (or juggled alongside) the need to solve issues on the run. There were few precedents to guide us, a limited number of experienced hands aboard ship, and a considerable disinclination to take advice, even from our own elders who were willing and able to offer it (such as Bentley Glass, the first academic vice president and a senior statesman of the academic establishment). We were all very busy; the whole place, in almost every aspect, grew virtually every year for 10 years. And besides that, we were all academics and we all thought we knew everything.

To give some structure, and perhaps some clarity, to the thematic approach, I offer here– before moving to the main tale – a condensed or summary narrative. This might clear the decks for more interesting stuff. As a history teacher of long experience I should have few illusions regarding student interest in the history of their university. Most students leave college with but a foggy notion of how a university works, let alone how it grew and developed. As the world goes these days, this is hardly a major problem, and I am quick to acknowledge that a blind spot about Stony Brook's past is neither shocking nor serious. Though I offer this book for its instructional value, and perhaps for some amusement as well, it is not intended to be anyone's required reading.

Some crude chronology, for a start. We can divide the years into a few major segments. The first might be the years at Oyster Bay, ending with the move to Stony Brook in 1962. Then there is a brief inter-regnum, from the move to Stony Brook to the selection of John Toll as president (1962-65). Then, rather obviously for our purposes here, we have The Toll Years (1965-78), a brief interval (1978-80) between Toll and Marburger, then The Marburger Years (1980-94), and a final coda on some aspects of the Kenny Years (1994—). For some of my discussion, I break the long Toll Years into two halves, mostly to simplify the complex tale of growth and also to separate the early turmoil from the calmer years after 1972. And as a user-friendly handout, I conclude with a time chart or tabular chronology; an escape from a lot of prose. Stony Brook's buildings - the physical campus we all know and love– are treated in Chapter 3 in a comparable fashion.

The first phase of SUNY Stony Brook was a complicated and troubled one, and it did not even take place at Stony Brook. The State University College on Long Island had a four year existence, as a four-year college, at Oyster Bay, in Nassau County. The College lived with a peculiar mission statement (as I explain at more length in Chapter 4) and it lived under sentence of an imminent move to the new campus at Stony Brook. The Oyster Bay years were picturesque, at least in memory, being played out on a lavish private estate, and the move to Stony Brook was accomplished without the guiding hand of a regular president for the University. This basic link in the chain of higher education was not closed until 1965, when John Toll was selected to preside over the (still-new) university center. These early years – our pre-historic days – are really told through a saga of two or three beginnings, like the two creation stories that never get edited out of the *Book of Genesis*.

In less than a decade a state college was created at Oyster Bay and then became a university center (with graduate degrees and a medical school) at an entirely new campus. The original mission of the State College had been to train teachers for high school science teaching and to do so by way of a liberal arts curriculum that emphasized inter-disciplinary learning and the continuity of the western tradition. By the early 1960s this had all been aborted, replaced in mission, campus, and identity by the university center at Stony Brook (in 1962). Neither the move nor the upgrade ended the rather inchoate legacy of Oyster Bay, and it was not until 1965, when Toll took office, that the research mandate could be implemented with some semblance of coordination and control. To sum up a lot of years and developments in a nutshell – with a fuller exposition to come in subsequent chapters— I suggest we see Toll's years as constituting the great growth phase, Marburger's those of consolidation and organization, and Kenny's those of community relations, publicity, and the amenities. This is a great simplification, of course, and each (and every) president is called upon to deal with the uncongenial and unwelcome as well as with those areas of great personal interest as he or she tries to arrange an agenda and a calendar.[6]

How did it all begin; or, we might say, where did it all come from? In putting on our larger-picture glasses, we see that by the late 1940s or early 1950s Long Island had become slated, by the powers that be in Albany, and those with a say about Long Island's development, for its own branch in the new State University system. The first two critical steps – beyond the creation of SUNY itself in 1948 - were the gift of almost a square mile of land at Stony Brook in 1956 by Ward Melville and the decision to open a temporary or interim campus at Oyster Bay in 1957, housed on the grounds of the Coe estate at Planting Fields (right smack in the glitzy section of Nassau County). The temporary home meant there was no need to wait until the permanent campus was ready for occupancy, and the first mission clearly was designed to fit the needs and resources of a small institution. By 1960 this role had outlived its usefulness, as the state formulated larger and more ambitious plans for the new university (as spelled out by the Heald Commission, 1960) – the third critical step.

Looking back, it was most unlikely that the original mission or purpose was going to hold up when forces for growth and development were brought to bear. It is safe to assume that in-house pressures for a university, with the concomitant dedication to research and graduate training, were likely to prove victorious – especially with powerful external allies to sing in harmony, whatever mix or clash of ideologies and goals was hidden by such an alliance. Bigger is attractive, if not invariably better, and bigger usually means greater visibility and a wider reputation. Long Island's political and economic "leaders" were happy to jump aboard the bandwagon of publicly supported higher education, which would also mean rising real estate values, new jobs, inexpensive education for the kiddies, etc. Nor were all the pressures for a university center those coming from developers of shopping centers and malls. The Oyster Bay mission, with its esoteric curriculum, had been formulated before the USSR launched Sputnik, the first space ship that worked. Sputnik was seen as a major slap in the face for the U.S., as we judged such things during the Cold War. The need to match and then top this great leap forward by a godless state was used to spur a great wave of public funding, especially in applied science; a new university was a logical component of our response. The future rested with big battalions and big bucks, and Stony Brook was set up to be part of this future.

When the college got its battlefield promotion to university status in 1962 and moved out to Stony Brook, many in SUNY Central in Albany, along with many at Stony Brook, breathed a sigh of relief that the Oyster Bay experiment was over. Never mind that the new campus was raw, unfinished, and ugly as sin. Never mind that it was remote from anything and everything. It was a new start, or at least an almost-new start. Life only offers a few such opportunities. From 1961 until 1965 the university functioned without a president. John Lee, the Oyster Bay president (appointed in 1961), had quickly been dumped because his short reign had united students and faculty who used their temporary alliance to ask that Albany intervene on their behalf – as it did. So SUNY Stony Brook came into the world under the eye – not of a president – but of an acting administrative head. Karl Hartzell, with a PhD in European history, had been sent down from SUNY Central to oversee things until they could be normalized. However, he never held full presidential powers, as he was only meant to be a stopgap until no longer needed. Over what turf did Hartzell reign? His friendly if not overly assertive rule covered a small but growing empire. The new University, when it opened its poorly-fitting doors, could boast of a medley of basic academic departments, mostly within a College of Arts and Sciences, plus the first inklings of graduate programs (in engineering, chemistry, physics, and biology), and a College of Engineering. The student body in 1962 was about 750, the faculty a little over 150. Since the faculty at Oyster Bay had numbered 14 in 1957, with about 148 students, demographic as well as physical growth was already an integral part of the game, though at a low level compared with what was to come. The first year at Stony Brook was one of great confusion and excitement, with some commuting back to Oyster Bay for biology labs.

But for all the problems Stony Brook was now home. Moreover, it was a home on which Albany and, at one remove, Washington, were now pleased to smile and to spend. Academia is close to a self-starting operation; we mostly work to replicate the system from which we ourselves have emerged. If you wind up a sufficient number of faculty members, or just a dean and a few department chairs and you give them a budget and authorization to hire, it is quite likely that some sort of university will emerge.[7] Red brick buildings, filled with prison-built desks and bookcases make it look more conventional, but state approval and some regard for the demands of the national accrediting agencies are about the only formal requisites.

The search for a full-fledged president came to an end in 1965, when it was announced that John Toll, chair of the Physics and Astronomy Department of the University of Maryland, would be the University's first real president. The Toll years (1966-78) were to be the years of major physical growth, and we could have anticipated the great waves of faculty hiring and of instant reputation that would result from such rapid growth. In fact, had Toll not been assured that the groundwork was in place, Toll would not have taken the post. That the Toll years largely coincided with a national concern for the expansion of public higher education made these lofty goals reachable. Governor Nelson Rockefeller (1959-73), made no secret of the fact that SUNY overall ranked as a favorite child and that Stony Brook ranked well even among his favorites.[8] Both Toll and Rockefeller liked big construction, big and ambitious plans, and grand statements. But it was not just the sunshine of good times and good money. Someone or other had to be the actual hand on the controls in those propitious years; someone or other had to make sure we grabbed virtually everything that came our way. And that someone was John Toll - a man of controversy, of limited popularity, of very powerful if restricted vision. From the beginning he leaned towards big science, research, and graduate education. He had been assured, upon accepting the presidency, that these were indeed the proper priorities. They were ones for which he had a strong personal and academic sympathy. Looking back, it seems clear that it was his determination and drive to push the new campus into a position of visibility and respect - overnight, if need be - that made him the final choice among candidates for the job.

In the first decade of Toll's presidency the university experienced (and suffered from) drug busts and days of student protest; the aura of a half-built, confrontation-oriented campus seemed to be our most singular characteristic. The Bridge to Nowhere (a walkway built to link the Union and the Library and left unfinished for almost a decade) was an appropriate if unofficial symbol - a source of sardonic pride and a symbol of some significance, however one chose to interpret it. In those years Stony Brook was establishing PhD programs in dozens of departments, developing a gigantic Health Sciences Center with a hospital and a medical school, setting up a community-oriented program of Continuing Education (CED), and trying to cope with a many-fold increase in students, faculty, and employees.

Physical construction was part of the University's life blood and daily routine. In Toll's first decade buildings were put up for a second campus, hard on the heels of that built for the 1962 opening. And inside those buildings the infrastructure of higher education was being put into place: offices and classrooms and labs and a library, along with people and space for the tiers of administration and services needed to cover admissions, budgets, human resources, travel reimbursements (paid slowly), grants and fellowships, student cheating, recording grades, the embezzlement of research funds, fines on overdue books, and whatever else goes on at a center of higher learning. When to build a medical school and how to eliminate cooking on hot plates in dorm rooms: both were pressing questions demanding answers.

The years of growth were rough and unpolished; the campus was a construction site as well as an ivory tower, and vocal segments of the local community were upset about the vast public institution that had sprung up in "its" neighborhood. Ward Melville himself – the founding donor - denounced the campus's appearance (and he probably was not too crazy about its social composition, either).[9] By the time Toll left to return to Maryland in 1978, we all knew that the days of vast budgets, fast-lane growth, and SUNY-friendly governors had come to a halt. As we say about U.S. history and the census of 1890, the frontier had closed.

The Toll years, appropriately, ended in controversy. When he left for Maryland his first lieutenant, Alec Pond - former chair of Stony Brook's eminent Physics Department and the University's EVP, and stand-in for Toll - agreed to serve for a year as acting president. During the course of the search for a new president (1978-79) a push to have Pond appointed president divided the faculty to a degree striking even for those divisive times. Would the university be best served by continuity, as represented by a Pond presidency, or was this the opportunity for a fresh start? The split grew so intense that Pond's appointment as president - probably never much favored by SUNY Chancellor Wharton in any event - became moot; Richard Schmidt, from the SUNY Upstate Medical Center in Syracuse, was posted here to serve a one-year term as acting president. Schmidt, with no interest in the presidency and no prior ties to the campus, brought a calming influence; there was life without Toll and without Toll's alter-ego. Like it or not, the campus was instructed to search again and to come up with a fresh-start alternative.

The second presidential search committee (1979-80, by now) finally recommended John Marburger, dean of The College of Letters, Arts, and Sciences at the University of Southern California. Jack Marburger, president of Stony Brook from 1980-94, came to New York at a time of harsh state budgets and of governors with little interest in steering resources to the system. He came to a campus that was almost fully grown in size and numbers and, at least in faculty circles, a bit tired. The years of agreeing with John Toll, or of opposing John Toll, had left most of the active faculty feeling rather battered; a respite was welcome, whether from loyal supporters or the spirited opposition. It was time to take stock.

To say that Marburger's years were largely years of consolidation is to damn with faint praise. In an era of state indifference and stinginess small steps were about all that were possible. As well as some years of genuine financial problems, state government in New York has to function under the puerile wars of Republicans and Democrats, upstate and downstate, and the executive branch and the legislative. So, at Stony Brook, physical growth would go on, but at a much slower pace, while the quality of student life would receive more emphasis, inter-collegiate athletics be upgraded, and a softer tone - on campus and in the community – would became the hallmark of the administration.

Some serious efforts toward affirmative action were developed, building atop what Toll and Pond had started (or talked about) but had never pushed with much attention. However, regardless of who was in charge, efforts to diversify the faculty – beyond the dramatic entry of growing numbers of white women— met with limited success. That amazing diversification of the undergraduate student body in terms of race and color and culture and ethnicity - now so much an accepted norm of academia - was just beginning to take off. In Marburger's years the university shifted from being a middle and working class white school to one with an impressive number of African-American, Latin, Near Eastern, Central European, and Asian-American undergraduates, though this is more a reflection of the changing American demography than of any enlightened policies on the part of Stony Brook.

Jack Marburger placed a great deal of emphasis on trying to move the university from its chaotic "growth mode" to an institution where administrative chains of command, structures of governance, and the delegation of authority would be part of business as usual. Of course, this was easier said than done, and neither the frantic style of the Toll years nor the desire of SUNY Central to control purse strings was easy to escape. Rapid turn-over among Stony Brook's higher administrators, especially in the office of the provost (or AVP) made educational planning a matter of stop-and-go in a way that Marburger had not anticipated. Serious financial problems stemmed from budgets that often fell below the rate of inflation, especially grim in view of the high cost of life, particularly housing and utilities, on Long Island. This meant some "down sizing" of personnel and programs, and while few were actually fired many who left went un-replaced. Marburger's problems came at a time when student numbers had roughly leveled off at 10-11,000 undergraduates, 5-6,000 graduate and professional students. It was a kinder and gentler university, but it proved no easier to build a consensus or to carry out long-range planning than in Toll's day, which I think of as the "robber baron" era of Stony Brook. Tougher times do not work in favor of high morale or cooperation, even if the president has a pleasant personal style.[10]

Marburger used to say that a decade was long enough for a university president; universities needed the periodic transition and stock-taking that only comes with change at the top. When he announced that he would step down after the spring 1994 semester, a search committee was constituted, representing far too many constituencies and reporting to the Stony Brook Council. After such foolishness as the use of a head-hunting firm, the committee offered a divided report. And when the dust settled and the differences between the search committee, the Council, and Albany had been smoothed out, the presidency was offered to Shirley Strum Kenny, president of Queen's College, City University of New York. President Kenny - with a PhD in English literature, rather than

Physics (like her predecessors, including the ill-fated John Lee of Oyster Bay days) - took office in the autumn, 1994.

Since the Kenny years are still being spun out, I am reluctant to attempt a full assessment. I have indicated that the Kenny Administration has put much of its money and energy into a commitment to a more attractive campus and to projects deemed student friendly: an activities center, a stadium for football, wider lawns and a fountain along the academic mall, elaborate signs for those who need help in identifying the library as "the library," and rented space at 29th and Park Avenue in NYC for "Stony Brook Manhattan." To be fair to President Kenny – many of whose policies have been greeted by faculty skepticism – much of my criticism stems from a different perspective. She may be correct about investing now to reap in the long haul – or she may be way off the mark, diverting funds from the academic sector now on the idea of a long-range payoff. This difference in perspective comes down to a case of alternative choices concerning priorities and planning, and it probably reflects the variation between an on-line faculty member and a CEO concerned with a future that may (or may not) be within reach. The jury that will render a verdict on which choice was the wise and/or profitable one has not even been empanelled, let alone authorized to collect evidence to move toward a decision. And in keeping with themes I will revert to throughout these pages, there is little reason to think that such a hypothetical jury will come in with a single verdict, let alone one reached with anything approaching unanimity.

A Time Line:
The State University of New York at Stony Brook

In 1948 SUNY was created and the State received the Coe Estate for the Oyster Bay campus. In 1956 the State Regents announced that a college would be built on Long Island, on the 480 acres at Stony Brook donated by Ward Melville, and that the Coe Estate (Planting Fields) would be its temporary home until the new campus was ready. The motto of the SUNY system: "Let Each Become All He is Capable of Being."

A Time Line: The State University of New York at Stony Brook

ACADEMIC YEAR	PRESIDENT	NOTABLES	EVENT
1974-75		Eliz. Wadsworth, VP for Student Affairs	Harriman College: Life Sciences (new bio) opens
1975-76			Education Department retrenched; Fine Arts, phase 1, opens
1976-77		Ward Melville dies	
1977-78	Toll Resigns		SBS building opens; bridge finally goes somewhere
1978-79	Pond, Acting President		New motto: "To Learn, To Search, To Serve"; Another self-study: "Stony Brook in Transition"
1979-80	Richard Schmidt, Acting President		Phase 2 of Fine Arts opens
1980-81	John Marburger arrives		Hospital opens; Coser v. Moore; Bach Aria summer music festival
1981-82		Homer Neal, AVP	
1982-83		Fred Preston, VPSA	
1983-84			Dube controversy begins
1984-85			Middle States re-accreditation, once more
1985-86		Homer Neal resigns; Jerry Schubel AVP	
1986-87			
1987-88			Sunwood burns
1988-89		Tilden Edelstein AVP	Grad Studets protest; Tent City on the Mall
1989-90			Marburger's "Decade of Refinement" Fine Arts Center becomes the Staller Center
1990-91			Honors College Established
1991-92			Indoor Sports Complex; DEC (Diversified Education Curriculum) established
1992-93		Goodby Edelstein	Grad Students vote to unionize (GSEU)
1993-94	John Marburger resigns	Bryce Hool, AVP	The "Patriots" become the "Seawolves"

A schematic discussion of the main buildings and the physical campus is given at the end of Chapter 3 ("Building the Academy").
The Kenny years (1994—) have seen a high turn-over of the high ranking administrative personnel, as in earlier administrations: 3 provosts, 3 deans of the College of Arts and Sciences by 2003. Buildings and major rehab projects, some begun under Marburger, have rolled along: Old Biology became the SAC (Student Activity Center), dorm rehab proceeded apace, the Wang Center was gifted and built (and opened in 2003, though still unfinished and mostly empty), the University took over the administration of Brookhaven National Lab (with Jack Marburger in charge), sports teams moved to NCAA Division I, and "Stony Brook Manhattan" opened at 29th and Park Avenue. The University was (finally) admitted to membership in the prestigious Association of Research Universities.

22

A Time Line: The State University of New York at Stony Brook

In 1948 SUNY was created and the State received the Coe Estate for the Oyster Bay Campus. In 1956 the State Regents announced that a college would be built on Long Island, on the 480 acres at Stony Brook donated by Ward Melville, and the Coe Estate (Planting Fields) would be the College's temporary home until the permanent campus was ready. The motto of the SUNY system was "Let Each Become all He Is Capable of Being."

ACADEMIC YEAR	PRESIDENT	NOTABLES	EVENT
1957-58	Leonard Olsen, Dean	Al Auster, Dean of Students	Oyster Bay opens: 14 faculty, 145 students in first classes: State University College on LI at Oyster Bay.
1958-59		Stanley Ross, Head of Senate, A & S	New Name: State University Center on LI
1959-60			Heald Report: Stony Brook to be University Center (when it opens)
1960-61	John Lee comes & goes		Students boycott classes: Gov. Rockefeller breaks ground for the SB campus
1961-62		Thomas Hamilton, Acting Admin. Head: Harry Porter, Acting Dean	First Oyster Bay graduates: 25 Bachelors' degrees are awarded
1962-63	Karl Hartzell, Acting Chief Admin. Officer		STONY BROOK opens: first graduate program: Muir Report (Let there be a medical school)
1963-64		Stanley Ross, Acting Dean of A & S	The "original" SB campus completed
1964-65	John Toll		Teams are the "Patriots" and State buys Flax Pond
1965-66		Bentley Glass, AVP C.N. Yang	First PhD awarded (in Chemistry)
1966-67			School of Continuing Education (CED) started:The bridge goes nowhere
1967-68		Alec Pond, EVP	Drug Bust (1/17/68): 24 students arrested
1968-69		Sid Gerbet, VP for Liberal Students	3 day moratorium in October; 2nd drug bust; Gate house burned: Library sit-in, 21 arrests
1969-70			HSC opens: DoD Debate: SB Union opens
1970-71			Library exansion
1971-72			Unionization of faculty, librarians, and professional staff
1973-74			Grad Chem building opens: Self-Study & Middle States re-accreditation

23

A schematic discussion of the main buildings and the physical campus is given at the end of Chapter 3 ("Building the Academy").

The Kenny years have seen a turn-over of the high ranking administrative personnel, as in earlier time: 3 provosts, 3 deans of the College of Arts & Sciences by 2003. Buildings and major rehabs, some begun under Marburger, have rolled along: Old Biology became the SAC (Student Activities Center), dorm rehab proceeded apace, the Wang Center was gifted and built (opened in 2002, though still unfinished and mostly empty), the University took over the administration of Brookhaven National Lab (with Jack Marburger in charge), the teams moved to NCAA Division I, and "Stony Brook Manhattan" opened, and Stony Brook became a member of the prestigious Association of Research Universities.

(Endnotes)
1. The very form of the name of the University offers insight into its complex identity. It was christened The State College at Oyster Bay. Then it became The State University College on Long Island, which deemphasized the temporary site. When the show moved to Stony Brook in 1962 the logical full name was now SUNY Stony Brook (The State University of New York at Stony Brook), paralleling the names of the university centers at Buffalo and Albany (and then at Binghamton).

In the early 1990s a movement developed to refer to Stony Brook either as USB (University at Stony Brook) or SBU (Stony Brook University). These changes supposedly would offer easy recognition on highway signs and the sports pages. But names have symbolic and historical importance; to call the university SBU or USB is to downplay Stony Brook as part of The State University of New York. Since I applaud the idea of being part of a public system, I will use SUNY SB or some variation as the proper name of the university. At present, "Stony Brook University" seems to be in the ascendant.

Along with the movement toward an autonomous identity the athletic teams dropped "Patriots" and became "Seawolves." The name, along with an ugly and predatory logo or emblem, heralded the new emphasis on athletics. Many on campus think this emphasis (and concomitant focus and costs) a costly mistake. "Seawolves" does seem to work in terms of selling sweatshirts, and even a seawolf looks better than a Georgetown or Michigan sweatshirt worn by a Stony Brook student.

2. A huge number of U.S. colleges and universities have their own "history." Harvard, as we might imagine, leads the way, with a host of publications written by (or under the aegis of) Samuel Elliot Morison, and as early as 1904 Columbia treated itself to a four volume historical review (written by a committee chaired by Brander Matthew: *A History of Columbia University, 1754-1904: Publications in Commemoration of the One Hundredth and Fiftieth Anniversary of the Founding of King's College*). Local loyalties are strong enough to support such volumes for smaller or more local-

ized institutions. We can range from Thomas G. Dyer, *The University of Georgia: A Bicentennial History, 1785-1985* (University of Georgia Press, 1985), for a prominent state university, to a small school's concern for its past: Walter Pilkington, *Hamilton College, 1812/1962* (Hamilton, NY, 1962), or Lewis Theiss, *Centennial History of Bucknell University, 1846-1946* (Williamsport, Pa, 1946).

3. Universities that see themselves as having a special mission are eager to proclaim this in stone – or in print. For the University of Chicago, with its combination of liberal arts and research, Richard J. Storr, *Harper's University: The Beginnings* (Chicago, 1966), and numerous works by and about Robert Maynard Hutchins. But Chicago took itself seriously from the beginning; for its 25th anniversary in 1916, there was a host of official publications, by or under the supervision of Thomas W. Goodspeed. For a different view of mission, Reginald C. McGrane, *The University of Cincinnati: A Success Story in Urban Higher Education* (New York, 1963). Cornell's land-grant roots (in which Ivy grew so well) can be followed in its own histories: Waterman Thomas Howell, *Cornell University: A History* (1905), and Morris Bishop, *A History of Cornell* (1962). For the Johns Hopkins University, Daniel Coit Gilman, *The Launching of a University* (1906), and Hugh Hawkins, *Pioneer: A History of Johns Hopkins University, 1874-1899* (1960). These references do not even scratch the surface of in-house and external histories of universities. Since I hold my degrees from the University of Chicago I will use that institution for various comparisons. However, such comparisons are not meant to put Stony Brook in the shade.

4. To give an idea of Stony Brook's early growth spurt I offer my own experience in the History Department. When I was interviewed (spring, 1964) there were 8 or 9 members of the Department and it was all very informal. Five new faculty (including myself) were hired that spring, on the heels of two men who had only come the year before. So in two years the department had jumped from six to 13. We then proceeded to hire one man the fol-

lowing year, four for the year after. This process soon exhausted itself and by 1969 or 1970 the department was at full size of almost 30, slightly larger than in 2000. The first woman joined the Department, at a very junior level, in 1966, and it was not until the mid- or late 70s that we had a significant number of women. By 1990 the Department was about 50% women, and by then they were moving up into the senior ranks.

5. The student photographs in the yearbook (*Specula*) for the first graduating class, that of 1961, show 13 women, 12 men (in a volume dedicated to Allen Austil, Dean of Students), and one student who looked to be African American. For this first graduating class, the majors listed were Chemistry, Physics, Social Science, Math, and Biology. For 1962 the yearbook shows 25 women (one African American), 45 men; for 1963, 47 women and 63 men (and all white - as best one can tell). Some graduates may not have shown up for their picture, but morale ran high in the early days and the chances are that these numbers approximate the entire class. Of course, growth came quickly and dramatically. If we turn to the yearbook for 1967, we can see how Stony Brook grew and grew. The 1967 yearbook covers the first graduating class that had begun its four-year life at Stony Brook; pictures of graduating seniors show 176 men, 145 women (and, once more, a single African American man).

6. The Health Sciences Center (HSC) - a teaching hospital and basic biological sciences, with schools of medicine, dental medicine, social welfare, nursing, and allied health - is beyond the purview of this study. In my preface I refer to the in-house history written by Howard Oakes. The full history of HSC is so vast (in terms of planning, money, employees, the politics of professional programs, etc), that it has to be told - if ever - by someone who either was involved in the process or who brings some knowledge of a very different aspect of higher education and scientific research, including the history of hospitals and medical schools. Good luck.

7. This view of the process ignores critical externals; the need for permission from SUNY Central (and a share of the SUNY budget)

accreditation from the Middle States Association, which gets renewed after an elaborate self-study and then a site visit, every five years: the approval of specific programs by professional societies that oversee fields like chemistry and engineering. A college or university must grant a degree that is recognized by professional associations, by the rest of academia, and by prospective employers; the various forms of external supervision are designed to guarantee that whatever the standards, the inherent quality of any given degree will be taken at face value everywhere and anywhere. A BA is a BA, no matter - as long as the school is accredited. This has been a basic tenet of western education since the origins of the system in the 13th century.

8.The governors who have played a role were Thomas Dewey (1943-54), under whom SUNY was created: Averell Harriman (1955-58), who looked with some favor on the new college at Oyster Bay: Rockefeller (1958-73), who ran Albany during Stony Brook's growth years: Malcolm Wilson (1973-74), who passed through too quickly to have much impact: Hugh Carey (1975-82), a lukewarm friend in an era of genuinely tough budgets: Mario Cuomo (1983-94), whose populist rhetoric never translated into support (financial or moral) for public higher education: George Pataki (1994—). The characterizations of the governors are my own, though they probably represent a consensus of the faculty "party line." Dewey, Rockefeller, Wilson (and Pataki) were Republicans. Pataki's treatment of SUNY has been hostile on two fronts: bad budgets for the system, and the appointment of conservative trustees who see intervention into rather than protection of the system as their brief. Pataki's "Rethinking SUNY" is an extension of his "Remaking New York," with the specter of privatization and divide-from-within (to widen the socio-economic gap between those who send their children to the university centers, or to privates, and those who are hard pushed to keep sons and daughters at the two- and four-year colleges).

9. When Ward Melville took the lead in rebuilding the Stony Brook village area, during and after the Depression, he imposed restrictive

covenants, still legal until 1948, against selling or renting houses to Hebrews, among those on the list of undesirables. When the University was built the northern parts of Long Island were not noteworthy for their racial or cultural diversity.

10. Marburger said, when taking stock of Stony Brook in the 1980s, that its history could be seen as a decade of building, a decade of consolidation (his first 10 years), and, now, a decade of refinement: roughly, 1962-72, 1972-82, and 1982-into the 1990s). In telling my tale I have ignored the dreams, schemes, and proposals that emanate from numerous "five year" and master-plan committees and commissions. Such wisdom, dreams, and projections about the future are a stock-in-trade for any large institution. Most of what eventually does get built on a campus can be traced to its inception (or public unveiling) in these various reports, though there is no guide to what is projected but never built, or to the interval between inception and completion (which, at the extreme, can be decades).

CHAPTER TWO

The Political Economy of SUNY: The Birth of the Baby

Where to begin - a common dilemma with historical narrative. As I frame the story, to trace the birth of the State University of New York at Stony Brook we should go back some years before the opening of the Stony Brook campus in 1962. To understand the conception and birth of Stony Brook I start by looking at the complex of social, economic, demographic, and political factors that were a major part of the public agenda of Post-WW II America. This tale involves weaving together a host of national and state commitments, projections about the imminent white flight to suburbia that would eventually be realized to an extreme degree on Long Island, and governmental response to a powerful public demand for affordable and accessible higher education. Both populism, in a progressive sense, and fighting the Cold War through university research (and the creation of a concomitant national ideology) are major players in the game.

The very phrase "political economy" is a loaded one. It asserts, implicitly, that the economic and political forces in our society are closely linked and that the former generally dictate to the latter, despite the forms and niceties of an electoral mechanism designed to express "the will of the people." And yet, the wealth and power of those who run the system are not invariably turned against popular interests, though such forces lead and shape the public agenda a good deal more than they bend to the dictates of majoritarian choice.

To bring this line of analysis into an account of the creation of SUNY, and then of SUNY Stony Brook in particular, is to remind us of the way the state's response to the growing demand for education was cobbled together by and with powerful interests that had a stake in economic development and real estate, construction and transportation, and re-election and patronage (which on Long Island was by, for, and of the Republican party). For its consumers, and would-be consumers, higher education is a goal, a socio-economic come-hither. It is also, as we have indicated, big business, and not just for those who teach at and/or administer universities and colleges. This line of explanation is not offered to caste a sinister shadow over SUNY or to argue that conspiratorial and manipulative forces pulled the strings. The historian's task, in discussing such matters, is to show how social forces play out in "real life," how the end results can be understood as the consequence of the contestation, interplay, and accommodation of different interests, different voices.

In the summer of 1945, when World War II came to a triumphant conclusion, most Americans had every reason to feel good about themselves and the collective national future. We had won a great and popular war; our troops, working with allies who had paid a far heavier price in blood and domestic devastation, had brought us victory on every front. It seemed reasonable now to believe that we - the American people - had earned the right to look forward to an era of economic expansion. After the Great Depression of the 1930s and the strains of war-time life, military victory and a hegemonic control of world economy should entitle us to an era of peace, prosperity, and global domination.

One of the most significant and popular forms of reward or pay-back offered to veterans was a open door to a college education: the GI Bill, as it is popularly recognized: The Serviceman's Adjustment Act of 1944. If no one in 1945 was thinking of a public university out at Stony Brook, many were thinking that it was high time for public higher education to grow by leaps and bounds. Colleges and universities were being called upon to accommodate hundreds of thousands of veterans, going (or returning) to college, and it was pretty obvious that the pre-war world of higher education could not meet the new demand.[1] By the same token planners should have been able to figure out that, some 20 years down the road (in the 1960s and early 1970s), another wave of growth and building would be needed to accommodate the babies those veterans were fathering (or mothering). Not all the lost time was made up in the library.

To put this into a "larger picture," we can see a national response in three stages or categories. The first was simply to enlarge existing (state) universities. The second was to build new schools and to "upgrade" old ones, mostly a process whereby two-year colleges became four-year ones and four-year colleges became universities, with varying ranges of graduate programs. And lastly, the separate states began to coordinate their colleges into systems, to mesh educational missions, growth and budget plans, and student numbers (whether with an eye on quality, race and ethnicity, gender, or fields of interest). New York State offers a prime example of this three-tier approach, as we shall see.

Sometimes a few years stand out as those that put a stamp on an era of major change in the social landscape. So it was with public higher education in post-war America. Less than a decade separates the establishment of the SUNY system (1948) from the creation of the college at Oyster Bay (1957), and another half-decade suffices to bring the new campus at Stony Brook into the picture. Our case study is but one example of a national trend. From the vociferous demand for credentials and training, from the need to deal with a growing population, and from a post-war belief in the value of research and big-science, came the landscape we now have for higher education. We might think of the late 1940s – the Cold War and the beginning of the McCarthy-Nixon witch hunts, racial segregation, and the Dodgers forever in Brooklyn - as the time when Stony Brook's parents met and began to keep company. The baby, however, was still far down the road when Harry Truman was completing the term in office he inherited upon the death of FDR in 1945.

What was the state of public higher education in New York State after World War II? Much of the answer lies in what we cannot say - or at least, in 1945, we cannot yet say. The State of New York had been a congenial home for institutions of higher learning well before the Revolution; Columbia University traces its origins to 1754, when it was founded as King's College. But through most of the state's history there was no major state university, let alone anything like a state system. The only major public college was the City University of New York (to emerge as the CUNY System in later years), with a famous CCNY campus in Harlem and worthy sister-schools such as Hunter and Brooklyn College. At the state level of public education, a lot of small, scattered, local and localized campuses is the best we can do, and not a PhD-granting one among them, though many went back well into the 19th century. Private universities dominated the scene, with little serious rivalry from those state colleges or from the numerous denominational schools (religiously affiliated) and small private colleges that dotted the map.

In the top tier of colleges and universities we certainly had worthy representatives of higher education, but they were all private colleges and universities, free to charge a market-rate tuition and to seek a student (and alumni) base that preserved their mission or their version of social reality. New York state was the home of nationally ranking schools like Columbia and Cornell, with a few others like New York University (NYU), Rochester, and perhaps Syracuse getting a foot into the elite door. There was also Vassar College, small, famous, and for women only (though it went co-ed around 1980). Coming down a step or two, in terms of academic prestige, New York was home to a wide range of private and secular or non-denominational colleges, largely tilted towards the local communities. Stony Brook's eventual neighbors come to mind: Adelphi and Hofstra and Long Island University, and they had numerous counterparts throughout the state (including the then-private University of Buffalo), especially in the greater metropolitan area. Many of these institutions had been offering varying levels of education, at varying levels of tuition, for generations. Most of them were in the small-to-medium bracket, in terms of size, and most of them by mid-century were coeducational

We did note that there were a goodly number of state schools, though not coordinated as a system and none, singly, of great stature on the national scene. These were the schools that were to be brought under a single administrative umbrella when SUNY was created in 1948, though by then many were in their fifth or even their 10th decade. Two-year institutions, mostly serving as normal schools to train teachers, were scattered across the state – local responses to local needs. Others were of the "aggie and tech" category, training people for local industry and agriculture. And at a loftier level, there were some genuine four-year (liberal arts) colleges, notably at Albany (with a Masters in public policy) and Binghampton (Harpur College). To generalize, the 11 teacher-training schools served the state well, but they had limited ambitions and limited resources, and they rarely went far beyond their local catchment basin for many of their students. The faculty were expected to teach, rather than to publish, and there was but a minimal focus on graduate training. It was a state-wide network of great value for many, but collectively the inchoate collection was not a major player in the world of higher education.[2]

Lastly, to squeeze a wide variety of schools into a few basic categories, we have a large number of parochial or denominational colleges. They were affiliated with religious bodies and churches - with varying degrees of autonomy or of oversight and support - and they ranged from large and prominent institutions like Fordham in The Bronx and St. John's in Queens to smaller and more church-oriented schools like Marymount or St. Francis in Brooklyn. Though most of these colleges were affiliated with the Catholic Church (and many were run and largely staffed by priests, friars, monks, and nuns), a few had different religious ties. Yeshiva College in New York had a tie with orthodox Judaism, and almost all its faculty and students came from such ranks. There were also colleges like Concordia, a "Christian liberal arts college" with Methodist ties, or Keuka Baptist College.[3] But except for some local recruiting, these colleges did not expect to attract students who would cross lines of faith. They also tended to be under the direct gaze of the denomination that supported them; a limited view of academic freedom for the faculty, perhaps compulsory prayer services, and much interest in or worry about conduct, dress, and inter-personal relations (sex).

So in terms of aggregate numbers, even without a major public commitment, we can see that higher education in New York State was indeed a good-sized affair, whether we talk of students, physical facilities, budgets, or public awareness. But it is all in context. New York State had not availed itself of the opportunities offered by the Morrill Act of 1862, at least not beyond Cornell as the land-grant university, and in 1945 public higher education was still a small timer in both the state and the national game. The great transition that would give birth to a system – and then to public research universities – and then to Stony Brook— was as yet down the road. But both demographic and political pressures were building; the walls of the dam would have to open to accommodate them.

This change was long-overdue. The great state universities of the land, known to the public as the university of the state (the University of Michigan or the University of California) had no counterparts in New York. The large and famous midwestern state universities had either come into existence or had achieved real prominence because of 19th century federal legislation (primarily by way of The Morrill Act), and they had risen to the top, in name-recognition and academic quality, in large part because they were not boxed out by prestigious and politically connected in-state rivals.[4] Supporting the state university was just an accepted part of the public agenda in Iowa or Indiana, regardless of election results or even the football team's record in the previous year. In contrast, as we have seen, public higher education had always been something close to a last resort in New York State. Though five of the colleges that comprise Cornell actually are public ones (like Forestry), it was not on their backs that Cornell's national prestige rested. The lesser status of public higher education had always been an accepted policy in Albany. As most of those who sat in the legislature were alumni of private colleges and law schools, they had no built-in loyalty toward public higher education, let alone toward any sort of state system. Neither did any of the state's governors - many of them famous liberal statesmen - ever make a state university system a serious priority.[5]

Pressure to blow this lid and to launch a public system of colleges was building even before World War II. By the late 1930s it seemed clear that, sooner or later, some sort of state-wide university was a-coming. By definition it was going to be built with, and then run with, money from state revenues - public funding, and it would either be free or have a very low tuition. Such social pressure – akin to that which led to the integration of baseball in 1947 and to the 1954 Supreme Court decision of Brown vs. The Board—rested on powerful support from the center as well as the left of the political spectrum. Labor unions and minority organizations (especially Jewish groups and the NAACP) were increasingly strident. Colleges were too few and many had a parochial mission and/or discriminated against a wide range or a large number of "others." The Great Depression had been an inhibiting factor when it came to creating and supporting a whole new sector of service, and after Pearl Harbor it was generally accepted that a state university system would be on hold "for the duration," as were other pressing questions in areas of race and labor.

This takes us to New York in the mid- and late 1940s. The war was over; it was time to move on. I am not going this far back just to criticize public officials and powerful conservative interests who dragged their feet for so long. Such criticism is a given; it need not be reiterated at much length. But I do want to stress the way in which institutions and social movements - like individuals - seem to have their time.[6] Economic and cultural factors, as well as political ones, had worked - sometimes openly, sometimes covertly, sometimes in the face of demography and social values - to deny or deflect the groundswell for public colleges. Such indifference or opposition had been easier to get away with, in part, because prior to WWII the proportion of college-age men (and women!) who actually went to college was small, whether measured against the entire college-age population or against the percentage of 18-20 year olds who would be going by the 1960s, when it stood near 50% of high school graduates. Beyond mere numbers, the bulk of the American college population had been male, white (outside of the historically recognized black colleges), and middle class. And while various forms of state colleges did serve thousands of New Yorkers, they rarely competed for the most accomplished high school students (except in New York City, where the City College system was a front-rank institution). For the most part the white middle class Protestant population sent its sons (and some daughters) to private colleges, both in- and out-of-state. Many students, driven by factors like quotas on Jews in the Ivy League, chose the public universities of the Midwest: the University of Michigan or Wisconsin.

Given this situation, we would hardly expect the privates of the state, let alone the professional schools, to look with great favor upon the creation of a competing system, one built with public money and running on much lower rates of tuition. The privates yielded, or concocted the best deal they could, when the pressures became too great, and when it became apparent that the pie was big enough for all. Nor did they come away without some special favors in return for their acceptance of a new reality. The power of numbers was a convincing answer, and one of the basic premises in the creation of SUNY was that the state system was not intended to put anyone out of business. Only a public system, with greatly expanded existing schools and some new ones thrown in, could cope with the social pressure that came from rising numbers and from a more egalitarian view of who should be able to go to college (and who should help pay for it).

Not all of the push was on behalf of a more egalitarian and mobile society. There were vested interests, of many sorts, that also favored an expansion of the network of higher education. The war had been the occasion for forging powerful links between government, industry, and big science, and universities proved to be the most efficient breeding ground for research, with costs shared between the interested parties (unlike the government labs at Los Alamos or Oak Ridge). We were calling for bigger and better bombs and "weapons systems," more medical and biological research, and a wave of consumer-directed discoveries in chemistry, engineering, and pharmacology. After all, it was the Cold War; the very years that saw the creation of SUNY and the expansion of public higher education were also years of loyalty oaths and Hollywood blacklists, of McCarthy and the House Un-American Activities Committee, of the mis-treatment of Paul Robeson, and of the building of the CIA. Post-war America is hardly being presented here as nothing but a land of open doors and of the free exchange of unpopular views. Against the vapid optimism of Jimmy Stewart in "A Wonderful Life" we can offer Arthur Miller's take in "Death of a Salesman." Racial discrimination and segregation were still the law of the land and the great burst of ethnic, cultural, and religious diversity that now marks urban America was hardly anticipated in those days. And on the local scene, Long Islanders were eager to sport bumper stickers to the tune of "America – love it or leave it," and "Get the UN out of the US and the US out of the UN."[7]

But winds of change were blowing; there was going to be a SUNY. Veterans and veterans' organizations, in concert with sympathetic politicians and others of like mind, were turning to the development of public higher education as a way of breaching old walls of class and privilege. Governor Thomas Dewey - beaten by Roosevelt in the 1944 presidential campaign and gearing up to run against Truman in 1948 - saw the writing on the wall by 1946 (whether or not he was wild about what the writing said). And lest he be outflanked by Mayor LaGuardia's own actions in this direction, Dewey appointed a commission to assess whether New York should create a state university (The Temporary Commission on the Need for a State University, chaired by Owen Young: TCNSU).[8] TCNSU's report– which of course was in favor of a state university - slowly snaked its way through the complicated maze of state government, and in the spring of 1948 SUNY was brought into being by the passage of the necessary legislation. The sprawling assortment of 32 four-year colleges and lesser institutions now became a system - a single university in a legal sense - with a vast and far-flung network of campuses. A new board of trustees, specifically designed to watch over all the units of the new system, now came into being as appointees of the governor.

In a sense the will of the people had triumphed. During the two-year interval between the establishment of the Temporary Commission and the creation of SUNY as a system, innumerable quarrels had been fought - quarrels instructive in pinpointing how Albany goes about the business of state business. We have a contentious tale of entrenched interests, insiders and outsiders, racial and ethnic agendas, etc, played with and against each other. The private colleges worried that they would be run out of business, or starved by the withdrawal of students and funds. Democrats in Albany, mostly from New York City, pushed for the creation of

SUNY, which made them peculiar bedfellows of Tom Dewey. The State Regents, who preside over all forms of education, and the State Commissioner of Education (on behalf of a legal fiction, The University of the State of New York), worried that they would lose the authority they held over all accredited higher education, and had held since the 1790s. All these issues meant months of fighting, much of it centering on the new creation, composition, and powers of the SUNY board of trustees. To whom would they answer, and what would be their powers – questions of interest to the existing state colleges, as well as to those who walked the corridors of power in Albany. Would they be the governor's men and women? Would they fight for or ride herd over the new system? Endless questions about their role, some with an educational component, many without.[9]

But the sands of time did run, and eventually the deals were made, muscles flexed, and SUNY created. Looking back, it seems inevitable from our distance that the TCNSU report was anything but a done deal from the start. Too many forces argued toward that end, whatever questions had to be resolved, whatever compromises (and sell-outs) were made along the way, whichever ones were left hanging for the future. Apart from what I characterize as liberal or populist pressure for a low-cost state system – a consumer interest, if we will— there was the state's own interest in rationalizing and controlling the patchwork quilt of two- and four-year schools, from Long Island to the Adirondacks and the Erie frontier. And Dewey needed some claim to liberal credentials, as an eastern Republican who – until the counting on election night in November, 1948 – was everyone's betting choice to whip Harry Truman.

The SUNY system was designed to accommodate large numbers in what we can think of as a geographical grid, with campuses spread across the state, and in a three-tier structure. This model, following that devised in California, puts university centers at the top, then the four-year colleges, and then the community (or junior) colleges, offering the first two years' of college work and awarding an Associate of Arts degree (The AA). And because the State entered the game so late, it responded to the call for university centers by creating Stony Brook from scratch, by up-grading Albany and Binghamton (Harpur College), and buying the private urban University of Buffalo and tucking it into the system. In addition, there were medical schools: Syracuse or Up-State (bought from the University of Syracuse), Down-State in Brooklyn, Buffalo, and Stony Brook. This was (and remains) a vast, costly, and impressive spread of higher education. We also like to think of it as good value for the public's money – both university centers and the other "members" of the system.[10] The tale of SUNY's gestation lends itself to the good news/bad news scenario. The down side to the creation of the system was that higher education now became the business of yet one more branch of state government. We tend to compare SUNY Central with the Bureau of Motor Vehicles, with perhaps far too many points in common for comfort. Jack Marburger used to say that the state's government had been designed by Alexander Hamilton in the 1790s and that a lot had been added since then but nothing had been lopped off.

In the early days SUNY Central really did help coordinate growth and development. And because the new state system was both well-funded and well-publicized, some figures of considerable stature and vision were happy to serve as chancellor. Samuel Gould, chancellor from 1964-70, had presided over the educational television corporation (and before that had been president of Antioch College). Ernest Boyer, chancellor from 1970-77, went on to serve as U.S. Commissioner for Education (1977-79) and then as president of the Carnegie Foundation for the Advancement of Teaching. The advantages offered to SUNY enabled New York to reclaim some of the ground it had long conceded to neighboring states and its own private colleges and universities.[11]

But as well as offering signs of instant quality and vast accessibility, there were factors that pointed to a down side, many being the consequences of all that negotiating. Cutting the regional pie is a familiar game in Albany, in this case not so much about the location of the few new campuses but more about the contracts for construction in the days of growth. It was not an accident or a mere coincidence that the construction unions endorsed Rockefeller in his gubernatorial campaigns. Another compromise, or buy-off, resulted in a scheme whereby the State subsidized private colleges and universities: Bundy money, which went directly to the institutions on a formula based on their graduation rate. Another concession was the unwritten but powerful and constraining "no poaching" agreement. Again, this is a de facto policy, though the horse trading was pretty open and the logic behind it not hard to appreciate. After all, in fairness, SUNY was not created to undermine the privates but to supplement them. These behind-closed-door agreements help explain why Stony Brook never developed the law school or business school that was called for in the reports of numerous task forces and study groups. A public, low-cost law school or M.B.A. program would be a threat to neighbors like St. Johns or Hofstra or C. W. Post, all heavily dependent on the tuition revenues generated by such professional and graduate programs. This probably was a factor in Toll's decision to retrench the Education Department in the 1970s, about which much more below. He met a budget problem and he jettisoned that which was so badly needed by our neighbors on Long Island.

A lot of background; time now to leave Albany and come closer to home. In the 1990s Long Island made much of the 40th or 50th anniversary of various post-war milestones, all noted for their role in the rapid development and commercialization of Nassau and Suffolk counties after 1945. Robert Caro's 1974 biography of Robert Moses, the Stalin of metropolitan-area planning and development, helped illuminate the way the planners imposed bridges and parkways upon communities, both for the sake of the auto and to make poor neighborhoods into service areas for rich ones.[12] But what drew the most public interest was coverage depicting the 50th anniversary of Levittown in Nassau County. This "event" focused interest on how the massive construction of low cost, uniform, and racially discriminatory housing had shaped post-war Long Island more than any other single factor under human control. Levitt's plan had called for some 17,000 mass-built houses - the price of $7900 being acceptable to banks and easily managed by a GI home loan. This was a stroke of genius, yoking new technologies for mass production (adopted from the Seabee construction techniques in the Pacific), the easy capital of the late 1940s, the nerve of a poker player, and an intelligent guess about demographic vectors and the lure of single-home ownership (with three bedrooms, a car port or garage, and no Negro neighbors). It was not hard to convince people that it made sense to own their own homes, and that these should be in the suburbs.

In retrospect, in 1997, much was made of the restrictive covenants and racism of Levittown, as well as of the imposed conformity of appearance (and of the behavior that accompanied it). Though Levitt was Jewish, his development would not sell to Jews, and it actively resisted black ownership well into the 1960s. But the racism and discrimination that strike such a strident note today were not really out of synch with mainstream white support for homogeneous residential communities as the best protection of one's investment. It was the 1940s – a decade in which Strom Thurman of South Carolina ran for president on an explicitly racist ticket and when something as tame as Jackie Robinson in the infield was considered a threat to the Republic. And to keep this discordant aspect of Levittown in perspective, the gigantic residential development did help make home ownership an integral part of the commodity we think of as the American dream. It was part of a post-war bundle of entitlements, alongside owning a car that ran on cheap gas and got one to the new shopping center. And truth be told, buying a home usually was a good investment.

Looking back, we can say that in 1950 Long Island was a development waiting to happen. While Levitt's housing can be thought of as the serious beginning of the process, it was located in western Nassau County, not that far beyond the Queen's boundary of New York City. But soon the wave of construction and/or migration would sweep far to the east, with Levitt's Strathmore development in Stony Brook a typical if ambitious part of the next great surge (eastward) in the 1960s. As with the growth of the University, this continuous extension of suburbia or "ex-urbia" was a trend in 1960, a full scale movement by 1970, and something that had already happened by 1980 or 1985.

The saga of migration and construction can be told in terms

of people, or of miles of expressways and highways, or in numbers of houses, as we choose. Nesconset highway (State highway 347) – today a ribbon of stop lights and re-paving - was opened as an express road from Hauppauge to Mount Sinai around 1960. Before that only old State 25 (Jericho Turnpike, becoming Middle Country Road) carried what traffic there was for the outer reaches of civilization. The Long Island Expressway (Interstate 495), part of the inter-state system of which Eisenhower was so proud, only ran as far east as Smithtown until the mid-1960s. Nichol Road, the main north-south feeder of traffic into (and out of) the University, did not connect the north shore to the south shore until the 1970s.

The towns and hamlets of central Long Island, relatively isolated and under-populated for so long, quickly grew until they touched each other. Semi-agricultural communities like Port Jefferson Station (aka Terryville) were now "home" to those leaving the City in droves. Potato fields and scrub pine yielded first to the bulldozer, then to the cement mixer, and finally to the carpenter (and then in turn to the home repair company). The new residents of Long Island, buying tract housing on long-term mortgages, thought they were escaping the problems of The City as they left its boundaries. In the suburbs everyone could own a house, vote Republican, and be oblivious to the relentless pressure of race, urban decay, and class structure. Many aspects of this suburban dream, now easy to poke fun of from the distance of four decades, were legitimately beguiling for the thousands of men and women who were quite reasonably in pursuit of a more comfortable life style. My parents, in Cleveland, were eager to go from renting in an old neighborhood of the city to renting in an old suburb to owning in a new one, and they made all these moves between 1946 and 1952.

That Suffolk County lay well beyond the older suburban belt of NYC now made it even more attractive, as well as more affordable. Moving that far out was almost a fresh start. The census returns for what eventually became Stony Brook's main student catchment basin indicate how empty central Suffolk County had been, and how relatively empty it would remain for some years. If we go back to the 1920 Census we find that while Brooklyn had about 2 million residents, and Queens almost half a million, neither Nassau nor Suffolk County was much beyond 100,000. After WWII, while Brooklyn was edging near 3 million, Suffolk had only grown to hold 276,000. But then came real growth: by 1960 Nassau was almost at 1.5 million, Suffolk at three quarters of a million, and many more yet to come: 1.3 million, for Suffolk alone in the 1980 census.[13] By the late 1950s much of this migration and expansion was predictable, or at least it should have been, and the plan to build a university center out in the wilds was a proposition supported by reasonable speculation about demographic movement and economic development. No one should have had to worry, either very often or for very long, about where Stony Brook would get a student body to fill the buildings that were always needed faster than they could be built.

I said above that though Long Island was the home of numerous colleges, long before the creation of Stony Brook, they had neither the size nor the resources to accommodate the future. All were private (except for SUNY Farmingdale, a small two-year aggie and tech school that still had cows in the barns in 1965). Many of these Long Island institutions could boast of venerable roots: Adelphi had been founded in 1896, Long Island University in 1926 (in Brooklyn: its C.W. Post campus in Nassau was established in 1954, its Southampton campus in 1963), Brooklyn Polytechnic in 1854, St. Francis in 1884, and Hofstra in 1926. Their student numbers were certainly respectable: 1956 enrollments were given as 2319 for Adelphi, 5500 for Hofstra, 2681 for LIU in Brooklyn, 6742 for St. John's - to cite the largest of them (other than Brooklyn College, with an enrollment of 17,239).[14] But even if they were willing to deal with the growing numbers, they lacked the facilities for the kind of growth that the state was now about to underwrite for its new university center. Only a Stony Brook, it seemed, could help solve what some sage referred to as "the Nassau-Suffolk education deficit."

It is hard to capture an idea of what either Ward Melville or the local community anticipated from the arrival of a small but fully-fledged university. It seems likely that the Melvilles must have expected that a state college, as a genteel campus of Georgian buildings and well behaved young men (and women), would add status to the area. It would certainly be good for real estate prices and local businesses, and it would hardly hurt the family image of philanthropic millionaires who gave back as well as took. The Melville gifting was one that would enable the university, and its students, to enjoy "the relative seclusion of a semi-rural setting" while being involved in big-time academia. And in addition to the 478 acres of virtually bare land for the main campus, the Melville family threw in "Sunwood," a mansion on Long Island Sound located a mile or two north of the university. This mock-Tudor house came with run down formal gardens but a useable beach. It served as a faculty club and social center, and it could house university guests. In fact, I spent the night there when I came for my job interview; a comfortable room but no food within miles except the private stores of the caretaker. A little touch of "great Gatsby" is fun for those of us who did not grow up in 40 room houses.

Building on Melville generosity and lavish state budgets, Stony Brook was born in the autumn of 1962, though calls for at least a state teachers college on the Island had been heard since the late 1940s. Its new location allowed the university to over-leap the growth of suburbia, at least for a few years, and it brought us into a community that still reveled in its older semi-isolation.[15] Though the 478 acres of the Melville gift today comprise only about 40% of the entire campus, they were more than enough for a very healthy start. Granted, as is often the case, the new baby was not much to look at, at least not unless you had some personal reason to find it attractive. But it did have good genes and doting parents (and a few aunts and lots of uncles), and it was going to do quite nicely, thank you.[16]

In taking this story up to the move from Oyster Bay to Stony Brook I do not wish to convey the idea that once Stony Brook stood on its own feet the State lost interest and the new university just blended into the local scenery. Not so. It is rather that my narrative's center of gravity will now shift, becoming focused primarily on the local scene. Were I to go through the SUNY Master Plans (designed to cover 5 year periods, like Soviet plans for industrialization) we would find wording that proclaims a sustained commitment to education and a recognition of how much the new university center was contributing to the common enterprise - as well as pervasive worries about budget stringencies and curtailed growth. This sense of commitment and dedication would also show through were I to turn to the piles of reports on affirmative action and diversity, or to those trumpeting the role of women in SUNY, or even to the faculty-staff union's own master plan (version 1990). All of these sanguine statements reaffirm sustained faith in the vision of inexpensive and accessible higher education. And in the roll call of such rhetoric, Stony Brook usually figures prominently.

But for all this faith and optimism, by the early 1970s money came to be the root of it all - whether we talk of plans implemented or of plans aborted. A grimmer and tougher slope was now set by state budgets and state politics. When NYS was rich and higher education a priority, and when Long Island was an exciting growth area, and when Nelson Rockefeller ran the show, SUNY prospered, and Stony Brook did so beyond its just deserts. Eventually things leveled off; governors had less money at their command and less inclination to pore it into Suffolk County. But through good times and not-such good times, the commitment to Long Island - a commitment to higher education that was always good value for the money - has been kept alive, though it sometimes takes a bit of faith to feel the warmth emanating from a pretty cold hearth. Walt Whitman (who hailed from Huntington, some 20 miles west of Stony Brook) still towers over us as Long Island's greatest writer. I like to think he would have found the traffic on Nesconset Highway, the crowds at the Smithhaven Mall, and the sheer numbers let alone the diversity of the students as they walk across the Stony Brook campus, well worth an ode of praise. Like beauty in the eye of the beholder, poetry is where you find it.[17]

(Endnotes)

1. Where my own reflections on post-war American needed professional support, I have relied on William H. Chafee, *The Unfinished Journey: America Since World War II* (4th ed., New York, 1999), and I was advised in this direction by Naomi B. Rosenthal.

2. The old state college at Buffalo is now the State University College at Buffalo (Buff-state), with an emphasis on training teachers. The Heald Report in 1960 called for the development of a state university, rather than just a larger Buff-State, and thereby gave the impetus for the purchase of the University of Buffalo. Buying a university is an unusual transaction, but as non-profit to non-profit it is a legal rather than an economic one. The new SUNY Buffalo campus – like that built for Stony Brook— is miles from anywhere. But while there may have been no alternative for the new Long Island university, SUNY Buffalo could have been located right in the old center-city, where real estate was going begging at knockdown prices. A flight to suburbia, surrounded by empty fields and white families in new housing, may well have been a factor in the decision about relocation.

3. This summary does little justice to four-year colleges with a national position (like Vassar). Nor does such a specialized institution as Rensselear Polytechnic (RPI, going back to the 1830s) get due recognition. On the other hand, the major role of New York University (NYU) is a fairly new development - coming, in great part, since the 1970s.

4. On the Morrill land grant act of 1862, William B. Parker, *The Life and Public Service of Justin Smith Morrill* (Boston, 1924), and Edward D. Eddy, *Colleges for Our Land and Time: The Land Grant Idea in American Education* (1957). For Cornell, Albert W. Smith, *Ezra Cornell: A Character Study* (1934), plus material cited in Chapter I. The Morrill Act was tied in with other legislation, like the homestead act, and was designed to bind the West and North to the Union cause. President Buchanan had vetoed such legislation,

but Lincoln was both more far-sighted and in need of regional support for the War.

5. The governors of New York, whatever their varying allegiance to SUNY, had no hands-on knowledge from their own student days. Farther back, of course, FDR was a Harvard alumnus; Thomas Dewey had a BA from Michigan and a law degree from Columbia; Harriman was a Yale graduate; Rockefeller a Dartmouth graduate; Malcolm Wilson had his degrees (B.A. and Law) from St. Johns, in Queens; Hugh Carey (B.A. and Law) from Fordham; Mario Cuomo also has his BA and his law degrees from St Johns; George Pataki has his B.A. from Yale, his law degree from Columbia. I have not tried to trace the education of the governors' children to see where they sent the kids. The state legislature has numerous SUNY alumni, but they have never worked to become a focused pro-SUNY lobby. There is some regional identification and cooperation, but while the Buffalo-Niagara area legislators have worked en bloc for localized interests, there has been little of this for Long Island.

6. Though many a reform - from left or right - never does. While an historian is not eager to argue that anything is "inevitable," it is not much stretch to offer this view of the development of post-war public higher education. And not to make the U.S. experience peculiar or essentially American, the phenomena I discuss here were duplicated across much of the developed world: some expansion in the 1940s and 1950s, and then a huge jump in the 1960s, with basically steady state or some reduction since then. My experience as a visiting professor at the University of Sussex (England) in 1973 showed me an attractive campus, but also one newly-built to serve the same socio-economic and political purposes as Stony Brook.

7. For a classic example of academic racism, covered as over as nostalgia while the world of academia was changing under his feet, see Carl Bridenbaugh, "The Great Mutation" *American Historical Review* 68 (1963), 315-331. This offensive homily was Bridenbaugh's presidential address to the American Historical Association!

8. This story is told in considerable detail by Oliver C. Carmichael, *New York Establishes a State University: A Case Study in Policy Formation* (Vanderbilt, 1955), and by Frank C. Abbot, *Government Policy and American Higher Education: A Study of the Regents of the University of the State of New York, 1784-1949* (1958). Also, as I acknowledge in my preface, Sidney Gelber's book and its thorough look at these early manoeuvres.

9. I referred in a note in Chapter I to Pataki's conservative trustees and their interventionist view of their role. To give credit where I have not always been overly generous, Shirley Kenny has been very outspoken against the trustees' attacks on Women's Studies and in support of the faculty's right to determine how U.S. history should be taught. It is also important to keep the trustees' public jeremiads in context, since their interest in publicity runs far ahead of their interest in education. However, despite their public comments that attack a diverse curriculum (and, by extension, against a diverse faculty and student body), it is on their current watch that Stony Brook's Africana Studies Program has been elevated to departmental status, as has Women's Studies. At a more personal level, a colleague of mine (Helen Lemay) whom the trustees singled out to criticize for courses on women, sexuality, and witchcraft, has been elevated to the SUNY-wide rank of Distinguished Teaching Professor. '

10. All SUNY bulletins give basic data on the system, and in the Stony Brook undergraduate bulletin for 1964-65 we learn of 3 university centers, 2 medical centers (Brooklyn and Syracuse), a "graduate school" of public affairs at Albany, 11 Colleges plus forestry at Syracuse, SUNY Maritime in the Bronx, ceramics at Alfred, agriculture and home economics and industrial and labor relations (all three) at Cornell (for a total of 18 SUNY colleges); plus 6 two-year colleges of the agricultural and technology stripe (including Farmingdale, on Long Island), and 28 community colleges (with Nassau CC and Suffolk CC on Long Island). If we look at the 1988-90 bulletin, for a system not anticipating much further expansion, we find 4 university centers, 13 4-year colleges of arts

and sciences, 5 centers for the health sciences (including the college of optometry in NYC), 8 colleges of technology (including Fashion Institute of Technology in NYC), 2 specialized colleges, 5 statutory colleges (ceramics, veterinary medicine, etc), and 29 community colleges.

11. When SUNY was first established its head was a president: Alvin Euric (1949-52), William S. Carlson (1952-58), Thomas Hamilton (1958-63), and then Lawrence Murray, as Acting Chief Administrative Officer (1963-64). He was followed by Gould (1964-70) and then Boyer (1970-77). After Boyer came James Kelly, Acting Chancellor for 1977-78, and then a long reign of Clifton R. Wharton (1978-87), with a background in international economics and old ties to the Rockefellers. After Wharton left to become CEO of TIAA (the giant academic pension fund) Jerome Komisar, of the SUNY central office, was Acing Chancellor (1987-88) and he was followed by Bruce Johnson (1988-94). Pataki's view of SUNY may be summed up by his appointment of Robert King as Chancellor. King had served in the State Assembly and as Pataki's Budget Director, among other public offices, with prior experience as a prosecutor and as executive of Monroe County, New York. His law degree is from Vanderbilt and he did some part-time teaching (mostly in the business program) at St. John Fisher, in Rochester, his only formal appearance at the front of the classroom.

12. Robert Caro, *The Power Broker: Robert Moses and the Fall of New York* (New York, 1974) continues to hold its place as the definitive muck raking treatment of Moses and the sort of planning he championed.

13. A little more census data on central Suffolk County, the University's most immediate catchment basin for students: Smithtown's population grew from 21,000 in 1950 to 115,000 in 1970, 123,000 in 1990; Brookhaven went from 45,000 to 245,000 to 426,000 in those years; Islip from 71,000 to 279,000 to 309,000 at the same time. In 1960 the "non-white" population of Nassue

Country stood at 42,000, that of Suffolk at 35,000. By 1980 the respective numbers were 117,000 and 99,000, with a great deal of growth (mostly Hispanic) in more recent years.

14. Student numbers are always given so to maximize the head count: part time students, one-credit students, etc. The number of full-time undergraduate students is always a good bit below the numbers given here; that number is given as the esoteric FTE (full time equivalents). But this inflation of number, or body counting, is done by every institution. When I say that Stony Brook had 5000 graduate students we have to remember that only about 1/3 of them were full time and only some significant fraction of those working toward a Ph.D.

15. The building of Strathmore gave us our own lesser version of Levittown. This development, also by William Levitt, was located off Nichol Road - some 2 or 3 miles south of the university's main entrance - and it too provided mass, inexpensive housing of reasonable quality and aesthetics just in time to coincide with the growth of the Stony Brook Campus, beginning in 1965. It eventually contained about 2000 houses and they sold for anywhere between $18000 at the bottom to about $25000 for the fancier models. These were reasonable prices for the mid- and late-60s, and a very small down payment ($1000 might suffice) was a major come-on. For Long Island suburbia, Barbara M. Kelly, *Expanding the American Dream: Building and Rebuilding Levittown* (1993); Barbara M. Kelly, ed., *Long Island: The Suburban Experience* (1990); Rosalyn Baxandall and Elizabeth Ewen, *Picture Windows: How the Suburbs Happened* (New York, 2000). Local pride: both Kelly and Ewen have their Ph.D.s from the Stony Brook History Department. A final note: Levitt was quoted as saying "No man who owns his own house and lot can be a Communist because he has too much to do."

16 Size is relative, of course, but Stony Brook was going to attract considerable numbers. At the start (1962) there were 782 students, including 22 full time graduate students. By 1967 we were at 5199, by 1972 at 12058 (with 4330 graduate students, mostly part-timers. Then total enrollment hovered in the mid-teens: 15006 in 1977 (with 1582 full-time graduate students), 14741 in 1982 (with 1730 full-time grad students), 16000 in 1987 (2700 full-time grad students), and 17,287 in 1992. By the turn of the century total numbers have run to about 20,000 – more than a comfortable maximum given the absence of new classrooms and the slight shrinkage of full-time faculty on the core campus.

17. An index of how well Stony Brook - as a fairly typical undergraduate school in the SUNY system - has served its public is found in some statistics about the entering class of 1988. Under "father's education," 39.4% of the fathers of the entering students were college graduates, against 56.3% for (all) U.S. public universities; for mothers, it was 28.4% for Stony Brook, 40.4% for the larger universe. Along this same line, for Stony Brook 24.5% of the students reported a parental income of less than $20,000 a year, against a mere 11.7% for all students in U.S. public universities. The value of a state system, as an avenue for mobility and opportunity, is readily apparent.

CHAPTER THREE
Building the Campus: Home Away From Home

Mud, noise, and confusion were the basic characteristics of the Stony Brook campus in its the early years, years of almost nonstop heavy construction. Anyone who had even the most casual contact with the University in the 1960s and early 1970s has memories likely to rest pretty firmly on these unlovely aspects of higher education. If you have ever lived in a house or apartment during extensive remodeling you have some vague idea of what life was like - except that remodeling is to heavy construction as a squirrel to an elephant (in both bulk and growth time). And for those not fortunate enough to have had such "interesting" experiences, the full impression of the confusion is hard to recapture. Today these memories of Stony Brook's growth may be grist for the mills of nostalgia but it was pretty hellish while it was going on. A good time was not had by very many.[1]

The chaos of expanding and building, after the initial occupancy of 1962, was just sucked up as part of business-as-usual; the faculty taught and kept office hours (albeit sporadically), students lived in dorms and hung out in the library, staff went about their many and varied tasks. To move around the campus often meant to negotiate an elaborate and ever-changing obstacle course – a problem compounded, a maze made more complicated, by the fact that in the construction phase of a SUNY building the site is boarded up and physically separated from the campus and in the control of the contractor, not the University.

Nor were the problems just physical. A contractor answers to the Construction Fund (in Albany), not to the local administration. The campus has no control over the rate of the work, or its quality, just as it had but little say in the building's design. Who knows what goes on inside the site? When the Wang Center was being built in the late 1990s the faculty-staff union (the UUP) sought assurances that it was by unionized labor. Assurances were given, though much of the work was covered by the umbrella of Computer Associates, Charles Wang's firm, and it was virtually impossible to get beyond bland assurances about compliance.[2]

Only when a building has been completed – or as close to completion as the contractor gets - does the university take possession. If the new building is not up to specifications or expectations, tough luck. Stony Brook was on the short end of this stick a number of times; the Physics and Math Tower, Social Science, and the Chapin dorms are but three glaring examples of sub-standard or semi-finished projects that were just dumped in our lap. This meant that the noise and confusion of construction might well be followed by disappointment, rage, and an immediate need to confront the costly challenges of rehab and repair. Until the construction barricades were removed few on campus had much idea of what it was going to look like (with architects' drawings an uncertain and often overly-optimistic guide).

Furthermore, these legal aspects of state university construction were not the only flies in the ointment. In the days when students were a radical presence, the construction workers were generally inclined to support the war in Vietnam and to display little sympathy for whatever voice was raised on campus on behalf of the civil rights movement. The physically segregated turf of a construction site came to symbolize the divisions of class and culture that plagued our society through Stony Brook's first decade. "Us" and "them" were in our faces, all the time, year after year, though in pragmatic terms the segregation may have been a good thing. Heavy trucks and bulldozers were an alien presence amidst the hallowed halls of the academy; they were often driven on walkways in a fashion intended to be hostile and even threatening. Though there were vocal confrontations and one famous punch-up (when a student got a bloody nose in a mix-up about a flag-lowering ceremony on December 7), at least no vehicular-pedestrian accidents or serious violence complicated the scene.

When I talk now about the physical campus I am moving, to some extent, from Stony Brook as a case study of larger social forces, to a more parochial tale. Certainly, scores of campuses, in every state and state system, were being enlarged in the 1960s and

1970s beyond all previous measure, whether we turn to budgets, the number of buildings, or campus demographics. Throughout the nation the overwhelming majority of these buildings were designed to be functional rather than decorative; quick completion over long term considerations of quality and/or aesthetics. Classroom and office buildings, libraries, dormitories, and space for the relentless growth of administration were the focal points, with student unions, gymnasiums (or gymnasia, to be pedantic), and parking garages a half-step behind. At least we got through the 20th century without a football stadium.

With these general considerations in mind, I hope my account of the Stony Brook campus - while admittedly a localized tale – can still be seen as one that retains some of my case study orientation. At the same time, I do not want to put too many eggs in the case study basket. Building a totally new campus was most unusual. While Stony Brook's physical shortcomings and dilemmas were common ones, a university arising in a decade or so on what had been virgin soil was an extreme version of the common destiny. Fortunately, it only had to be done once.

The building of the physical campus is a tale that does carry its share of lessons in a thematic treatment of public higher education. Though there are a number of ways in which I could tackle this tale, I want to get through it without an overwhelming mountain of factual material, and I want some themes and contextual considerations to shine through as we go along. A simple but uninviting approach would be a year-by-year, building-by-building narrative. While this might touch all the facts – or at least far more than we are interested in telling – it would convey little about the logic behind the planning and building of the campus and it would open few windows on the successes or the failures. A second approach is geographical; and I follow this to some extent; what went where— breaking the campus down into zones or circles. A third line of approach is an academic one, that is, in terms of functions and the spatial relationship of buildings linked in terms of use and purpose. We might think of these three approaches as the chronological, the geographical, and the functional. Of course, no matter how and where I begin, the modes of explanation are intertwined.

No university, whether large or small, ever has a campus that is finished – beyond the reach of new plans, new needs, new buildings. And in keeping with this generalization, there are always going to be mistakes of planning and of placement. Every constituency and unit of the university, be it the central administration, the statistics department, or the squash team, is invariably in need of more space; we can take this for granted. Furthermore, all these claims are likely to be legitimate, though centralized planning and chance, in about equal measure, dictate how the queue of humble petitioners is arranged. Ideally, a university would like to cluster buildings of related purposes, just as it would like to keep buildings from stretching too far out in one direction while the campus remains empty or under-built or another. So in a very real sense the competing agendas and the mixed messages of the planners and architects have to come together into some sort of livable community. When you add the extra ingredient – that Stony Brook has to seek Albany's permission to build - it is a wonder the campus is not even more helter-skelter and shoddier.

Whether it was conceptualized in the planning stages or merely a descriptive comment formulated afterwards, it has been said that Stony Brook was built like a modern city. The center of the campus is downtown; busy workplace buildings, mostly occupied from 9 to 5 (or 8:20 until 5:45, or whatever). Then, after the working day, people leave the center for their residential neighborhoods, primarily their dormitory rooms but also in living quarters in the extra-mural world that surrounds the campus. And because almost no one can get to the campus on foot (except from the train station), the urban pattern of going to work for the entire day is the norm for students, faculty, and staff. Even for many who live in the dorms, the trip to city-center is a once-a-day affair, with mid-day food and leisure space being found in central buildings, rather than back "at home."

Stony Brook began as a small campus, its buildings clustered near each other, roughly surrounding the library, the largest building at what we can think of as dead-center. In a world of cold logic, each compass point around the library and the space beyond might have been designated as the growth area for a given academic unit. Thus the biological and health sciences might have started at the library's north corner and moved steadily northward, into the outer reaches. This would have linked buildings in terms of function. But it would also have meant that each new biology building was farther and farther from everything else – except the previous biology building. Such a scheme may be fun to play with, but it carries planning, not to mention convenience and travel time, to and beyond a logical conclusion. So while there was clustering, it was never carried out as boldly (or as doggedly) as in this model.

A final perspective, before we get to some buildings. As well as the city-suburb model we can visualize the campus as a series of concentric circles (or ovals). If the city-suburb model imitates modern urban life, in which mechanized transport moves workers from home to workplace and back, the concentric circle model is that of a medieval city: originally within the walls and combining workplace and residence, then newer neighborhoods, perhaps within an extended wall, and finally housing and work below (sub-) or outside the city (and hence, sub-urb). Of course, this sensible model is more a function of Stony Brook's need for space than to its desire to emulate 12th century Paris or London.

Talking about physical construction emphasizes space, whether used wisely or haphazardly. But a campus is built in time as well as in space – to raise another set of hurdles. Given the barren nature of the site and the small size of the original campus, it made sense for the original buildings to be fairly close to each other - clustered settlements in the wilderness. Thus new buildings steadily tiptoed farther and farther from the center, usually with some regard for the functional links between old and new. This pattern or process of ever-outward expansion is not so serious for those who work within a given cluster - say, Humanities and the Library, or the seven-story world of Math and Physics. But what about the poor student, parking in the South P lot, or with a dorm room in the old H dorms and an 8:20 am class in Heavy Engineering? A campus bus service was in place by the early 1970s, but "in place" can also mean stationary.

What was the physical campus that Stony Brook presented to its public, first to those brave souls who arrived in 1962 and then to the tens of thousands who would follow in succeeding decades? This question implies "agency" on the part of Stony Brook in such matters. Alas, local in-put was minimal at first, though it has grown over the years (if always within the constraints of state planning and funding). A building on a SUNY campus requires legislative approval (in terms of the budget), an ok from SUNY central, and a green light from the State University Construction Fund and the Dormitory Authority (regarding bonds and contractors). Each stage has to be negotiated, though they all fall together often enough, and readily enough, so campuses do get built, rehabilitated and rebuilt, and even – to a limited extent— landscaped and prettied-up.

Authorization for a SUNY building comes with funds for its construction, and usually for some start-up costs like furnishing. But even in the best cases the burden of maintenance and repair gets subsumed into the campus budget. Of course, in theory, that budget gets increased as more obligations are accepted. But the State is not always so generous or so logical. I have referred to contractors who could not be brought to heel, and such peculiarities as the Bridge to Nowhere stood for years (before its demolition in 2002) as a reminder of how low-bids for construction might be followed by well-timed construction bankruptcies. The early buildings contained asbestos, as a matter of course; later to be removed at great cost. And given the intemperate climate of the Northeast, an early predilection for flat roofing was going to be a costly and bothersome mistake; subsequent dorm rehabs including adding a pitch to the roof.

The campus that one sees is, obviously, the campus that was built. But we should remember that over the years planners and committees argued on behalf of projects that never were (or as of yet have been) approved – what we might think of as an alternate or virtual-reality campus. Some plans, as for a law school, have probably been shredded beyond recall. Others still await their turn; as I write the old Humanities Building, vintage 1961-62 and hard-used for decades, is getting the major rehab first bruited in the 1970s. The Ad Bldg will never get the additional wing it was designed to accommodate; that space was claimed, around 1980, by the parking garage. Where would Stony Brook have housed Journalism or Business, had such schemes survived the great leap from committee report to bricks and mortar? Additional causalities, sleeping if not dead, include a hotel-cum-conference center and perhaps a humanities tower; the Wang Center may double for the first, the rebuilt Hum Building for the second. To be fair, every large institution has more buildings on the drawing board than on the ground, and stagnant indeed would be the university not eager to show you its plans for an even grander tomorrow.

But a discussion of the layout and process of building has to be steered towards the actual buildings – what was built, and when, and (perhaps) why. The full story of the physical plant can also stretch to such pedestrian matters as heating and air conditioning, the co-generator plant for some independence from LILCO, a sewage plant, miles of roads and walkways, countless acres of paved parking, street lamps in bright and dark corners, tunnels beneath and aerials above, and the 14 acres of woodland between main campus and the south campus, preserved in memory of Ashley Schiff.[3] Though one is hard pressed to grow sentimental about the Stony Brook campus, it is a city that works almost around the clock. It pounds its buildings hard and is always running behind the needs of its physical plant. Door hinges break, windows fall from their frames, and rain finds new and interesting ways to make its presence known on lower floors of high buildings.

Stony Brook's first incarnation, on the Coe estate at Oyster Bay, was a fairy tale in terms of physical setting. An old estate was turned over to the fledgling college, and whatever academic chaos reigned, the setting was compelling. Pictures in the first yearbook (1961) show a movie-land college: cute, tiny, virtually all-white. Though the problems that befell the College proved to be very real, its location and setting whispered of a romanticized view of college life; absent minded professors with jackets and pipes, co-eds in matching sweater sets.

Ward Melville's gift of 480 acres for a new campus had been announced as far back as 1956. When the newly-promoted state university moved to its new home in 1962 it brought its personnel and students to a sprawling complex that was almost completed; the first, or original, Stony Brook campus. Confusion and inconvenience were accepted as part of the birth process. Though only two wings of the G dorm complex were ready, they just managed, with some improvisation, to handle the students. Mud and temporary walkways and boarded-off sites seemed a natural part of this brave new world. But to counter these factors - and perhaps keeping them from become serious drawbacks - was the fact that the education was a bargain and that students came, in ever-increasing numbers, until full growth was reached by 1980.

What was the campus to which hundreds and then thousands of students came, and which drew almost instant criticism from those responsible for its size, shape, and functioning? A student arriving in the autumn of 1962 would have found a large square three-storied library, and then, radiating outwards, or roughly encircling it, a variety of pseudo-Georgian red brick buildings: Humanities, Physics, Chemistry, Biology, Engineering, two dorm complexes (G, almost completed, and H, still under-construction); the infirmary and gym were almost completed. The buildings had been built in a common style; rectangular, devoid of cosmetic touches (except for marble window ledges), and standing nude on a barren landscape (the contractors having bulldozed the land pretty heavily). It was a raw and ugly campus; the red brick was closer to bright pink, and no tree was brave enough to assert itself. There was a great deal of unused land, pushing up against the edges of what had already been staked out - a frontier town, somewhere just over the Cumberland Gap in 1770. A dairy barn, left from some bucolic past on the site of the Kelly dorms, did add a rustic touch.

The diagram from the early catalogue, shown among the illustrations of this book, brings home the idea of one of everything. It also illustrates what I said about clustering and about concentric circles and city-suburban paradigms of spacing and usage. This original campus was only intact for a few years before the second building phase, the construction of the mid-1960s, got underway. As the original agenda had been for one of everything, and in some sort of working condition by 1962 or 1963, so we had a humanities building, a chemistry building, a library, a dorm complex, etc. The basic set of buildings had just been thrown down, and those in charge had to arrange for doubling-up and for the configurations of use. The academic buildings combined offices, classrooms, and laboratories, and the administration was mostly squeezed into a library that for a few minutes had more space than books. This was the campus I saw when I came, by way of the old Penn Station, for my interview. It was not impressive but it was clearly gearing up for business.

By later standards, the original Stony Brook campus was small. There were but few of us and we thought nothing about being squeezed together. My first office, along with the rest of the History Department, was in a wing of Humanities that we shared with Political Science, some of the Education faculty, the first hire or two in Anthropology, and an odd sociologist here and there. There are two aspects of this building that remain as vivid memories. The wall strips in each office that were designed to hold shelving for books (no bookcases yet) would give way, from time to time, though picking the books up did facilitate their periodic rearrangement. The other memory is of a men's room built so the door would bark one's fingers when pushing it open. I do not recall if the adjacent lady's room presented the same challenge, though I must have asked at the time.

No one was certain what the final shape or size of the campus would be, let alone how it would look. This made long-range planning a guessing game, at best. Early in its history – in those glorious bygone days of great optimism and big spending– there was talk of a Stony Brook that would reach student numbers of 25-30,000 (with an appropriate faculty of 1500+). Though this was never to come about, such projections always loomed over us and clouded serious thinking about how big was "big enough." Both Albany and John Toll suffered from an addiction to gigantism. Each original building was dwarfed, in turn, by its younger (discipline-related) sibling (or it was out-numbered, as with Engineering), and most departments were well advised to keep a supply of moving cartons on hand. As faculty increased and buildings proliferated, we realized that moving around was likely to be part of life. Counting the shared wing of Humanities as my department's first home, History had three more moves in its future before coming to rest on "our" floor of Social & Behavioral Science, where we presumably will remain until the end of time. This may have been a move or two above average, but it has made for an adventurous record.

Though such issues will be enlarged upon when I come to the academic sector, the size factor loomed large in all considerations. While it was becoming apparent that the largest projections were but talk, the university was in the continuous process of approving new Ph.D. programs. Nor was the commitment to big time research, especially in physics and chemistry, ever scaled down in terms of the size of the faculty, labs, and buildings. By the final leveling off we did have a university of significant size; by the 1980s numbers stood as about 10-12,000 undergraduates and 5-6000 graduate students, taught by a faculty that in the College of Arts & Sciences ran close to some 800 souls (who comprised about 80% of the main campus faculty). While this seems big to many students, especially to those who began life at Suffolk Community College – and it has inched up another 10% or so at the turn of this new century - much of this perception is colored by the towering lab buildings, rather than by mere numbers. We are but half-sized compared to the great state universities of the Midwest, and the campus charts or diagrams included in the illustrations give an idea of the leaps in, as well as the limitations upon, the physical expansion that we can trace through the 1970s up to 1980.

Having covered the original campus, and several stages of its expansion and development, I will call quits to this narrative approach. A building-by-building survey is offered in the appendix to this chapter; the rest can be left unsaid. Rather, I turn to two case studies of buildings and their use; the main library and the dormitories.

The main library of a university is usually among its pride-of-place buildings, a hub of campus life in intellectual and, perhaps, in social terms. Often it is the physical center; it is usually one of the larger buildings. At Stony Brook the library, as a building, has always been much more than just a library, in terms of use. It offers a sober tale of bad architecture and wayward planning. Though multi-use buildings are found at most universities, the Melville Library is an extreme case – and this had probably been anticipated, or at least accepted, from the start. Whether we made a virtue of necessity, or vice versa, is open to debate.

The original library, the inner core of the present building, was just (more or less) ready for students and faculty in 1962. A three-story red brick rectangle (or square), perched on a slight knoll, it was the largest building of the new campus, not counting the sprawling dorm complexes. It ingested the Oyster Bay collection, and very soon - thanks to lavish budgets and a large staff including many cheerful but poorly paid part-timers, mostly women - it housed a respectable collection of books, journals, microfilms, and government documents. Acquisitions were so rapid that they far outstripped cataloguing and shelving; they had to be stored in an empty supermarket in nearby Setauket. The library building also held the academic administration: the president (when John Toll arrived), vice-presidents, deans, and support staff. There was no other place for these offices, since not only was the dedicated Ad Bldg a few years away but it too would turn out to be too small from the day it finally opened. Of course, from a faculty perspective the growth of an academic department is a good thing, that of the administration an indication of administrative bloat.

Even before John Toll arrived the Stony Brook administration was trying to enlighten Albany about the inadequacies of the library, especially about space. As enrollment grew steadily for over a decade, the university soon fell well below accepted standards. For example, the library of a residential university should be able to accommodate 25-30% cent of its students at any given time, whereas by 1970 barely 10% of Stony Brook's students could fit in at one time, had they tried. By the late 1960s Stony Brook managed to get to the head of the queue in Albany marked "new library" or, as it turned out, "immensely expanded old library." Good news and bad news. What Stony Brook was authorized to build turned out to be not a new building, on a new site, but rather a huge square donut that would surround and tower over the original building (five stories in the new, but three in the old). The old building would be the inner core of the new complex, only distinguishable today if one already knows how they were fused. In the short run this plan had some virtues. The library could continue to function during construction. Furthermore, no additional chunk of land would be chewed up and center point of the campus would still be commanded by this large symbol of our love of books.

But the serious bad news, apart from that of living with such a vast construction project, became apparent as the work neared its end. We had been saddled with one more vast and ugly building, serviced by vents and blowers more befitting a runway at Kennedy than a tower of learning. The building was vast; almost a NYC block in external dimensions. And in a world of shrinking budgets and diminishing concern for books as the medium of information, the Melville Library (named for Ward Melville's father, Frank) is so large that it will hold the University's acquisitions into the third or even the fourth millennium. Bigger did not turn out to be much good, let alone better. Access has always been a problem, with the stack entrance on the third floor, and building security means sealed doorways and locked lavatories. Who knows if the automatic alarms on the fire doors work any better than the elevators.

This is an unfriendly exposition of an unfriendly building. At the same time I certainly want to acknowledge that the librarians and administrators showed up for work, every day, amidst the turmoil of construction and re-shelving. These hardy souls ran from John Toll and the director of the library to scores of more humble (and lower-paid) employees. The library, as a working library, never closed during the 18 months or so while its giant wrapper was being built and attached. Dust or mud, noise, and a long treck on a narrow wooden pathway in search of a working entrance, were all stoically accepted. Librarians remained as cheerful and helpful as ever; a sort of Battle of Britain mentality kept people on even keel.

Because the main library is both central and gigantic, it invited the presence of other offices, functions, and units from the start (if not before). Furthermore, the Melville Library was not the only library on campus, though whether this eased the squeeze or allowed us to duck the problems is open for debate. At first many buildings had space for a specialized library, particularly in the sciences, where large buildings and a library of a narrow focus seemed a natural match: a chemistry library, one for engineering, for earth and space, for math, and the like, with biology even getting a special building when the new Life Sciences opened in the late 1970s. Branch libraries made sense back then, days of lavish spatial resources and a still-growing faculty. No one worried about duplication of books or budget, let alone of what do when space would run out and become a contested issue. In effect, Stony Brook did for its library collections what SUNY did for its campuses; it scattered them all over, accommodating local needs and interests. That this generous policy would come home to roost, as contraction and over-crowding became the orders of the day, was some 15 or 20 years in the future.[4]

Some additional considerations. One is to pay tribute to an impressive tale of collection growth; the other goes to the multipurpose uses of the building. The first is really related to academic growth, not construction, but it seems to fit here, illuminating the links between physical growth, budget realities, and academic development. It also offers a balance to my barrage of criticism. In Stony Brook's early days the president's annual report carried statistics on the number of volumes added that year. Such numbers were a point of local pride and a basic datum for the Chancellor to take note of - a sign of growth and scholarly maturation, alongside the listing of faculty publications. The figures about the library are very much part of the world of big budgets and grandiose visions. The holdings for 1967 were given as 175,000 volumes: for 1972 at about 600,000: for 1977 at 1,123,000: for 1982 at 1.374,000: for 1987 at over 1.5 million, and for 1992 at over 1.75 million.[5] Unfortunately, such numbers give no hint of the tortuous interval between acquisition and shelving, or the likelihood of incorrect reshelving. Nor, by themselves, do they look at the appalling inflation in journal costs, especially in the sciences (where journals were often bought in triplicate for the various specialized libraries). But the main problem with such numbers is that they seemed to create of norm of scholarly commitment which has not been sustained, and in recent years the University has fallen quite dramatically in terms of volumes, expenditure, and full-time employees. The jobs handled by 160 librarians in 1972 were covered, 30 years later, by about 110 trained employees.

In addition to its basic collections and services, a university library is the repository for special and specialized collections. In the latter category we can consider the music library: records, disks, sheet music, and tapes, plus the usual assemblage of scholarly books and journals.[6] Special Collections, housed behind locked doors, contains an eclectic body of books and manuscripts. It is there that the University's own archives, plus many of its in-house and student publications, are stored. There is also the need to accommodate a stream of gifts and donations. These vary widely in substance and value, and the huge collection of papers covering the long public career of Senator Jacob Javits, presented to Stony Brook in 1981, shows both sides of the coin. The Javits Papers are not a great treasure (consisting of printed materials), but they are of value for a student of American political history. The collection was more or less forced upon the university, along with some early funds for rough cataloguing but nothing by way of a permanent supplement to maintain and showcase it.[7] This is a universal problem among libraries and museums; donors over-estimate the value of their gifts and have little regard for the obligations that attend its storage and accessibility.

A final aspect of the library as a building: its multiple-purpose role. As it was built, almost no collection of books was likely to need all that square or cubic space; other uses were clearly envisioned from the start - whether related to a library or simply in regard to necessity. To illustrate how people, units, and functions were put into the building I turn to 1975-76 campus directory. At that time my department occupied the back of the 4th floor and part of the 3rd – our home between our stay in a prefab on south campus and our move to SBS. Though historians like to think that they and a library have a special affinity for each other, this was a space decision, not an academic one. This 4th floor space is now occupied by Purchasing and Procurement (sic), and it has been so reconfigured that only by an act of conscious visual recollection can I recall a time when it was home to seminars, oral exams, and job talks.

The directory tells us that in 1975-76 History was only one of many units housed in the building, above and beyond the library collections. The rump of Education, after its retrenchment, and some inter-disciplinary units were our neighbors, as were various language departments. The latter, as humanities units, have been long-term residents; one can never say "permanent" in this context. For decades the Library has been the principal home of the array of western language departments: French and Italian, Hispanic, German and Slavic. Nor should we overlook minority-centered programs then housed in the library: Chinese language, Ibero-American Studies, Asian Studies, and Puerto Rican Studies. These units never received much independent support, and their existence owed something to their academic credibility and something to a political climate that made them seem valuable as bridges between a conservative curriculum and new social concerns and identities. There was also a small Classics unit to be found (Greek and Latin), still one more area that has always been short-changed.

These academic units were mostly small to medium size (other than History). In addition, the library has always held a part of the administration, just as it did when I came for my job interview in 1964. At least by 1975 it was mostly the academic administration; managerial areas were either in the Ad Bldg or scattered in odd corners of the campus (though some were to return). In the Melville Library one could find the Undergraduate Studies universe; a dean, those overseeing Equal Opportunity, the Challenge Program, undergraduate advising for Law and the Health Professions, and more. Nor are we finished, for we can spot a few programs that stood in relative isolation (Comparative Literature or Communications), or various institutes with at least a nominal claim to office space (Colonial Studies), or such long-term occupants as Career Development (in the basement; hard to find). A bit later the bookstore (which had also been ping-ponged around for years), a travel agent, the photo I.D. office, and the meal-plan office all showed up, using dreary basement space that somehow had been bypassed in the search for prime real estate.

In conclusion, we can choose to see the Melville Library as Stony Brook in a microcosm. Its history encapsulates many of themes of the 40-plus years: a too-large building, mixed messages and missions and uses, limited money for upkeep, spare change at best for the amenities. At the same time, as a library, it worked. We went from a collection of some thousands of volumes at Oyster Bay to over a million volumes in 10 or 15 years, though the growth rate had plunged alarmingly by the 1990s. The library staff has a reputation for being helpful. Many librarians are up-beat about leading classes through the intricacies of the building and the computerized catalogue. In an effort to remedy some of the ambience of the Port Authority bus terminal, the ground floor now has a small art gallery and a make-shift coffee and donut bar, while Special Collections mounts photos from the University's past. Students can gaze at the oil portraits of John Toll and Jack Marburger that hang from the brick wall of the atrium as they drink their weak coffee and trade chemistry answers. Since I trust that a portrait of Shirley Kenny will eventually join this august team, there will be gender equality as well as a nod to the Humanities.

This look at the library is intended to tell how Stony Brook coped with one set of spatial problems and needs.[8] Basically, there was the original library and then the "new" attachment, and that was it. Other than a lot of minor tinkering, the die had been cast. For a contrasting picture of how the university tried to move with the times and to learn from its past, we can turn to the dormitories. These were built unit by unit over several decades. This meant that changes could be made, new modes of dormitory building and living accommodated. A map of the campus shows the dorms ringing the inner or academic space on about 2 1/2 or 3 sides; a working city center, surrounded by residential neighborhoods and then, farther out, by suburbs. And as is the case with suburbs, we can move farther and farther out, ultimately reaching the Chapin apartments - the Pluto of this solar system. Downtown supplies the basic *raison d'etre* for the whole affair, though many who focus on the outer regions rarely go into the heart of the metropole – just as many Suffolk County residents pride themselves on years without Manhattan. When the State University College on Long Island became SUNY Stony Brook it could count an almost-finished G quad among its buildings, with the H dorms about a year behind.

The race to have a dormitory ready for the first students had been won, if in a close contest, and G dorm was now ready for about 600 students, though each block (and every subsequent unit) was designed for about 1000 residents.[9] Floor plans and spatial arrangements would vary, from complex to complex; from long corridors and separate rooms for the doubles in G and H (with tripling always a threat), to suites in new dorms comprising a living room and two or three bedrooms. Like all the original buildings, G and H had to be there as soon as possible. Then came Roth in 1966-67, Tabler in 1968, Kelly in 1969, Roosevelt Quad by 1970-71. Almost nothing after the 1970s; the exceptions were Chapin in 1981 (with 811 beds), and the Schomberg graduate student units in 1990 (a mere 200 beds).[10]

The early dorm complexes are much in keeping with 1960s dorms around the world, and except for their impressive size they could be exchanged with those on any other SUNY campus. They were red brick rectangular buildings, functional-ugly, and with long halls, small rooms, with bathrooms down the hall and shared on some ratio of N students per toilet/sink/shower. Eating was in the traditional dining hall; cooking in rooms was a major no-no (for safety and to preserve the sanctity of the mandatory meal plans).[11] Life in the dorms came with many rules and regulations; forbidding hot plate cooking went side by side with injunctions about visiting hours, curfews, sleeping arrangements, and the like. Dorms were sexually segregated though-to the dismay of those with supervisory responsibilities - the legal drinking age in New York still stood at 18.

Since Stony Brook has no neighborhood in the urban or college town sense - unlike many of the upstate four-year colleges - it was clear that the undergraduates would live in the dormitories or at home.[12] In fact, freshmen (and freshwomen) had to live on campus if they did not live at home; another of those rules that were tolerated, if not appreciated. Off-campus housing of any sort has always been in short supply near the university, which meant that what was available was expensive. Thus a combination of SUNY policies and local economics assured that the dorms would usually be full, and in many instances this amounted to being full beyond their designed capacity. Because the state lagged in building dorms, and by the 1970s was pretty much moving out of that side of the construction business, a squeeze on dorm rooms has been a regular feature of Stony Brook. Graduate students, with cars and perhaps a bit more money, generally gobbled up the lion's share of what off-campus housing could be found; undergraduates tended to concentrate on getting better dorm rooms or moving, with friends, from rooms to suites.

Within limits the University tried to make the dorms more attractive, more "user friendly" and less like factories or low-security prisons, though the considerable amount of tripling (in double rooms) made much of this an uphill climb. Newer complexes were built on edges of the campus, spots that had escaped the brutal bulldozing so characteristic of the first campus. Thus the new sites themselves, as well as their buildings, were less forbidding (if still a bit short of scenic). In contrast to the stark geometry of G and H, the Roth and Tabler complexes or quads consisted of 5 separate or free standing buildings arranged rather loosely around a dining hall. Roth centered around a pond, while Tabler, with a slight dip in the terrain that escaped the back-loaders, could boast of an open courtyard.[13] Separating the buildings - even while the complex held its quota of 1000 – made them more inviting and less monumental after a hard day at the mill.

The move to more intimate architecture was not the only new idea in the area of resident life. By the late 1960s the university had bought into the idea of a Residential College Plan (RCP) – to be instituted in or imposed upon each hall or dorm wing. This was a scheme whereby the dorm had faculty master, a group of associated faculty, a staff person, and a budget for cultural and social events (pizza, donuts, and movies). This was all in pursuit of a sense of community and identity, a way of fighting anomie by encouraging on-site activities. Cultural and social life, if not academic life, would bridge the gap between classroom and residence, between home and away. Each unit, under its master, was now to be designated as a (residential) college.

This sounded like a good idea, and by the late 1960s we were hearing far too much about alienation and the virtues of what was dubbed the living-learning experience. In some instances the RCP had reasonable success. But – as I saw it, as a college master for two rather unsatisfactory years – it was another top-down scenario, like mandatory play time at camp. Students and faculty often had trouble grasping their roles. At a time when internal dorm governance was rudimentary, and when the RA's (resident assistants) were chosen with virtually no student in-put, the populist facade did not really translate into reality. Many students found the presence of faculty and faculty-organized activities in "their homes" particularly disquieting. In a few cases students took to the leadership of such masters as Ashley Schiff of Political Science (master of Cardozo in Roth), but events were often poorly attended and of limited relevance to student interests. There were some bonuses for the campus; the dedication ceremonies at Sanger College featured Linus Pauling (Nobel laureate in Chemistry and in Peace) and Alan Gutmacher, head of Planned Parenthood. I only got a good house in Joseph Henry when we promised free pizza at an event – even though we never provided more than donuts and cider.[14]

If the RCP was a limited success, at least it showed that Stony Brook was interested in going along with new ideas, and was even willing to put some resources into its commitment. Though the original idea of the RCP ran out of steam in the 1970s, it was but the first of numerous attempts to link student living with learning and to aggregate students with common academic or cultural interests. Later efforts to house Honors College students together, or to create theme-halls (around interests like international studies) were more rewarding than the uniform but random RCP of the late 1960s. In contrast to simply declaring a dorm to be a college, residential groups with a particular focus, like AIDS Awareness, or Environmental Studies, or Sexuality and Gender, were linked with a faculty supervisor and a budget. With only the committed (or those who had thought they would be committed), such efforts realized enough success to merit a minor place in the budget. Diversity in the profile of student life, as of physical structure, has always been badly needed.

This account may paint a dim picture of dormitory life, focusing on the under-funded problems of communal living. As such, it hardly tells the whole story. Home is home, be it ever so humble, and most college dormitories, whether at fancy privates or venerable publics, are every bit as crowded and as functional as those at Stony Brook. Over the course of 40 years thousands and thousands of students have lived in the dorms and enjoyed the experience. Within and around these complexes students have had new adventures (if not ones to write home about), built friendships, played intra-mural and pick-up games, done some studying and a fair amount of sleeping and partying, and tested the wiring against appliances as yet un-invented when I went off to college with a portable typewriter. There is a lot of dorm pride and identity. Students go to college to embark on a new phase of life, not to have a luxury vacation - or so we hope. Stony Brook students are generally realistic, if not wildly enthusiastic, about coping with a bread-and-butter campus that is their way station to higher education, independence, and adulthood.

I end this discussion of the physical campus by turning to a peculiar aspect of the buildings– their names or labels of identification. It is only in the university's dorms that we have a link with the political culture of New York State. Naming a building is to impose symbolic significance upon bricks and mortar, and to name a building is to determine whose name lives on, and conversely, who has been omitted from the pantheon of famous mothers and fathers.

The buildings of the original Stony Brook campus reflected its basic functionalism in naming that was commensurate with their use and style: Physics, Engineering, Humanities, etc. This was like naming a dog "dog," or a first child "baby #1." For the academic buildings it has remained the pattern; subsequent construction gave us a Physics and Math Tower as the successor to Physics ("old physics"), Life Sciences as successor to "old biology," etc. Private institutions, or public ones with rich alumni, name buildings for benefactors (read donors of big $) and local heroes. Presidents and academic luminaries get commemorated, as do millionaires whose bequests helped them earn such an honor. The University of Chicago has buildings endowed by Ryerson (Inland Steel), Swift (meat packing), and Rosenwald (Sears Roebuck), for external philanthropy, and Cobb (university planner and architect), Goodspeed (theologian and early historian of the University), and Harper (first president) for internal glory. This is a pretty standard pattern, at least when there is money to turn memories into stones.

By obvious comparison, Stony Brook is too new, its founding figures too-much alive for such pieties. Nor, with a few exceptions, has the university uncovered wealthy alumni or benefactors who yearn to express their appreciation for a job well done - at least, not at this level. Though the exception would seem to be Charles Wang's Asian-American Center (opened, amidst much skepticism, in 2002 and named by Charles Wang for his favorite philanthropist), the basic story is of eminently neutral structures like Grad(uate) Chemistry. There should be a Bentley Glass Hall (the first AVP and very prominent biologist), perhaps with its Robert Sokal and Larry Slobodkin lecture halls or laboratories (to single out two other distinguished biologists).[15]

When the University did strike a deal to honor a patron saint, it rarely got much by way of returns. Naming the main library for Frank Melville seems fair enough, in exchange for the Melville donation of the land. But re-naming Social & Behavioral Sciences (opened in 1977) for Ward Melville (in 1987) was a case of shutting the barn door after the horse had chosen to leave; no further Melville gifts have ever materialized. To name the College of Urban & Policy Sciences in honor of Averill Harriman (in 1976) was to pay tribute to a distinguished New Yorker: governor of the State, the envoy sent by FDR to assess whether the Soviet Union could hold out against the Nazis, and the developer of the Sun Valley ski resort. But whereas Harriman gave Columbia University $10 million for Russian and Soviet Studies, Stony Brook put his name up in block letters on Old Physics and received some poster sized photos of Harriman with Roosevelt and Churchill in return. The Javits Lecture center was named to please and honor a former Senator, not to extract a gift. Nor was one forthcoming, unless the Javits papers in the library's special collections can be thought of as a fair return. Beyond this, the Staller Center for the Arts (with a concert hall and a recital hall) - named in honor of a family that made a fortune developing Long Island real estate - was mostly built with state money and then dedicated to/by the Stallers after completion. While they did give several million dollars (out of a total of about $12 for the complex), they topped up the project, rather than paying for it from the start.[16]

The dorms offer a more interesting aspect of the name game.[17] Perhaps to give some individuality to the buildings, as well as to honor various heroes and heroines, dorm wings and the buildings were separately named, given approval of the Stony Brook Council. Though the complexes were named for their designers or builders (Roth or Tabler: no Mr. G has yet surfaced), people of note were suitable candidates for smaller units. The original dictate was that they meet three criteria: dead, New Yorkers, and not too partisan, though it was not put this baldly. This bland approach led to such safe and unobjectionable choices as Keller, Gershwin, and Mount - named respectively for Helen Keller (1880-1968; no reference to her socialist sympathies); George Gershwin (1898-1937: a musician, I believe), and then local boy and major 19th century artist, William Sidney Mount (1807-68). Benjamin Nathan Cardozo (1870-1938) must have been a close call; a great lawyer and justice, but one who sided with social reform and the downtrodden. In balance, it was hard to be on safer ground than Othmar Ammann, designer of the Whitestone and Throggs Neck Bridges. In one celebrated instance student culture did assert itself against orders from above. What began life as Joseph Henry College in Roth Quad was eventually accepted, semi-officially, as Jimmy Hendrix College. Joseph Henry (1797-1878) had been a pioneer of American physics and we already honor him with the Henry, a unit of electrical induction. By contrast with the long dead, Jimmy Hendrix actually played on campus.[18] Eventually time heals most wounds, and even Eleanor Roosevelt (1884-1962) no longer threatens conservative sentiments; hence a quad in the great lady's memory.

Appendix: The Physical Campus

This appendix offers a survey of the clusters of buildings, linked by purpose and chronology (1961-2 through 2000). The original campus– as in the plan in the 1964 bulletin - is the starting point. It was a total triumph of red brick: all right angles (except for faulty construction), little ornamentation, no air conditioning (except for window units in labs for equipment or animals). Landscaping was a foreign art. A recent New York Times article referred to it as "faux colonial;" our characterization is "neo-penal."

The original buildings were Humanities, Biology, Physics, Chemistry, the Library (in its first incarnation), plus Engineering. The G dorms, and then the H dorms, are of this vintage, as is the old Gym, now re-christened the Pritchard Gym. The Infirmary, which once housed some administrative offices, was also an early building. Lots of parking for faculty and staff, and lots of open ground; the Tabler dorms went up gently rolling wooded land, still with the old barn. This early campus was designed for about 3-5,000 students, which meant it would suffice for about 3-5 years but no longer. Obvious problems: no student union, no public transportation (other than the LIRR across the fields), no easy access to stores in Stony Brook or Setauket. Nothing but functional, purpose-built buildings.

The Engineering Quadrangle

Southwest of the central core is Engineering (College of Engineering and Applied Science: CEAS), mostly contained within its own complex. In addition to the original Engineering building came Light Engineering, Heavy Engineering (now undergoing extensive expansion and rehabilitation), and the Computer Center, all in place by 1970.[19] These buildings enclose the quad; a pleasant small space, with its slight dip in the lawn and a gift of statuary, Chong Hee Kim's "Korean Village" (1992). Computer Science has moved to the adjacent Lab Office Complex, while Applied Math and Statistics is in the Math Tower. The Computer Center was the scene of a sit-in in the late 1960s, protesting military recruiters on campus. The building was seen as a symbol of our link to the military-industrial complex and Defense Department-funded research.

Physical Sciences and Math

The original campus had a Physics-Math building. The first new science building, after 1962, was the Earth & Space Sciences Building (1967). Governor Rockefeller turned the first spade of earth. ESS's structural concrete was a dramatic departure from red brick, and the terrace, fountain, and trees were also novel. The large tower buildings for Math & Physics (1972-73) and Chemistry (1973) showed how big Big Science could be. Old physics was turned over to Philosophy, Harriman College, and a medley of orphans and strays. Old Chemistry continued to house undergraduate labs plus Korean Studies, Women's Studies, and the faculty-staff union. ESS united Astronomy, Geology, and Oceanography, and it houses The Museum of Long Island Natural Sciences, a small museum designed for school parties and curated for some years by Steve Englebright, a lecturer who went on to become the local state assemblyman (on the Democratic slate).

As well as its own library ESS boasts a collection of fossils, some shabby dinosaur heads (in paper mache), and cabinets where moon rocks and other treasures occasionally show up. Physics has display cases with material on the history of physics, though no one seems commissioned to dust, let alone change, the displays. Pictures of C. N. Yang and Toll and Marburger are likely to be seen, and the University was very proud when it installed a Van De Graf generator in the 1970s. The large Chemistry Building has a dining hall on its second floor; the University Club boasts one of campus's few liquor licenses. It also has a display trumpeting the work of Paul Lauterbur on MRI, work begun at Stony Brook and leading to his share of the 2003 Nobel Prize in Medicine.

Biology and the Life Sciences

Because of obvious links between "west campus" and HSC, biology has moved toward Nichol Road (a shorter walk and a symbolic link). As the life sciences have come to the fore, so has their claim on space. Genetic engineering, cloning, and the like are superseding nuclear physics and space travel as research priorities, and they carry a potential bonus in the form of patent dollars for the university. The Life Sciences Building ("new biology") was opened in 1974, with a separate one-story building for a handsome library (later slated for teaching labs and now the temporary home of English). In the late 1990s Life Sciences was complemented by the Molecular Medicine building. Old Biology was gutted to become the Student Activities Center. A small greenhouse once gave Old Biology an exotic touch. The Incubator Building (1992), across Nichol Road, links academic research and industrial development, and biology is the field most active in this kind of enterprise.

Humanities and Social Science

The Humanities Building originally held all the "soft" disciplines. By 1980 it was down to English and various writing clinics, plus the usual miscellany of tenants and guests. The first social science building (now Psychology A and B) was opened in 1967 - shoddy from the start - and the social sciences left Humanities. It soon became clear that Social Science (as a building) would not hold all its departments, that division being the largest in the College. SBS (Social and Behavioral Sciences) opened in 1978 and is home to all the relevant departments except Psychology (which took over old Social Science). SBS was well built by local standards; air conditioning, a floor for each of the larger departments, and elevators that work. Psychology A houses various clinics and therapy programs, and in SBS one can find the School of Professional Development (created as Continuing Education: CED) and a day care center.

Humanities – now a shell undergoing total rehab and expansion – always held the English Department, and more recently the writing programs and clinics. Until they got kicked out in 2002, space was divided between a small cafeteria, the religious groups and chaplaincies (into the old Union in 2000), and such offices as the campus community advocate (as the ombuds office came to be known), the Office for Disabled Students, and Orientation. Other humanities departments are scattered: languages in the Library, philosophy in Harriman, the fine arts, theater, and music in their own headquarters in different sections of the Fine Arts Center.

Administration and Student Services

The Administration Building (1970) was never adequate for all its sprawling functions, and various units continue to be housed in the Library, including most of the academic administration below the level of the Provost. Student service buildings have generally been of less regard. The Union (1970) was too small from opening day (nor was its "bridge to nowhere" connected to the Library until 1977). The Union is a maze; many levels and half-floors. Moreover, as the campus spread to the south and west it lost its central position, though it remains the home of student organizations, publications, and the radio station, plus an assortment of cafeterias and delis, and more recently, the student religious organizations.

Other student service buildings are the old gym, attached to the much fancier Indoor Sports Complex (1990), and the Infirmary. The Student Activities Center (old Biology rebuilt and enlarged) is more the center of student life, but only since 1997. It holds a large auditorium and cafeteria and many meeting rooms and the Dean of Students' suite, but no classrooms.

There are lots of other buildings, some of obvious purpose, others just used as needs dictate. The Javits Lecture center was built in the early 1970s; the dedication to Javits came in 1984. This compact building - looking like the elephant house at the London zoo – has the only large lecture hall on campus: Javits 100, seating about 700, with a balcony and with students still dozing from last semester. Lesser lecture halls there run as small as 75-100. Lecture rooms in Javits were to have elaborate audio-visual systems in conjunction with the Instructional Resources Center (IRC). This was an over-blown idea, and the buildings now house the Grad School and Computer Sciences. No food in this major center of teaching, except for machines and a pretzel and bottled water vendor.

South Campus

Distant and rarely visited by students or faculty. The "south campus" consists of 11 high quality pre-fabs that will stand until Long Island washes into the sea. Though the History Department spent a few years in the early 1970s in this exile, the regular residents now days are the Dental School, Marine Sciences (MSRC), and some administrative and business-related offices (like telecommunications). Except for MSRC these units have little connection with the life of students and faculty, though the dental clinic will have a go at student teeth.

Miscellaneous Buildings

In the university's annual bulletin there used to be a grand tally of buildings. I have not tried to determine how much of this count rested on such as storage sheds, outhouses, the parking garage, service buildings, the heating plant, or the sewage plant. Though Stony Brook is too young to have much record of demolition, the barn on the Tabler site was burned during a night of protest, May 1970, as was a short-lived gate house near the main entrance. A day care center opened in 2001, located at about the farther edge of the campus (Hawkins Road, even beyond the South P lot).

The Melville family gift included the Sunwood mansion on the shore of Long Island Sound (with its beach). Until it burned in 1986 it housed visitors, and it could be booked for university events (Christmas parties, departmental retreats, and even weddings). It was out of a Great Gatsby set, with formal gardens going to seed (literally), a vast library and dining room, and a two-level driveway and car port. For a small fee faculty and staff can still use its beach and swim. It has been rebuilt (2002), combining a home for President Kenny and a small social-academic center.

To conclude, it seems safe to say that there will continue to be construction, rehabs, and endless quarrels over claims to space. But this is tantamount to saying that life goes on and that taxes will have to be paid. Nor is the development necessarily linear or progressive. The $25,000,000 Wang building, the Asian-American Center, makes some of the earlier buildings look tasteful, modest, and pleasantly tucked into the landscape.

(Endnotes)

1. In the program for the 1965 graduation there is a boast that within the next 27 months 27 buildings will have been built or at least be under construction! In his report for the 1966-67 year, Toll did comment on the chaos of construction and crowding, protest rallies, and saturated library space: though the campus had been "orderly and ordinary pursuits were difficult to maintain in the face of this activity." A masterpiece of under-statement, as he went on to say that 3 students had been turned over for arrest because of drug problems.

2. The gift of $25 million from Charles Wang of Computer Associates was the largest Stony Brook has ever received, and the Asian-American Building that consumed all of this money (and probably needs more) finally opened – to limited and ill-defined use – in 2002.

3. Ashley Schiff (1932-71) was an early member of the Political Science Department, and one of the first faculty to die. He was an energetic and charismatic master of a college in the Residential College Program, while his scholarly work helped link environmental interests to public planning and policy: *Fire and Water: Scientific Heresy in the Forestry Service* (Harvard: 1962), plus well regarded papers in *Administrative Science Quarterly* (1966) and *Natural Resources Journal* (1966). Frank Myers of Political Science furnished this information on his old friend; Schiff came to Stony Brook the same year Myers and I did (1964).

4. In 1997-98 the main library (The Melville Library) began consolidating the branch libraries, after much discussion and over the objection of departments and areas that stood to loose their own library. Physics and Chemistry have kept their libraries in their buildings, while that from Engineering has been given space on the ground floor of the main structure. Engineering seems happy to use the free space for offices that "outreach" LI businesses.

5. In addition the library was receiving 12,455 periodicals and serials in 1977, 18,579 in 1982. The number of documents (mostly from state and federal government) and microform materials is usually about equal to the number of separate volumes, though it is easy to run up big numbers when all the sets of pending legislation in Albany and Washington are counted in. The tale of recent years is, however, a very lugubrious one; cutting journal subscriptions, buying fewer books, a focus on other forms of data storage and retrieval, and more of the like. The annual rating of academic libraries as published in the *Chronicle of Higher Education* tells a grim tale – one badly out of synch with the public relations releases of the University itself.

6. In 2000-01 the Music Library moved from the 2nd to the 1st floor of the Melville Library, to occupy a large stretch of attractive, rehabilitated space. It has up-to-date facilities for new technology, and its holdings in books, journals, and scores have always been well managed.

7. The Yeats Papers, another major special collections holding, are not the literary manuscripts of the poet. Rather, they are a collection of his miscellaneous and personal papers, plus microfilms of literary materials. But they are the largest and most accessible such collection in North America (and perhaps in the world). Also to be found in Special Collections are such L.I. collections as that of the Environmental Defense Fund, the papers of Robert Cushman Murphy, the naturalist and environmentalist (who lived in Setauket), materials relating to the L.I. Rail Road, and odd gifts of children' books and literary manuscripts. The Javits family donated some memorabilia: the Senator's desk, portraits and autographed certificates, etc. These were set out in an attractive small conference room on the Library's second floor - the Javits Room.

But this room too suffered from lack of attention and some of the items were removed lest they be stolen or vandalized.

8. When the new addition was added to the Melville Library in 1971 John Toll boasted that Stony Brook had the largest library building of any U.S. university. If he was correct - and no one wanted to check - the best response seemed to be "yes, the more's the pity." In terms of collections, the data in the university bulletin offer guidance. In 1965, referring to the original structure, the party line was that the building was designed for 350,000 volumes and could accommodate 700 students, with 2000 periodicals and 20,000 volumes arriving and being processed each year. By 1969-70 the new building was on the horizon and there were already 4 outlying science libraries. Periodical subscriptions were up to an amazing 5800, with 100,000 volumes being added yearly, for a total of about 430,000 volumes, 100,000 documents. A music library had come into existence. After the growth years, the 1979-81 bulletin told of one million bound volumes, 1.2 million microform items, 5 branch libraries. It also referred to the "architecturally distinctive Melville Building," which is certainly true if (deliberately) misleading.

9. Two of the "colleges" or wings were open, those later named for Washington Irving and Eugene O'Neill. They held about 600 students, which sufficed for 1962.

10. There is some new construction and a lot of serious rehabilitation of the older dorm complexes: G quad was re-done in 1999 (with the flat roofs replaced a few years before), H quad in 2000, Roth renovated in 1992-94, Chapin (the worst of the lot) made handicapped accessible in 1997, when some patios were also installed, and so forth. Some dorms carry an elective option for the residents of being a "quiet house."

11. Such innovations as a table with peanut butter, raw vegetables, and yoghurt, as alternatives to the prepared entrees, were not available when I lived in a dorm in the early 1950s. Our option was the drugstore at the corner, though that meant spending almost $1 for

lunch, close to $2 for dinner.

12. The 1969-70 Bulletin displayed a sense of irony rarely found in official publications: "Stony Brook is located in a region of wooded hills and small villages on the north shore of Long Island... Despite its long history and nearness to great centers of population, the area retains a pastoral character with a distinctive New England flavor."

13. Apple and cherry trees were allowed to stand in the Tabler space, though the old barn was torched during the days of political troubles (as was a newly-built wooden gatehouse by the main entrance to campus). In the good old days when winters were really winters one could skate on Roth Pond - just large enough for young children and parents with weak ankles.

14. I put in a 2-year stint as master of Joseph Henry College in Roth (later student-christened as Jimmy Hendrix). Movies, accompanied by food, drew a reasonable crowd, but I found little student interest in the RCP experiment. I held my lecture class on medieval history in a dorm lounge and invited dorm students to audit. They told me that they appreciated the effort but they came back to the dorm as a relief from the classroom. We (Kate Lopes, my administrative assistant, and I) drew a crowd when we presented Ingmar Bergman's "Virgin Spring" as X-rated. An enterprising dorm student, Jim Frankel, began a science fiction library in the college basement; this took off and Frankel went on to success in science fiction publishing and marketing, while the student activity still exists on campus. But my overall impression was that the dorm residents really didn't care. I never found a comfortable role, and though the position carried some extra money, I stepped down after two years. Each college had a small apartment, an attraction for would-be masters who were getting divorced. Since I was not so occupied the apartment in Henry was used for a while by Kofi Awooner, a distinguished African writer who was teaching in

English. He was a wonderful addition to a white-bread campus, and Stony Brook came to his defense when he was jailed as a political prisoner in Ghana in the 1980s

15. With or without official permission, some departments have named departmental libraries or seminar rooms to honor someone connected with the department. Sociology named its own reading room for Lou and Rose Coser, faculty of considerable distinction, Philosophy has a memorial library, and Physics is about to name its common room for Peter Kahn.

16. I will return to some of this when we look at town-gown relations and the university's contact with the non-academic community. In 1999-2000 there were 5 members of the Staller family listed among the "pacesetters" and five more among the Center's "benefactors." Money from the William and Martha Pritchard Charitable Trust went, in 1991, to rehabilitate the old gym; only then was the building (re)named in their honor.

17. Ann Brody - whom I thank several times in this volume - was especially helpful in passing along a memorandum put together in 1987 by Les Johnson of the Division of Residential Life for the University's 30th anniversary (or birthday).

18. John Dewey Hall, in Kelly, was to honor the famous educator and philosopher; in student usage it was tagged Harpo Marx. An exception to the naming of quads for their architects is the Chapin Apartments, named for the Long Island folk singer and philanthropist, Harry Chapin. He was killed in an accident on the Long Island Expressway in 1981, and his generosity toward the Island's cultural life, plus the tragedy of his death, sufficed to overcome reservations about his leftist political stance. The G Dorms were finally given a name in the 90s – Mendelsohn Quad - for Harold Mendelsohn, a popular dormitory administrator who died while jogging on campus.

19. The dating of buildings is chancy. Most of them have a dated

cornerstone, but that might have been put in place well before the building actually was completed and turned over the Stony Brook. Also, the difference between calendar years and the academic year can be the source of further confusion. I have followed the cornerstone, where I have been able to find it. That failing, various publications or authorial memory.

CHAPTER FOUR
Building the Academy, Part I:
Filling the Faculty Offices

To build a large campus that can house a comprehensive university, and to do this from scratch in a few years, is a mammoth undertaking. If one goes today to some top floor, such as the 7th story of SBS or Chemistry, and gazes down at what rolls out below, it is most impressive. There are two things to keep in mind when looking down upon the sprawling complex of buildings, parking lots, roads, greenery, and athletic fields. One is that none of this was in existence in 1960. The other is that it was all built by the lowest bidders.[1]

But clearly a university is not primarily "about" buildings, large though they loom, much though they figure in our memory, and first as they have come in my exposition. A university is a special institution, and has been so ever since its European origins in the 13th century. It is about faculty and students, curricula and degrees, training and vocationalism, research and scholarship - at least when we focus on its more cerebral side. In many ways the tale of the building of the academy, by which I now mean the development of the academic and intellectual side of Stony Brook, is one in which experiments and new departures have been blended into − or poured on top of - a conservative or traditional model. Many agendas and goals were juggled; faculty and administrators often had to make decisions with little guidance and on short notice, picking one or another of the various uncharted and poorly illuminated pathways. Even those with considerable experience in the academic world had but a limited idea of how to shape and plan so much future. When it is put this way we might wonder that Stony Brook grew and functioned as well as it did.

One way to frame the story of academic birth and growth is to think of Stony Brook as a pampered and pushy newcomer among the ranks of research universities. Though we were coddled and praised and publicized, probably beyond our deserts, we also returned fair dividends almost from the start. Millions and millions of dollars went into the campus. Stony Brook came on stage in a day of heady rhetoric about education, research, and social opportunity – a rhetoric almost a reality, thanks to state and federal dollars. This was the era of Kennedy and Johnson and civil rights and public spending. The "Berkeley of the East" was our unofficial slogan, and for a few years it seemed as though this inflated boast might have some substance. Even settling for less, as we eventually did, put us into pretty respectable company in a very short span.

Whatever the limits of Stony Brook's mission or freedom of decision-making, once the university wended its way from the formal gardens of Oyster Bay to the scrub pine of Brookhaven Town, and whatever credit must go to lavish external support, the almost-instant success of Stony Brook is still a tale hard to recapture. Nor it is going to be replicated.[2] Quite the contrary; in the mean spirited America of recent decades, with an anti-intellectual agenda, a zeal to reverse the social visions of preceding generations, and a vision of world domination, Stony Brook's heroic origins are the stuff of legend. I look back to governors who embraced SUNY, to legislatures that doled out money, and to a time when faculty hiring and program development had been there for the asking. It's a bit much to go around saying'"Nelson Rockefeller – where are you when we need you," but there is some substance beneath this facetious nostalgia. Nevertheless, from the beginning a basic intellectual and institutional conservatism was built into the new academic structure. In the quest for instance success and recognition the most traveled paths of higher education were the easiest to follow. This meant a conventional curriculum and an academic-cum-intellectual structure that would center almost wholly on discipline-oriented departments and units and that fit into traditional molds.[3] For example, though my own department had a serious commitment to Latin America, our mainstream emphasis on Europe and the U.S. were typical of the conventional channels of hiring, teaching, and scholarship. Both administrative vision and departmental or disciplinary ambition steered most of us in this direction.

In 1960 a study group called the Heald Commission had recommended a comprehensive university center on Long Island (as well as counterparts in Buffalo, Binghamton, and Albany). This was the charge or mission statement, and Stony Brook was developed in response to the call for excellence, and size, across the board. On the ground, the mandate took shape through the process of signing on waves of new, and newly-hired, and mostly young, faculty—along with hoards of Long Island and New York City students. How had the structure that would "educate" these students, and challenge their teachers, come into place?

When the State of New York authorized a university to be established at Stony Brook many of the great debates about the nature and course of public higher education were long past. Though the list of such battles could be lengthened considerably – like a list of Civil War memorial sites— I will focus on areas or issues directly relevant to Stony Brook's actual situation. Coming with the mandate of being a state/public university (rather than a private and/or a college) in New York State, it was accepted without even the most perfunctory debate that the institution would be: 1) co-educational, 2) offering a mix of liberal arts or general education and discipline-oriented training at the undergraduate level, 3) offering both undergraduate degrees and a variety of graduate and professional degrees, and 4) integrated or non-discriminatory on racial lines.

1). That women could go to college with men was, in the 19th century, a fairly radical (and threatening) idea. As the movement for women's education grew, one response was the women's college – a logical one in a world of men's colleges that had dominated the educational scene since the beginning (which might be marked as Harvard, 1636). But a second response, and one much easier to pull off in terms of the expenditure of resources and the struggle for recognition, was to "integrate" existing or new institutions, so they admitted both men and women. The establishment of state colleges and universities in the mid-19th century, and then their rapid expansion in numbers and size after the Civil War and the Morrill Act, made them a natural site for coeducation. Though women were hardly treated equally, and though many majors and fields of study like elementary education and home economics were heavily emphasized as women's fields, women on campus and pursuing degrees were a major presence. Early studies indicated that women did at least as well as men, in so far as academic fields could be compared. Nor did they take their degrees and simply sink into passive domesticity, as critics had claimed they might do, thereby wasting the public investment devoted to their education. And when some privates turned to co-education, as Chicago did in the 1890s, the superior work done by the women actually frightened a university president who generally thought of himself as a bold and innovative leader.

Women's colleges, ranging from prestigious national ones like Wellesley and Smith to small and local (and often, denominational) schools can still be found. Many have resisted the push for co-education on the idea that they have a special tradition, and it seems quite likely that women continue to do better in some fields, especially science-related ones, when they are not set into a competitive situation with men. Loyal and wealthy alumnae have made the single-sex future of some of these colleges reasonably secure, in an uncertain world, and in a nation where about 90% of the institutions of higher learning are now co-educational, there seems to be a small but accepted niche for those who have bucked the current. There seems to be less sympathy, at least in liberal academic circles, for the Citadel, the military college in South Carolina, in its recent efforts to block the admission of women. Nor, as we know from the rapes at the Air Force Academy or the continuing attacks on Title IX provisions for equality regarding athletics, is even an old and good fight safely won beyond dispute and counter-attacks.[4]

2) Liberal arts and specialized training at the undergraduate level. The first colleges in Anglophonic North America were for men, of course, and they were mostly to offer humanistic education (the Classics) so young men could go forward into the ministry or law. The curriculum rested heavily on Greek and Latin authors, as well as Christian fathers and – as these schools were virtually all

Protestant – the heroes of the Reformation of the 16th and 17th centuries. Some science, as an extension of liberal arts or intellectual history, was covered, but it was not to train people for futures in the laboratory. This was a gentleman's education – useful as a start in life, perhaps of practical value for what he would do, perhaps not.

By the 1820s and 1830s a movement was underway, led by many of the old elite schools (with Amherst, Brown, Yale, and Harvard all involved) to open up the curriculum. It should be made broader, more practical, less focused on humane letters and classical education. This call for a broader education was eventually heeded by most American colleges, though it took about two generations before it was the accepted model. But from this struggle, or movement, or reform, came the accepted idea of college as having two components or segments: a couple of years of liberal arts and general education, and then a couple of years of more focused training in a more specialized area (be it Greek literature, mathematics, or New Testament studies). This is the working norm of almost all schools today, and even those with a strong bias toward engineering or fine arts try to meet it half-way. It is usually presented in terms of two years of general education, two of more specialized work as defined by a departmental or disciplinary major.

3) Mixing undergraduate education and graduate training. A four-year college offers a bachelor's degree, usually with the mix of work spelled out in #2. A university offers training, for more advanced degrees, in addition to the Bachelor of Arts (BA) or Bachelor of Science (BS). The idea of specialized training in a field, ultimately capped by a research project (as in a doctoral dissertation) also goes back to the mid-19th century, and it was imported from Germany to American universities after the Civil War, with the Johns Hopkins University in Baltimore taking an early lead. Established schools like Harvard and Yale now began to put significant resources into graduate training, in a wide variety of fields, and competition for scholars, for funding for labs, and for a list of faculty publications became another part of the contest waged by each school against its rivals.

Training for professional degrees in fields like law and medicine came around the beginning of the 20th century, not so much out of a quest for a research environment, as in response to a growing impetus toward national professional standards. The impetus was fueled more by the emergence of professional associations than by universities, but the latter quickly became integral links on the chain whereby doctors were expected to meet uniform standards of training and competence, lawyers to pass state bar exams, and so on for other comparable fields (such as dentistry or library science). Virtually all American universities offer a mix of undergraduate and graduate training, though some professional schools (e.g., Brooklyn Law School) confine themselves to a second or professional degree. Usually the same faculty teach students at all levels, though in practice research-oriented senior faculty have less to do with undergraduates than their junior or non-publishing colleagues. Stony Brook has always avoided a two-tier model for its faculty, but obviously my generalization about the hierarchy of work and prestige fits the bill to a considerable degree.

    4) Non-discrimination. Though Stony Brook's record of attracting minority students or faculty, or of developing programs designed to foster scholarship in such areas, or of fighting for a local community that was closer to color-blind is not a record to win awards, the University has made some effort to accommodate this aspect of its mission. The percentage of African-American students has hovered around 10% for decades; not very impressive, but near the national census figure. And though their success record is a checkered one, innumerable programs – mostly based on state or federal funding – have been developed to encourage applications and to support students who have come. But at least race as such has little explicit role in admissions, grades, or graduation rates. In a race conscious world, Stony Brook probably would get a decent grade for its role and its efforts, though it comes in well short of earning many honors.

    This quick run-through of Rosenthal's historical survey of higher education sets the table for a good deal of what follows regarding that peculiar aspect of the University – courses, teaching, and faculty research. I hope that much of what is to come flows in some fashion from this running start.

So from the perspective I have offered here, the academic creation of Stony Brook was primarily a matter of learning to wear basic cuts of fairly standard clothing. We were not inclined to cut strange fabrics into fancy or odd patterns: the Oyster Bay experience indicated that the State's approval, and its dollars, rested more on doing the conventional things well– and being seen to do them well – than on being different. This meant that the task of building a university only needed people, buildings, books, administrators, and a lot of money. Virtually any and every existing state university that could offer some sort of success story would be an instructive model, if we could decide what to imitate, and why. While we aimed at being an imitation of the University of California at Berkeley – which certainly sounded pleasant when it rolled off the tongue – any other school would have done as well. The real excitement, and the real novelty, was that it was so new; we were doing it for the first time. That was more than enough.

The pedagogical history of Stony Brook takes us from the Oyster Bay focus on interdisciplinary education to the conventional, state college/state university model. The Oyster Bay world was one in which a core of faculty taught a cluster of inter-disciplinary liberal arts courses to very small classes. This was an expensive and eccentric model, not destined for long life under the bright lights and budgetary competition of a research-oriented university. The transition to stand-up lecturing and to graduate training was also sign-posted by a shift in faculty identity; from being a part of the social science or humanities or natural science staff, one was now hired as an historian or political scientist or biochemist. The common syllabus for the Oyster Bay course, taught by an interchangeable staff, went out the window. In lieu of small discussion groups around a table, the new demographics, alongside the commitment to research, meant lecture classes and Teaching Assistants. Perhaps by the student's third year, when he or she had chosen a major, there might be an opportunity for smaller and more intensive courses, individualized work, and even an occasional discussion (or oral report).

There are some features peculiar to SUNY (and especially to Stony Brook, given its location) that also affect this conventional model. One is the SUNY-wide commitment that admits, to a four-year college or university center, any student who has earned the two-year degree (The AA: Associate of Arts) at a community college. As a result of this policy – commendable in political and social terms – many upper-level Stony Brook courses have larger enrollments than lower-level ones, due to the flood of transfer students now entering as juniors. But this inverted pyramid of student need is in contrast to an educational logic designed to lead one from the general and introductory to the specialized and labor-intensive. In addition, given our emphasis on the sciences, few who come from a community college are able to make the fiercely competitive grade. Thus there is a steady flow of students away from science, running largely in the direction of social science, secondary school teaching, and majors like history and English. I mention these issues, not to denigrate transfer students, but to indicate that their needs make it even harder to draw a firm line when explicating the break between liberal arts and career-oriented training - between culture and applied or market place skills.

The faculty and administration have gone back and forth on the rigidity, or flexibility, of liberal arts requirements. Each department has some discretion in defining its major within general boundaries. In the 1990s Stony Brook adopted a new set of regulations governing general education; the distribution of fields, the amount of work at upper levels, the need for written work regardless of major, and more of this sort. In keeping with national trends, we focused on basic skills (writing and math), and on exposure to the humanities and social sciences and with some introduction to the wide world: non-western traditions in addition to Euro-American ones, science and society, American pluralism, and the like. Of course, by the 1990s Stony Brook - like everyone else - was trying to cover both old strengths and new interests, and doing so with fewer faculty.[5] The idea behind the adoption of the DEC was to maintain or return to some basics and, simultaneously, to open the door for multiculturalism and a social content that moves away from Eurocentrism and its emphasis on dead white men[6]

This takes our tale to its near-past, to the curriculum of the 1990s and the present day-despite, so far, the worst wishes of our SUNY trustees. Let us take a longer look at our youthful, frivolous, and experimental days, and then pick up the evolutionary trail from there.

The rapid demise of the Oyster Bay curriculum and style of teaching signals how readily Stony Brook moved from the unorthodox and inter-disciplinary to the white bread and discipline-oriented. At Oyster Bay the liberal arts courses had been modeled on those of the University of Chicago, with an emphasis on the integration of the large fields of knowledge (the "big questions"). For example, the year-long course in Social Science incorporated sociology, psychology, and anthropology. This approach was replicated for the humanities (where the effort was to integrate art, music, and literature) and even, to some extent, in introductory science courses. But this was an expensive and labor-intensive way of teaching, and it depended on a faculty with a deep commitment to undergraduates and little concern for research and graduate training. That the college at Oyster Bay had been prone to factionalism and scandal hardly helped the cause. It turned out that the path to the platonic academy could run through a minefield. This exotic form of general education was what I had been exposed to (with very limited results) at Chicago, about a decade before I came to Stony Brook. Though in my undergraduate days I was fiercely loyal to the values and concepts of this curriculum, much of the actual efforts to integrate large and complex fields of inquiry passed over my head. Eventually I came to realize that I was more at ease when teaching focused historical material. Some of us have trouble dealing with the big questions; some reflection on the smaller ones is more than enough to keep us busy.

Somewhere on the pilgrimage from Oyster Bay to Stony Brook the old curriculum fell off the back of the truck, though interdepartmental or interdisciplinary courses had a few more years of life before the plug was finally pulled. An early Stony Brook bulletin (1964-65) shows their last flickers. For the Humanities; 12 lower-level courses, all taught by "staff:" the classical tradition, the

Judaeo-Christian tradition, and the philosophical classics. In the social sciences there were seven courses: topics in cultural and behavioral science, foreign policy, and teaching methods. The mix of physics and chemistry (on the track to the B.S. in Physical Science) was still in place, a vestige of the mission to train high school teachers. But the days of such courses, as of their core staff (and the accompanying round tables that accommodated about 20 students), were numbered. All gone by 1967; neither the courses nor the tables were ever mentioned again. It was like showing up at the Supreme Soviet under Stalin and asking if anyone had heard recently from Trotsky. Faculty from Oyster Bay mumbled about a sort of underground resistance, with esoteric passwords like "Hum II" (Humanities II), as early Christians drew the sign of a fish to indicate fellowship while under Roman persecution.

On the new campus, in keeping with the new mission for a comprehensive university, traditional departments, disciplines, and a commitment to research were the unquestioned order of the day. In 1964-65 there were 16 academic departments, plus the three holdover interdepartmental programs. And because the University was still so small, there were clusters rather than departments for Theater Arts, Biology, and Foreign Languages. The first eventually split into Art (and then into Art History and Studio Art), Music, and Theatre (note the affected spelling of "theater"). Biology (now, in 2003) consists of three departments, plus pharmacology (a bridge-unit with the HSC), and they carry heavy student demand due to the burden of the pre-med teaching. Of the languages, more below.

Because quick success and visibility were deemed so important, fitting the new University into the standard model of higher education made sense. This meant academic departments, each the home of a recognized discipline and with its own chair (appointed by the administration at first, though gradually election by faculty became the pattern). Generally an academic department houses and presides over a self-contained major, though the line between departments and smaller programs can be fluid. Nor was it just administrative conservatism that shaped this course of development. Hiring faculty is much easier when job descriptions are conventional and discipline-defined. Early hiring worked mostly through contacts (the old boy network); little emphasis in the 1960s on public ads or open searches (which really came in with Civil Rights legislation).[7] When the Oyster Bay faculty units were dissolved and people relocated within departments, fields like anthropology achieved an autonomous existence. The old liberal arts courses had placed no premium on the focused training needed to produce PhDs and the university faculty of the next generation.[8]

The power to grant a degree is conferred on a campus by The University of the State of New York (the State Regents). New degrees, like a Ph.D., or a new B.A., need official approval, though Stony Brook was able to set up a vast range of programs with little delay and little hostile inquiry. Most students work for the bachelor's degree, and the departmental majors and the various options converge at the final rendezvous - graduation day— though many will walk away with a B.S. (bachelor of science) or B.E. (bachelor of engineering). The authority to grant bachelors' degrees had carried over from the Oyster Bay mandate.[9] But the B.A. was only the foreplay for the new university's faculty (and administrators). A major goal of the new mission was to have graduate programs in place across the board– designed to train people for advanced work leading to masters' degrees (MA's) and doctorates (PhD's), and the march in this direction began early. An aspiring department needed a critical mass in terms of faculty before it could embark on this high road toward research and the prominence it was expected to bring, and external visiting committees came to campus to endorse the proposal for a PhD program or to indicate what was still needed for the fairy godmother's kiss.[10] To get the go-ahead there had to be adequate library holdings or laboratory facilities, and the program would need enough glamour to attract enough (subsidized) graduate students to fill its seminars. They in turn would be apprentices in their craft; a genteel way of saying they would also be TAs (teaching assistants) in the ever-growing undergraduate courses. We can chart the development of the graduate university by the dates when departments were authorized to move ahead. When Stony Brook opened its doors Physics, Chemistry, and Mechanical Engineering had already been cleared for the PhD, though it would not be until the late 60s that the first dissertations were being defended by the proud survivors of our semi-controlled experiment in higher education.

Though I was involved in this version of academic imperialism within my own department, the breath-taking pace of the entire process was harder to see, given the need to focus on each unit's programs and growth. Behind those first departments authorized to offer the PhD, the parade marched in close order drill: a PhD for Applied Math in 1963, Biology in 1964, History in 1965, Psychology and Electrical Engineering both in 1966, English, Math, and Material Sciences in 1967, Sociology and Earth & Space Sciences in 1968, Economics and Anthropology in 1969, and so forth. Seven more PhDs programs were authorized in the 1970s, along with a wide range of MAs – sometimes more than one MA program per department, as different streams of students and different levels of training were being accommodated.

In the lavish days of the 1960s a lot of money was available, through the office of the graduate dean, and departments were able to hand out fairly generous TAships to a large number of graduate students. A full assistantship covered tuition and gave a cash stipend, beyond that, of $2575 (and $2700 for advanced students). Most full-time doctoral candidates received some sort of support, a return for their presence and labor. Though the stipends were reasonable – as they had to be to attract students to a no-name university – they were soon to fall behind the rate of inflation and of those offered by our rivals and competitors. The lavish hand grew tighter; $2800 (and $2900 for second year students, and then $3000) was pretty thin by 1973-74, and even $7600 in 1988 was limited comfort for students hanging on in an expensive corner of the world. Articles about the high cost of living on Long Island were hardly news to those who had to drive a car, pay an inflated rent, and hope to eat. The rate for the early years of the 21st century - $11,200 - is, as always, a stretch; every department complains that it has trouble reeling in the best applicants when they receive more lavish offers from schools that we like to think we can top in terms of quality.[11]

How does a university grow? How does it go about filling

the buildings - faculty offices and labs - being built in anticipation of the waves of new hires? In one sense the answer is by replication. Faculty already on the ground (and hired at first by the administrators) were then authorized to bring in others, usually much like themselves. Senior faculty got on the phone, wrote letters, talked to friends (usually of their own sex and age-cohort), all in pursuit of promising graduate students and young colleagues whom they could interview and to whom – all going well – they would make an offer. It is a chancy and imperfect process - especially when so much emphasis is on untested futures - but trial and error can actually return a reasonable success rate, and even a newly-minted PhD comes with an academic track record through graduate school to cut down the element of guess work.

Despite my resolutions about limited hard data, a few numbers help convey the rapid rate of hiring that went on for about a decade.[12] Moreover, as so many of those new hires were just beginning their careers – coming as instructors and assistant professors – data about promotion rates show how quickly Stony Brook became a medium sized university with a good sized tenured faculty. In his report for 1966-67 John Toll said that 27 new professors had been hired; eight more had moved up by way of in-house promotion. In addition, there were eight new hires as associate professors and 10 such internal promotions. But the big number, and the most revealing one in terms of the youth of the faculty, was the 55 new assistant professors – truly an astounding number - along with six such promotions for lecturers or instructors already at Stony Brook. Also, down at the base of this pyramid were 38 new instructors, many waiting to move onto tenure-track lines upon completion of their doctoral dissertations.[13] Of course, this growth rate was soon to taper off; for 1974-75 we get a more conventional report. By then we were down to six new hires at professorial rank and 11 promotions to that level, 15 associate professors promoted from within plus 21 new hires, and (a mere) 41 new assistants, 31 lecturers.[14]

To put some comely flesh on these numerical bones I will look in more detail at some of the early glamour departments. First in line comes Physics, and we can cross the campus to look at English, for the Humanities, and then Psychology, for the social and behavioral sciences. What is of importance in offering these data and in drawing some comparisons? Certainly, departmental size and the identification of a particular focus for hiring and research can be considered. We also can look at the number of graduate degrees awarded. These departments were large, and their ability to maintain their status rested on their ability to attract faculty with name-recognition and to present a focus or a recognizable identity so as to claim a professional and/or public niche. In the latter regard the English Department may have lagged behind Physics and Psychology, though it had the advantage of a public outreach, as the gatekeeper and guardian of our literary classics.

For a university that was never to grow beyond medium size, how large is large? Physics began with several advantages, and it has always remained among the largest of Stony Brook's academic units. One advantage, in terms of attracting new faculty, was the proximity of Brookhaven National Laboratory, about 15 miles to the southeast. This facility was already famous for government-sponsored work in physics and other forms of non-classified research. Another advantage was the 1965 selection of John Toll, a physicist who came from the chair of a large physics and astronomy department at Maryland. And perhaps the most important of all was Toll's success in recruiting Chen Ning Yang as The Einstein Professor (a prestigious and high-paid professorship, only bestowed by the SUNY Trustees).

When Toll persuaded the 1957 Nobel co-laureate to come to the new campus, away from the Institute of Advanced Study in Princeton, he pulled off what stands out over the years as the most important single stroke in establishing Stony Brook's academic credibility. It gave the university an academic world figure. That C. N. Yang was already an active spokesman for science (and the first Chinese to win a Nobel Prize) all enhanced the value of this high-profile appointment; Yang's travels and policy statements would now be those of a Stony Brook faculty member.[15] But Yang hardly stood alone, whether it was in the Old Physics Building or, after 1971, the new Physics and Math Tower. In 1964-65 Physics already had 16 full-time faculty: seven professors, five associate professors, and four assistant professors.[16] By 1972 the numbers were, respectively, 29 (including Toll and Alex Pond, the EVP and former department chair), 12, and 15. By 1982, when departments on campus were pretty much at maximum size and leveling off, Physics numbered 42 full professors (with Marburger now added and Toll and Pond still on the books), nine associate professors, and seven assistant professors (plus 50 TAs). Such size and prominence were seen as the norm for Physics in those days. A high public profile, lots of money, and a powerful image meant an academic generation (after World War II) in which Physics was the undisputed lion-king. Since the building of the bomb in 1945, it had been THE field (along with astronomy, its close relative). SUNY Central publications, designed to laud state support for research, focused on Stony Brook. Both *SEARCH*, in 1977, and *SUNY Research*, in 1985 (issue 3/4), in its illustrated "Stony Brook/Fermilab: Superpartners in Physics," gave kudos to Stony Brook's most visible research unit. Those of us in other fields heard much about our colleagues across the campus; we were envious, though a good deal of it was true.

What about the Humanities and Social Sciences - English and Psychology? Within the Humanities, English was indeed the big fish. Its numbers, once more, show how quickly full growth was achieved. In 1967 there were 23 regular faculty in English and then as many as 41 in 1976-77; down a bit to 37 in 1987-89.[17] If English had no counterpart to C. N. Yang or the Institute for Theoretical Physics, there were big-name hires and reasonable support for public show-and-tell enterprises (such as poetry conferences and writers' workshops) that bring renown, sometimes beyond academic circles. To broaden or compliment the scholarly work of the main-line faculty, creative writers and literary critics were recruited to fill out the ranks. Much was made of the fact that Alfred Kazin and Louis Simpson were drawn to the new university, and the proximity to New York City was of value in hiring for the fine arts and music as well as for literature.[18]

If English departments are expected to lord it over the Humanities, it is not surprising that Psychology - straddling social science and hard science, with links to physiology, neurology, and statistics - is likely to be the largest department of its division.

Furthermore, it usually ranks among the more popular undergraduate majors, just as it is apt to lead the social sciences in external funding. Such funding is a boon to the university as a whole, but particularly to departmental recipients whose research grants are counted on to subsidize laboratories, doctoral and post-doctoral training, summer stipends, and travel and equipment – far beyond any stretch of the state budget. Psychology at Stony Brook did not mean talking to a shrink about your desire to kill your father and sleep with your mother (or vice versa). The emphasis, and the quick and noteworthy road to prominence, was by way of a focus on behavior modification, though there were also sub-groups in social, clinical, and experimental (with a bias toward biological research). Though the faculty in each unit went its own way in many of their endeavors, their collective size and weight made the Department a power to be reckoned with in university affairs.[19]

These mini-sagas of disciplinary and departmental growth and coming-of-age were being repeated, on a reduced scale, across the university. I could pick other departments and tell a similar tale, though with smaller numbers, fewer dollars, lesser names.[20] Many academic areas, both old and established ones and some that were newer and trendier, were easy to put on their feet, given the resources available. Across the land the 1960s were a golden age for academia, as young and not-so-young scholars were readily identified and lured to an emerging school that was receiving a lot of publicity (and paying respectable salaries and benefits).[21] Of these legions of new faculty, some stayed for the long haul while others just passed through. By the 1966-67 academic year, when Stony Brook might have been celebrating its 5th birthday, there were departments in most of the usual areas, as well as a few interdisciplinary programs (some destined to disappear), and such fused areas as Romance Languages. Higher education was still a coming field.

If we look at the changes between 1967 and 1983, we see that change, albeit at a slower pace, was a regular phenomenon. By 1983 Biology had undergone fission; separate departments of Biochemistry, Biology, Ecology and Evolution, and Neurobiology and Behavior. Another alteration of the academic landscape came from the creation of programs and inter-disciplinary units – lesser units than departments in size and autonomy and with a smaller investment in personnel and dollars. By 1983 there were clusters of courses in such fields as a liberal arts major, Judaic Studies, a business minor, classical languages and literature, Chinese, and various secondary education programs (still viable despite the retrenchment of Education), to pick from a larger list. Most of these units catered to undergraduates, as did such endeavors as the Federated Learning Community and an interdisciplinary program in the humanities.

In terms of basic structure the University had reached full growth by 1980, if not before. Of course, full growth in numerical terms does not end the tale of faculty life and academic development. In the next chapter I will turn to other activities that occupied these august and lofty minds; grants and fellowships, publication, and faculty governance and academic administration. A vow of silence regarding one issue of perennial faculty concern; parking.

With the growth of graduate studies in American universities came the need for internal organization and structure that could exercise oversight and yet not infringe on departmental and disciplinary autonomy. One common approach to this organizational or educational problem was to divide the disciplines into divisions: Social Science, Humanities and Fine Arts, Physical Science and Math, and Biology are the customary big four in a college of arts and sciences. Though this separation was primarily for administrative reasons, it did reflect the university's approach to the main categories of academic endeavor. In a small college there might be little need for such a formal separation; one dean or VP might preside over the entire scene. At Stony Brook the idea of lumping the departments into divisions was becoming useful, if not absolutely necessary, by the late 1960s, when size and complexity called for some intermediate level of organization. There were too many departments for one administrator to remember names and faces, let alone to keep track of what was going on.

Though on an individual basis faculty seem to do more or less whatever they please, from an administrative perspective the university is a hierarchical institution, and it runs – or is run - accordingly. A department is presided over by its chair, who reports to a dean, who reports to an academic vice president, who reports to the president. Faculty and departments can make deals with each other, but most decisions involving personnel or budget or the curriculum at least get cleared at a higher level – and few serious decisions fail to touch at least one of these three areas. A dean, working with the budget given him or her from above, makes decisions about or between the units of jurisdiction: new faculty positions, the allocation of TA lines, and the endless stream of special requests and favor-seeking that transcends departmental boundaries.

Academic departments are relatively fixed stars in the firmament; who ever heard of a university without an English or a Math Department, and I have already looked at some of the largest and strongest of the departments. But as well as fixed stars there are shooting stars and eclipsing variables, as we see if we turn to the foreign languages. Here we have a tale of organization and reorganization, over the course of 30 years, of changes that illustrate what I have said about the search for pragmatic arrangements, and of the need to adapt to changing currents of student demand, scholarship, and resources. If we turn to the 1964-65 bulletin we find the foreign languages to be one department. The faculty consisted of a full professor, two associates, five assistants, and eight instructors; the offerings: 16 courses in French, 16 in German, four in Italian, 10 in Russian, 12 in Spanish, and three in language-based teacher-training.[22] The heavy use of junior faculty – instructors, unlikely to stay for long or to be offered tenure-track positions - is common in the languages, where basic instruction demands a large staff for which the PhD does not seem essential.

How would the foreign language offerings of 1964-65 develop, as numbers grew and then stabilized, and as graduate programs developed? The answer is a mixed bag. In 1993-94, at the end of the Marburger years, there were departments of English (which we should think of as a language and literature field), of French and Italian, of Hispanic, and of German and Slavic (an oil and water mix to an historian, but not an unusual one). Hispanic Languages and Literature was so named to indicate a focus on a world touching both sides of the Atlantic (and elsewhere). But this is only part of the story. The languages mentioned are those of Europe (though hardly all those of Europe, or those of all of Europe). The Department of Linguistics, dealing with language as a process or phenomenon, had left the Humanities. It broke away from the English Department in the 1970s and eventually came to rest in Social and Behavioral Science. Nor is this the only example of linguistic diaspora. Korean, as language and literature, was covered by a sub-program housed within Comparative Studies (which itself had begun life as Comparative Literature). Chinese was offered through Social Science Interdisciplinary, a quirk explained by the home base of the instructor in the fallout from the retrenchment of Education. Hebrew and Yiddish, like Korean, were based in Comp Studies (in Judaic Studies: history and biblical literature as well as language). Yiddish had once been housed in German— a close match, philologically, if not culturally. Stony Brook had no classics department for Latin or Greek; a single part-time Latinist shouldered this burden. And beyond what I have listed, a student with sufficient energy could dig up instruction in Portuguese, Arabic, Japanese, and various Indian languages. But these languages (and literatures) - spoken by some perhaps 30-40% of humanity - had no regular home, no full-time faculty commitment. Exotic languages, they were often taught by faculty spouses, native-speakers who wound up at Stony Brook for obvious personal reasons. For a research university with a commitment to globalism, this is an uninspiring tale.[23]

If the languages are one of the most noticeable victims of wavering commitments and changing fashions - a case study in thwarted rather than in arrested development - we should note that other units were threatened with comparable fortunes, though they usually had better luck, more clout, and stronger friends. In the early 1970s there was a short-lived effort to combine math, applied math, and statistics; a division of mathematical sciences. This was quickly dissolved; math remained in Arts and Sciences, the other units survived in Engineering. Such matters are relatively esoteric. Students notice them when courses are not offered or are over-enrolled and registration is closed ("un-met demand" is the euphemism for the waiting list). Such problems are felt most keenly in fields where progress has to be lock-step onwards, as in languages or math; one cannot take second level calculus or French until the first has been completed, and so forth.

To some extent this story of limited commitment and confusion may reflect the second-class citizenship accorded the Humanities at a university that puts most of its grade-A eggs in the science basket. But this only part of the story; we can always feel sorry for ourselves. Some of the problems of these units are of their own making. Language departments, and perhaps humanities departments in general, seem particularly prone to internal divisions and disputes, often along predictable fault lines. With foreign languages, we have polarities of native speakers vs. "Yankees," language teachers vs. literary historians and critics, plus the competition between different languages, whether in the same or different units. Those who work on 17th century Spain may feel limited fellowship with colleagues studying 20th century German expressionism. Nor do I wish to single out the foreign languages; English and Philosophy were deeply divided in the 1980s and 1990s over the "culture wars:" post-modern and structuralist criticism, feminism, administrators who preferred heat to light, old vs. young, left vs. right, and more of the same.

There can be structural as well as personal reasons for academic problems. Some departments write by-laws for internal governance, either before a major blow-up or afterwards; they at least try to confront the issue, even if the wisdom is the bitter fruit of hindsight.[24] That language departments often had a high proportion of women, while being chaired by men, was hardly an irenic factor; harassment, discrimination, chauvinism and old-boy bonding had a long turn at bat. Furthermore, peer review in personnel cases is probably more subjective in soft fields than in empirical ones. Men in the language departments often treated their women colleagues with condescension; the women often felt - with justice - that they were paid less, pushed into more university service, given heavier teaching loads, and denigrated as serious intellectuals. Snobbery and a stereotype of the women as "mere" language teachers run deep.

Telling the story in this way, with such an emphasis on the

negative aspects of language teaching and language departments, undervalues the considerable volume of excellent (and even prize winning) scholarship that the departments have produced. Nor does it credit efforts to introduce innovative teaching methods, including an early exploration of the potential of "learning machines" (with some German department faculty making an effort to get Stony Brook towards the front of the line). The impulse to study foreign languages, let alone literature, in its original tongue, has diminished across the nation, despite the internationalization of business and trendy talk of a globalized economy. Enrollments in foreign languages have been in decline for years - a datum used to justify the reduction of faculty and graduate programs.[25] The Stony Brook situation was exacerbated because historical factors scattered the languages all over the place. They straddled two divisions and never had a single or collective lobby to argue on their behalf, at least not beyond their own faculty and a few allies. No one was ever in charge of all such teaching, and no one ever drew up a coherent plan for their present, let alone their future. Orphans and foster children rarely get their share when the goodies are handed out.

The creation and growth of departments is a guide to the way new areas of research are identified and given institutional life. In the creation or configuration of new units lies an opportunity to yoke new styles of intellectual fellowship - when we have the vision and resources to go in this direction. An example from Stony Brook's history that shows to advantage is the Department of Earth and Space Sciences (ESS). This unit came into existence in the mid-60s; the idea was to combine astronomy, oceanography, and geology, with strong links to material sciences in Engineering and eventually to Marine Sciences. Housed in its own building, with a library and museum, ESS was a rather bold educational step. The astronomy unit– with strong links to physics - was very large in comparison to astronomy at much larger universities. Old disciplinary boundaries were to be leaped, perhaps in a single bound, and ESS's team approach (also reflected in its undergraduate major) was well suited to the study of our planet: under it, upon it, and above it. ESS was largely put together by a founding-father chair, Ollie Schaeffer, a geologist who had come from Brookhaven Lab. And for many years, at least as it appeared to an historian, this strange ménage a trois seemed to work.[26]

So even in most hectic days of growth, when expansion and quick results were at a premium, there was some room for experimentation. If early priorities demanded departments with traditional labels and a hook on instant recognition, the university did recognize the value of new departments and new majors – along with a wide range of minors - as the years rolled along. The College of Engineering moved as the currents carried it: from its original four departments it came, by the late 1990s, to house no fewer than 10, including the pseudo-business programs of Harriman College.[27] Two large catch-all majors - Social Science Interdisciplinary and Multidisciplinary Studies (formerly, Liberal Studies) – served as a welcome and necessary home for hundreds of students who found no comfortable departmental major. And to indicate faculty interests and entice students toward a smidgen of unorthodox work, minors have mushroomed in such diverse fields as dance, Korean studies, Journalism, Judaic Studies, Child and Family Studies, Middle Eastern Studies, Optics, and many more. Some of these are popular and draw well; others are just paper entities in the bulletin, often to the bewilderment of interested students.

Other aspects of faculty life remain to be discussed in the next chapter. But if we pause to take stock, we can offer some judgements and even distribute an occasional compliment. Where did Stony Brook stand at various points along the way? One rather harsh way of assessing this mid-way progress – and we are always midway between the start and some subsequent point— is to think about what the University does not have, provided we don't go overboard. This approach does emphasize opportunities missed or roads not taken. It may be less than supportive and it relies heavily on wisdom gained after the fact. Still, a tally of missed opportunities helps pinpoint weak spots in the academy and in the political economy and master-planning of a state university. Where might a different vision or different chemistry of administrators and faculty and state resources and community interests have taken Stony Brook?

One glaring black hole is that of professional schools and other alternatives to the arts and sciences. From the heyday of aircraft production by Grumman and Republic in WW II through the end of the space race in the 1980s, Long Island was one of the main centers of air and aero-space production, only behind California and Boeing in Seattle. Grumman Aircraft had been the Island's main industrial employer for decades, with a World War II workforce that ran over 25,000 men and women, working in two or three shifts a day. At first, of course, there were airplanes: the Grumman "hellcat" and other models used by the armed forces. When the national goal became the domination of space, components of vehicles that rolled across the moon said "made on Long Island." Given this, the failure (or inability?) of Stony Brook to build a major college of Engineering leaps out as a big-time missed opportunity. This may go back to the political balance that shapes the contours of higher education: Columbia University and Brooklyn Polytechnic, and lesser technical schools, cast a watchful eye on growth in the public sector and colleges of engineering are not sprinkled casually across the map. In addition, physicists tend to look down on engineers, and the most important voice among the Stony Brook faculty was that of a Nobel laureate who presided over an Institute of Theoretical Physics. One may wonder how seriously great theoreticians take the aspirations of engineers. Our culture, since the Greeks, has valued pure science over applied.

The absence of various kinds of professional schools is not hard to understand; Stony Brook came late, costs were prohibitive, rival schools easily upset. Hence, no law school, no business school (though Harriman College and the Economics Department, with an Institute of Decision Sciences, have tried to fill this supposed vacuum, though as yet with little success). Both law and business received the endorsement of numerous study groups, and at one time there was even a budget for law journals and court reports. Nor were serious steps ever taken to do much about the oft-professed concern for journalism, though some flirtation has continued from time to time. As the years pass the value of training students for print journalism, as we now call it, has been superseded by a focus on electronic media, now well beyond Stony Brook's expertise and budget. A few courses taught by adjunct faculty in English are about the sum total of any commitment to training students for careers in the media.

Ethnic studies programs are barometers of political ideology and campus identity, rather than of professional and academic necessity. Over the years the University has blown hot and cold about putting resources into such areas, and minors– rather than departments— have been the usual response. The variety of programs that have appeared over the years usually rested on a small number of faculty plus adjuncts and friends from other units. Neither budgetary support, nor scholarly sympathy, nor graduate recruiting can be depended upon, and these are all essentials in elevating a program from the politically correct to the academically self-sustaining. There was a program in Puerto Rican studies in the early 1970s. When it was eliminated, as a budget casualty, I was dismayed to find out how little outcry there was.[28]

The great exception, in terms of survival and eventually of elevation, has been Africana Studies. This began in the 1970s as Black Studies, more in response to student pressure than to faculty or administrative sympathy. Racism and collegial condescension were serious obstacles, and both the academic and the social sides of the matter had to be addressed. AFS never got much support; few faculty, limited resources. Despite the presence and even the chairmanship of Amiri Baraka (Leroy Jones), the most significant creative writer to serve on the faculty, AFS was allowed to withdraw from mainstream campus life, though the courses always drew a good mix of students in terms of color and background. An external review of 1999 and some new hires fueled a successful campaign for elevation to departmental status, and the tale may be one of those with a happy ending.

Another possible direction for growth and inter-disciplinary work – mostly one not taken – was area studies. During the Cold War, with its heady days of government funding, such programs brought money to campuses and drew together faculty from the Humanities and the Social Sciences. Perhaps because of the need to build strong departments, these inter-departmental endeavors rarely were pushed with any enthusiasm. Since we eventually learned how much of area studies was subsidized as a personnel pipeline to and for the CIA, Stony Brook was probably fortunate that it never went in that direction. Nor was the potential of the Instructional Resources Center ever realized, for all the 1960s talk about technology and teaching; a wired lecture hall, built-in audio-visual gadgets, and whatever gimmicks would help supplement an older methodology, that of reading and writing. The planning was expensive smoke and the building has long been a home of mixed uses and casual tenants (including a retail computer store). "Smart" classrooms have never been a high Stony Brook priority.

But this litany of what Stony Brook did not develop should not set the tone. Common sense tells us that no university – let alone one built on the run and relying on public funding - is going to match the programs, resources, and traditions that come with centuries of big checks and powerful friends.[29] All faculty push for new departures of value to their own agenda, whether this is a subscription to *Norfolk Archaeology* (for me) or a linear accelerator (for the experimental physicists). We all cast a jealous eye on the grants, endowments, and initiatives at other universities, as well as elsewhere at Stony Brook. But while the menu cannot be changed on a daily basis, over the longer haul there is considerable turn over of educational offerings, carrying away some of the old, bringing in some of the new.

Clearly, there has been a lot to do in 30 or 35 or 40 years. Some of it has been done; some of it even has been done well. Other things - well, we didn't get around to them. And for some of those schemes and plans on the drawing board - truth is, we never will. But in life we never get around to everything - whether we refer to personal or institutional matters. The original SUNY motto was "let each become all he is capable of." In those words a noble dream is tersely summarized. Reality, as we look back on 40 years of ups and downs, may be a different story. But that too is a history we have helped to shape.

(Endnotes)

1. This generalization about lowest bidding may not pertain to the newly redone central mall, completed in 2000 with a fountain and a spill-way. Supposedly the project cost something in excess of $3 million.

2. Founding a new campus is a lost art. Between 1870-1899 about 430 new colleges and universities came into existence in the United States. The number fell to 323 for the years between 1900-1929, and between 1930 and 1959 it was down to 116. Since 1970 there have been very few new universities; most growth now comes from upgrading, from small to large, from two-year to four-year, from college to university, and so forth. It is a measure of New York's early commitment to SUNY that, in addition to Stony Brook, there were new colleges founded at Old Westbury on Long Island, and at Purchase in Westchester County. In addition, there was the commitment to build Empire State College: see next note.

3. Though Stony Brook did become conventional in its basic undergraduate curriculum, the SUNY system maintained a commitment to diversity in form and function. The four-year college at Old Westbury was founded for inter-disciplinary ends, and after a good many growing pains (comparable to the Oyster Bay days of Stony Brook) it turned instead to attracting the "traditionally bypassed," which meant students of color and older students. The College at Purchase emphasized the performing and studio arts. Empire State College, the "college without walls," has its learning centers (either on other campuses or in rented space) all across the state. Since it was started around 1970 its has delivered by way of individual learning contracts and student-tutor sessions rather than classes.

4. If early yearbook pictures show classes of substantially more men than women, a fully-grown Stony Brook was pretty close to gender parity. In 1974 the University indicated an enrollment of 7670 men, 6523 women (or 46% of the total); for 1984, 8022 men and 6593 women (45%), and for 1994, 7648 men against 7028 women (48%).

5. The current version of the DEC shows the effort to cover as many bases as possible. Students must do work in or be exposed to various skill and culture areas (such as writing, interpreting texts, mathematical and statistical reasoning, and understanding the fine and performing arts); then there is "disciplinary diversity," which means selecting several courses in humanities, social science, etc; finally, "expanding perspective" through courses in cultural awareness, diversity, the implications of science and technology, the world beyond Europe, etc. There are not many ways of getting out of these requirements, though they are trimmed a bit to fit some of the most cluttered departmental majors.

6. In the late 1990s the SUNY Trustees began attacking the multiculturalism incorporated into the DEC, as I have already indicated. Though the trustees call for a return to basic (conservative) U.S. history was aimed at all SUNY campuses, Stony Brook took a commendably hard line in resisting this assault on academic freedom. As of this writing, the "enemy" has been held at bay but the war goes on. It is not unusual in the world of public higher education for state trustees to launch such an attack, though it was without precedent in the generation-plus history of SUNY.

7. The 1971 Faculty Handbook set out fairly straight instructions for hiring procedures, first within the unit conducting the search and then in steering choice forward (or upward). In this official advice the emphasis is on executive responsibility and the chain of command; internal democracy was not a point of much concern.

8. Small units could not really offer graduate work, or, if somehow authorized (perhaps when they had been larger), were often hard

pressed to cover their commitments. In 1990 the full-time faculty of some of the smaller units in Arts & Sciences ran as follows: Africana Studies, 4 faculty; Anthropology, 14 (and in trouble: saved by a de facto merger with primatologists and anatomists in the HSC): German and Slavic, 12 (and later merged with French and Italian): Linguistics, 8 (and hanging on, with a PhD): Religious Studies, 7 (and an odd mix, eventually set into Comparative Studies). As indicated elsewhere, the main campus faculty had reached 685 by 1972 and it has stayed at or slightly above the 700 mark ever since.

9. A university offers a wide range of degrees, though most graduates are covered by a few big umbrellas. The graduation program of May, 1990 lists candidates for the Bachelor of Arts (BA), Bachelor of Engineering (BE), Bachelor of Science (BS), Master of Arts (MA), Master of Arts in Liberal Studies (MALS: the degree from Continuing Education [CED], to become the School for Professional Development[SPD]), Master of Music (MMus), Master of Science (MS), and Doctor of Philosophy (PhD). In addition there are the degrees granted in HSC (MD, DD, MSW, etc).

10. When the History Department was being considered for this sort of "promotion" in 1964-65 the Dean arranged for 3 external examiners, one each in U.S., European, and Latin American history. The first said it was wonderful, the second took a look and said maybe, the third confined himself to a telephone interview and then gave us thumbs-up. On this basis we were authorized to declare ourselves a Ph.D. granting Department (though the first degree was not actually awarded until 1971– when there were 4 or 5 - such being the rate of progress in the humanities.

11. When the graduate programs were launched, around 1966-67, a TA ship paid $2575 (plus a full waiver of tuition). Though fairly healthy for the day, this stipend (if it can be so characterized) hardly went up to match inflation or academic competition. In 1974-75 it was only $2800: $2900 for 2nd year students, and then $3000 thereafter, up to the regulation four years of support. In 1980 it

might be up to $5137, to quote the bulletin, but most TAs were getting something around $3600. In 1986 it was still pushing $6000, and by 1998-2000 it had risen to $9900. Poorer departments, with many grad students but a limited number of TA lines, were often driven to dividing the TA lines, so half of the stipulated amount was all the paycheck reflected.

12. In chapter 6 I look at the size of the full-time faculty, over the decades.

13. The pendulum swings both ways; as well as the new hires and promotions, Toll reported one retirement and 36 resignations. Retirement only became common in the late 1980s, when many of the older new hires of the 1960s were now in their 60s. In 1991 mandatory retirement because of age was abolished in the public sector by act of Congress. Nevertheless, few faculty have stayed beyond 70, though the big pensions that made retirement so easy may be a thing of the recent past, depending on the stock market.

14. Far down the road, in 1986, there 35 new hires in Arts and Sciences, 10 in Engineering, 7 in Harriman and Marine Sciences, plus 2 promotions to distinguished professorships, 15 to professor, 21 to associate professor (and 2 librarians granted tenure and promoted). No tally given for resignations, retirements, and terminations.

15. Chen Ning Yang (1922-). The first Asian to win a Nobel Prize in Science, he received his PhD in 1948 (University of Chicago) and had been a professor at the Institute of Advanced Study at Princeton since 1955 when he agreed to come to Stony Brook. The Nobel Prize, shared with C. D. Lee, came in 1957, for work on the "nonconservation of parity in weak reactions."

16. As I indicate elsewhere, the numbers for Physics were about double those for History. Given how many more undergraduates take history courses than physics courses, we can see from the start how scientific research, accompanied by external funding and the

glamour of mystery, helped set the priorities. Not a complaint; just a reflection on the world.

17. English is virtually always the largest department in the Humanities. In 1967, of 34 faculty there were 6 full professors and 7 associates; in 1976, it was 40 in all, 16 and 14 at the higher ranks; in 1987, 39 faculty and 15 and 13 at the top two levels. In 1998 the Department listed 8 professors, 9 associate professors, 3 assistant professors, and 2 lecturers (a tally that does not count President Kenny but does include two professors who were really tied up with their duties in the Writing Center and The Humanities Institute). We might compare English with Philosophy, larger at Stony Brook than at most schools our size. In 1966-67 Philosophy had 9 faculty members (4 at senior ranks), 23 in 1975 (14 seniors), and around full growth at 26 in 1987 (25 now senior and with tenure).

18. When Tom Flanagan came to Stony Brook in 1978 he lived locally, as did Louis Simpson, whereas other distinguished writers (June Jordan: New York City, and Amiri Baraka [Leroy Jones]: Newark) were commuters, which cut their involvement and accessibility. Baraka was a faculty member of Africana Studies (which he chaired for a while in the 1980s); neither English nor Theatre offered a joint appointment to this towering figure of American literature. When June Jordan died (spring 2002), her substantial obituary in the New York Times did not mention her Stony Brook years, whereas much was made of her senior status at the University of California, which came after her Stony Brook years.

19. Psychology was comparable in size to English. In 1967 the department had 8 senior faculty out of 15; in 1976, 37 seniors out of 52; in 1987, 36 seniors out of 42. For comparison, we can look at Economics:10 faculty in 1966 (with four senior faculty); 20 faculty in 1975, with 14 seniors; in 1987, 16 seniors out of 28.

20. To follow the saga of these 3 departments: at the graduation in 1976 Physics presented 17 PhDs, and 16 in 1989; English, at those

same ceremonies, presented 15 and then 21 new doctorates; Psychology, 18 and 26.

21. Various national bodies and publications put out rankings, as do sport writers and coaches. From early on - for whatever such evaluations are worth - the Physics Department stood very high, and the ratings show how much harder it is for humanistic fields to break into the upper ranks. In 1986 national ratings put Physics at 11th place on the charts, Sociology at 14th, Psychology at 25th, Math at 18th, Geoscience at 17th, English at 29th, Computer Science at 19th.

22. The catalogue listed faculty for the courses in what now seems very quaint language: Elementary French, for example, was taught by "Mr. Mills and staff," which meant Leonard Mills and whoever else was on hand when the course had to be scheduled.

23. To compare Stony Brook's record to its disadvantage, in 2002-3 the School of Oriental and African Studies at the University of London advertised instruction in 59 languages (and all from the geographical range indicated by the College's name) on posters in the London Underground.

24. Departmental by-laws are for internal guidance, having no currency beyond the faculty who made the compact. My department wrote by-laws in the early 1970s after a terrible split warned us that we had to agree on some basics (such as a chair not being eligible for consecutive terms) if we wanted to be able to function as a unit.

25. In 1998 the Dean of Arts and Sciences ordered a merger of the foreign language departments (other than Hispanic Languages and Literature). So in 1999 there was now a department of European Languages and Literature, embracing French, Italian, German, and Slavic, and the university's one Latinist (who had moved over from Comparative Studies).

26. Astronomy is now joined with Physics, and students can study Planetary Sciences. Majors are available in Marine Sciences, Atmospheric and Oceanic Sciences, Environmental Studies, Geoscience, and other variations on the old ESS union.

27. In 1963 the College of Engineering consisted of departments of Electrical Sciences, Material Sciences, and Thermal Sciences (plus a computing center staff). In 1964-65 Engineering Analysis was added. In 1989-91 the College (CEAS) covered Applied Math and Statistics (24 faculty), Computer Sciences (27), Electrical Engineering (22), Material Sciences (18), Mechanical Engineering (25), and Technology and Society (11).

28. Early in the 21st century we have acquired a unit dedicated to Asian-American studies, in keeping with the $25 million gift of Charles Wang. However, putting this unit on firm academic feet is more than the Administration (or faculty) have yet been able to manage.

29. Being a new university is not all bad news. In recent years research, much of it conducted by Yale graduate students, has revealed Yale's complicity in and profits from the slave trade. Stony Brook, so far, has only sold off monopoly rights for vending machines and for related advertising and signing to Coca Cola, which in comparison seems a venial sin, and probably not one to return anything like a comparable return on the investment.

CHAPTER FIVE
Building the Academy,
Part II: What Else Do Professor Do?

Academic departments are hardly the whole story of faculty life, central though they may be. We can look at other areas where the history of the university can be explored in terms of ripples (or waves) running outward from a faculty center. Many are areas that students, alumni, and the general public rarely know or care about, which may be just as well. There is research and publication - the famous or infamous "publish or perish" hammer of the modern university. The curriculum - not very sexy, but the master or mistress to whom every student is in bondage – gets another touch. And faculty governance, at least at some critical moments in Stony Brook's dramatic past; this can serve to remind us that the ivory tower is not all that disconnected from "the real world."

Research and publication are terms that roll easily off the tongue (or the computer screen), and in their dire guise of publish or perish they stand as a pair of grim alternatives that stare every young faculty member in the face. Students mostly know of this world when they are told that such activities compete - in faculty focus and university resources - with undergraduate teaching and student-oriented commitments. Some truth, no doubt, and a lot of exaggeration.

What is academic research, and what can we say to explain the energy spent on the process and the publications that result therefrom? The idea behind research is that knowledge - applied or theoretical, a new breakthrough in virology or a different way of looking at a Picasso - is one of the special products or preserves of an institution devoted to higher learning. Universities – or so we like to think - are not meant to stand in place just so they can transmit accepted ideas and long-received techniques. Higher education is meant to be more than mere packaging, or pre-packaging, and delivery. Universities are created and subsidized to train students and to advance the frontiers of our understanding of the world - be it the natural universe or the socially-constructed one in which we live. Such work demands time, dedication, and acquired skills, all set within a nurturing environment. And, for the most part in our society, this nurturing environment is the heavily subsidized institution of the university.

The huge costs of and the physical facilities demanded by research, especially for scientific research, are supported to a limited extent by the state; a regular portion of the annual budget. However, state funding rarely comes to 50% of what it costs to teach undergraduates, let alone to train graduate students and conduct research. So to keep the research engine running there have to be grants from the government, private donors (mainly industry - the profit or private sector), and non-profit foundations. Though the costs behind lab research are the most obvious and the highest, scholarly endeavor in the humanities also requires time, travel, libraries (and London is preferable to NYC), and contact with peers at other institutions. Such humanistic research might be inexpensive compared to high energy physics or biochemistry, but each discipline is also competing within itself. A University tries to provide a comfortable environment for all fields of research, as their cultures and the endless chase for hot topics dictate. The National Endowment for the Humanities (NEH) may be but a sapling beside the mighty oaks of the National Science Foundation or the National Institute of Health (NSF and NIH), but subsidization for research is needed at many levels.

Academic research catches the public eye when it is dramatic or of obvious economic value or, perversely, when it is at its most esoteric and remote extreme. Usually it is somewhere in between, though Stony Brook has had its share of cutting-edge moments. A professor of chemistry (Paul Lauterber) played a major role in the development of magnetic resonance (MRI); this brought him a good deal of kudos and, eventually, an offer from Illinois in 1985 that was too good to turn down, and a Nobel Prize in 2003. A breakthrough in particle physics - the search for the top quark– was led by Paul Grannis of Physics and his team, working at the Fermi Lab outside Chicago. This too made the science sections of serious newspapers. Important work in hot fields in the Life Sciences, providing new information regarding AIDS, breast cancer, organ and tissue transplants, Alzheimer's disease, lyme disease, recombinant DNA, and reproductive technology, helps justify the costs of basic research and a teaching hospital. Nor is the University's public relations office shy about blowing our collective horn.

At the other extreme, in terms of whetting public interest, *The New York Times* gets considerable pleasure from attending a meeting of the Modern Language Association and covering the most esoteric papers; transgressive sexuality in Milton's "Comus," or a Marxist reading of Victor Hugo's winter imagery. But most academic research - like most detective work - is a process of accumulating details to set against insights, guesses, and lucky dips into cultural and social sources and/or the structure and behavior of the natural world. We hope that the theoretical and the empirical - the general and the specific – converge to offer a satisfactory (and replicable) synthesis or solution. Then comes publication–announcing ones findings and contributing to the current state of the question.

Except when an occasional professor makes the news, or when he or she assigns something he or she has authored, undergraduates have little direct contact with faculty research.[1] A striking characteristic of most such work is that it is, in direct terms, unpaid. It is part of the job, an expectation the faculty accept in return for light teaching loads, the opportunity to train graduate students, and tenure. This is in contrast to SUNY's 4-year colleges, where there is more teaching and fewer demands about publication (though they too are ratcheting up the standards). Some scientists and engineers, and such applied social scientists as economists and sociologists, do work as consultants, and they expect to earn fees for their extra-mural expertise. This additional income can run from the minimal (reading a manuscript for a university press) to the exceedingly handsome, though only for a very few faculty are these extras a serious supplement to the state pay check. There are supposed to be limitations on how much outside activity faculty can engage in, in terms of time, if not income. Lucrative patents that result from work done in University labs, on publicly funded grants, raise tricky legal questions, though few medieval historians are lucky enough to have such problems when they fill out their tax returns.[2]

Some faculty turn to writing a textbook; this might be instead of publishing "original" research, or alongside it. In a few lucky instances these texts get widely adopted; the sale of thousands of volumes in five or ten years means a significant side income. And once in a while a creative writer, like Tom Flanagan of the English Department, produces a string of high-quality historical novels that win prizes and also get snapped up by the general public in airports and supermarkets.[3] But these are odd cases; a few hundred dollars from royalties, a few hundred for reading manuscripts, and perhaps another few hundred for a talk or two is a fair year for most of us in the humanities and social sciences.

Like all serious universities that take pride in faculty research prowess, Stony Brook brags about publications, prizes, fellowships, and research dollars. In John Toll's yearly reports to the SUNY Chancellor he included an item-by-item listing of faculty publications. We can take a look at what was reported from our old friends - Physics, English, and Psychology, for 1966-67. For English, 13 faculty were listed, with an emphasis in those days on creative writing and belle lettres: a novel by Jack Ludwig, an article in *Life* by Jeremy Larner on Wilt Chamberlain, essays by Alfred Kazin in *The Reporter, Commentary*, and *The New York Review of Books;* for traditional scholarship, Richard Levin in journal of *English Literary History,* among others. Physics, of course, was mostly represented by short and specialized articles: C. N. Yang in Physical Review, and others in *Bulletin of the American Physical Society, Physical Review Letters* (for fast breaking items), and *Nuclear Physics*, to name some of the outlets for the 24 faculty who were listed. Psychology reported 13 faculty, and again most of the work was in specialized journals, rather than in books or general presentations for the lay public that thinks psychology helps you cope with life: *Journal of Abnormal Psychology, Journal of Consulting Psychology, Psychonomic Science,* and more of the like.

As the university grew the point of tabulating this data diminished. In a hard-nosed sense scholarly publishing was, after all, what faculty are paid to do. That so many of them did so was gratifying but hardly out of the ordinary. In the early 1980s Jack Marburger, in an effort to laud scholarly achievements and boost faculty morale, initiated an annual "authors and editors" reception. Faculty who had written or edited a book or a scholarly journal contributed a copy for a display (and then donated it to the library, if they chose); scholarly articles were too numerous to merit a free drink. Faculty who met the standard of publication were named in a glossy brochure and invited to a wine and cheese reception in their honor.

The last such event held on Marburger's watch was that of 1994 (for work produced in 1993). The brochure prepared for the occasion listed 105 separate items; 60 books (written, edited, or translated), 45 scholarly journals edited by Stony Brook faculty. For the first time the list included recordings and art exhibitions - in recognition of diverse achievements and a widening definition of "to publish." While many publications were appropriately obscure, much was made of the fact that John Gagnon of Sociology co-authored *The Social Organization of Sexuality*, a follow-up on the famous Kinsey Report of the late 1940s. Gagnon's book received attention in national media like *Time* and *U.S. News and World Report,* as public interest in what Americans were (and were not) doing in bed pushed sales and whetted national curiosity. My own role, as co-editor of *Medieval Prosopography*, got me some munchies but little by way of media attention.

Counting publications is a guide of limited value regarding the impact or shelf life of scholarly work, and scientists rarely produce full-sized books except as texts and general surveys. Books vary widely in quality and impact, and they are written for different purposes. Textbooks, apart from the monetary attraction, can be thought of as a contribution to pedagogy and the classroom, though many might think this a charitable assessment. Years of research can result in a difficult monograph, published at a loss by a university press in a run of 400 or 500 copies. Some consolation for those of us in humanistic fields is at least that our works do not age as quickly as those of our scientific colleagues, or so we like to say.

We can look at three distinguished faculty members, as they are listed in the Melville Library's on-line catalogue, to get an idea of the scope and variety of academic contribution. I take C. N. Yang, Nobel Prize in Physics, Louis Simpson of English, a Pulitzer Prize winner for poetry, and Robert Sokal, a biologist and member of the National Academy of Sciences. Numbers of publications here reveal more about the culture of their disciplines than about the eminence or productivity of the men (and the numbers I report may also reflect short-comings or eccentricities in the catalogue). C. N. Yang, beyond doubt Stony Brook's most distinguished faculty member, is listed for nine items. The language of theoretical physics is a compact language; *Yang's Elementary Particles: A Short History of Some Discoveries in Atomic Physics* (1961) presents his 1959 Vanuxum Lectures and runs to 68 pages. The *Weyl Lectures of 1985*, where he appears as one of three authors, runs to 119 pages in all. Only his *Selected Papers, 1945-80* (1983) is a full-length book, bringing together his major work as published over a third of a century, and such a collected volume would not be of lasting interest except for a scientist of such distinction. Clearly, major contributions in science do not depend on the number of pages and concision is an integral part of the game.

Louis Simpson, by contrast, is listed for 52 "records" in the electronic catalogue. This includes many volumes of his own poems (including numerous editions of collected works as he continued to write and his overall corpus grew over the years), criticism, and video lectures on major works of English and American literature. From *At the End of the Open Road* (1963) through several volumes published in 1995, Simpson - now retired, as a distinguished professor from the English Department - remained productive. A teaching career that ran to literary criticism as well as creative writing was very different from one that trained a small number of young physicists, in terms of public impact and mode of presentation.

Robert Sokal, from Ecology and Evolution, was an early leader in the use of statistics for taxonomy and classification. His nine "records" in the library catalogue run, chronologically, from his 1963 *Principles of Numerical Taxonomy* through his 1987 revision of his more general (popular?) 1973 volume, *Introduction to Biostatistics*. In this case, his scholarly contributions were a mix of short technical papers and more general work in which an advanced methodology that he helped develope was now explicated and applied to relevant data. Sokal did not rest on the laurels of just his specialized papers, and yet without them as the foundation for his expertise he was not likely to have turned to the production of his larger publications.

So we see that many roads lead to Rome. To look in a different direction, one common way of gauging collective faculty achievement is to aggregate the major prizes and fellowships collected across the campus. Admittedly, this tally combines grants awarded for proposals that might never see the light of day alongside honors marking long careers of sustained achievement. But at least the various fellowships are won in direct competition with scholars from other schools, year by year, and therefore they - like books that catch the public eye or scientific discoveries reported in *The New York Times* – seem legitimate trophies to mount on the wall.

Prestigious fellowships and awards are spread across the academic spectrum; Guggenheim Fellowships, among the most glamorous of all, have gone to Stony Brook faculty in most departments of the university. Many scholars have been subsidized and honored with fellowships from the NEH, the NSF, the Social Science Research Council, the American Council of Learned Societies, Fulbright Fellowships (from the government), and the like. The list of private, industrial, and governmental foundations and granting agencies - all with something to give away - is so vast that merely to list them fills a reference volume. Scholars in the humanities and other soft fields usually are content to apply for a fellowship, an award that subsidizes a leave or supplements a sabbatical. Scientists, as we can imagine, require a good bit more than just a salary supplement; they rarely apply for less than a six-figure grant. Scientific research - even in a low-tech field like math, where chalk and a board once sufficed - now requires access to high speed computers, and social scientists who do quantitative work often qualify for grants of this sort, alongside their big-budget colleagues.

Because the sciences are competitive and fast breaking, serious research is usually accompanied by money for travel. Why pass up a chance to attend conferences, arrange consultations, and visit friends. In addition, ever since the advent of big science on the Manhattan Project, much of the work is done by teams - sometimes (as in high energy physics) running to dozens of researchers, from the seniors who obtain the grants down to flocks of technicians, post-doctoral researchers, and graduate students now being blooded for what awaits them. Obviously, work at this level is beyond the university's funding capacity, and support on this scale has to come from the Department of Energy or the NSF. Such considerations add up to a fairly firm line between the sciences and the humanities.[4]

When Stony Brook marked its 25th anniversary in 1982 scorecards of faculty accomplishments and honors were compiled for their public relations value. At that time Stony Brook boasted of an Einstein Professor (C. N. Yang), four Distinguished Professors (plus one in HSC), 32 winners of the Chancellor's Award for Excellence in Teaching, plus recipients of other SUNY honors. In addition, there were already 51 Guggenheim fellows (at some time or other in their careers), plus 40 Sloan fellows from math and physics. Robert Cess of Mechanics had been awarded the Heat Transfer Memorial Award of the American Society of Mechanical Engineers, and Lawrence Alloway of the Art Department had received the Frank J. Mather Award of the College Art Association - to pick two colleagues, at random, from a long list of those tapped for achievement. Every university makes much of these matters, and regardless of how much politicking lies behind an award for distinguished teaching or service, it is better to have faculty win such honors than not. Some 20 years after this 1982 list we could virtually double the numbers (though without an Einstein Professor), and most faculty collect some such golden apples during their careers. My own record is about par for the course: a Fulbright as a grad student and then grants from the Social Science

Research Council and the NEH, while at Stony Brook, plus a batch of minor fellowships and grants-in-aid. While I certainly did not get everything I applied for, the grants I received were especially valuable when I was beginning a new research project.

External monies awarded to SUNY faculty are paid by the granting agency to the Research Foundation, the branch of SUNY authorized to receive and disburse external revenues. Even when "the check is in the mail," it does not go directly to the faculty recipient, the principle investigator (the PI) who applied for the grant or fellowship. The amount actually needed by the PI - say $1,000,000 for a large engineering project - is inflated by institutional overheads into a figure that may be almost twice that. Then, if the money is awarded, overhead is skimmed off by the university. Some of it covers benefits for the team, if not for the PI. And some of it goes into general university coffers and may wind up as travel money for the music faculty or summer grants for minority students, even while the grant itself had been to study moon rocks or a cockroach's memory. The institutional overhead greases many wheels.

The Stony Brook branch of the SUNY Research Foundation, in conjunction with the Graduate School, published a newsletter with vital information on grants, both those available and those now funded. This also served as a useful form of in-house boosterism, proclaiming our successes (more than our failures). The issue of February, 1970– when dollar amounts were still on the small side but every victory worth crowing about - announced that 173 grants had been funded between February, 1969 and January 1970 (an average of 16+ a month). They totaled $6.175 million; of this, $993,751 would be held as indirect costs – for use elsewhere in the University. The monthly average intake from indirect costs had been $82,812 - 16% of the grant money. No one in January, 1970 really struck it rich, important though the money was: $16,000 from the Navy for studies in stellar atmosphere, $56,000 for computer assisted indexing of UN documentation (from the UN), $46,300 from the NSF for work on the larval firefly, and some smaller items. To set these sums into a comparative context, when I was chair of my Department in the mid-70s the annual History budget was around $1 million. This covered the salaries of about 25 faculty and 4 staff, TA lines for over 30 graduate students, and such incidentals as postage (before e-mail) and mimeograph supplies (before the Xerox and the fax).

But, like almost everything else at Stony Brook, the world of grants and grant money got larger and larger, trying to keep pace with growing expectations and costs and with the need to attract and support doctoral and post-doctoral students. If neither Stony Brook's size nor its status enabled it to challenge the really big guys of higher education, money did roll in to subsidize the enterprise. For the 1980 fiscal year, federal funding amounted to $20 million (and another $3.5 from other sources); by 1985 the respective sums were $36 and $6 (in millions), by the mid-1990s we were up to $74 and $15, respectively. As well as the aggregate dollars, the percentage of applications funded is a guide to how well Stony Brook proposals stacked up in a competitive world. The Research Foundation reported in 1975 that 299 applications had been funded, out of 445 submitted. And though I refer to research in any and all academic fields as basic to a comprehensive university, we should note that for 1976 – to take a typical year - 87% of such funds came in by way of science and engineering. Alas; the social sciences accounted for 12% of the external funding awarded, the humanities about 1%.

I talked above about the creation of new departments, minors, and programs - innovations that reflect changes in student demand and in faculty interest and expertise. The research analogue is an institute or an organized research initiative, set up to cut across departments and disciplines, or – ideally— to bring them together. Though the most successful and best known such initiative in Stony Brook's history has been the Institute for Theoretical Physics, run for many years by Max Dresden and C. N. Yang, the ITP is but one of many such creations.[5]

In much of the above I have talked as though "big science" has invariably been heavily privileged. Though I think this is true, it is also proper to emphasize that, on a proportionately lower scale, other fields and enterprises have had plenty of opportunities to engage in empire building. If few ventures outside the sciences have been able to put down deep roots, a fair share of the fault lies with the departments and faculty involved. Many faculty in the humanities and social sciences turned out to be less than entrepreneurial, with very little interest in developing an organized base for collective and team research. They either eschewed the collective (and big-money) route, from the start, or they tried, only to discover that it was a game for which they were not particularly well suited.

When we turn from the vast complex of colleagues and support staff needed to conduct work on sub-atomic particles to the solitary labors (and joys) of research in a library or an archive, the distinctions of culture and methodology seem to make sense. Few will take umbrage with the idea that deciphering Beethoven's revisions of a sonata is more likely to be an individualized project than cloning a rat or tracing the half-life of a sub-atomic particle. The Institute for Colonial Studies (in the History Department) had a run with state money in the 1960s and 1970s, with a major conference and the useful project of acquiring colonial records (on microfilm). The idea behind the Institute was that comparative colonial studies would be a natural for Long Island, with its 300-years of European settlement. But eventually interest waned and the Institute was defunded; no one in the History Department suffered much from its demise. Economics housed the Economic Research Bureau, also with a strong focus on Long Island and the Metropolitan region,[6] and more recently (in the early 1990s) Economics was the base for an Institute for Decision Sciences, though that proved very costly. The English Department had money for summer poetry conferences and writing workshops. Sociology has housed an Institute for Social Analysis, largely under Mike Schwartz, and there were conferences on "Social Problems in the Suburbs" and "Long Island: Politics, Economic, Culture, and Society." The Anthropology Department maintained a University Museum for a while, with exhibitions on such items of interest as Long Island colonial gravestones. But when considered as a collections of enterprises, these ventures came and went as faculty interests and resources waxed and waned. They needed an active organizer and some sort of god-parent in the form of a supportive dean or affluent department chair.

The creation of an institute allows faculty from different fields to work on common ground; what we like to refer to as interdisciplinarity. Such ventures help the university attract faculty, drawn here by a chance to escape the constraints of their previous home. And, to sweeten the pie still more, those being recruited are frequently given special concessions: little or no teaching, especially of undergraduates, money for start-up costs, extra travel funds, etc. Because competition for name faculty is always fierce, relief from the regular teaching load - light as this is – is a trump card in negotiations (as is a healthy jump in salary). An extreme example of how the University can get stricken with recruiting fever was the series of extravagant concessions made in the early 1990s by the provost to lure people to an Institute of Behavioral Neuroscience. Huge salaries were bad enough, but when the spending stretched to fancy carpets and over-size desks, it verged on the scandalous. Good news in this instance: such cost-overrun foolishness helped lead to the quick dismissal of the provost responsible. But again, while it is easy to point to excesses that get authorized, institutes are a window of opportunity, a way of tapping into new fields of research without making the full commitment entailed in the creation of a department.

Stony Brook's most successful institute, outside the sciences, has been the Humanities Institute (HISB), established in 1988-89 under the active leadership of Ann Kaplan. Ironically, the humanities qualified for a serious extra-department institute in part because the new language of literary analysis - drawing on structuralism, psychoanalysis, and linguistics – had become so opaque that it merited (or necessitated) special treatment. Despite having a distinguished international board of advisors (including Jacques Derida, Stewart Hall, Fredric Jameson, and Julia Kristeva) the HISB has made major contributions through its long and ambitious list of programs; films, speakers from Stony Brook and elsewhere, visiting scholars, fellowships, and conferences. Some of the colloquia and conferences, on themes like autobiography and French philosophy, have resulted in published volumes. Some of the talks can be followed even by a medieval historian, though many focus on the conundra of post-modernism and show how far the humanities have come since I was an undergraduate working my way through Jane Austen.

Another way in which the universities make a statement about the centrality of the research mission is by hosting conferences and workshops, especially during the summer when the dorms are empty and registration and room fees bring in cash. The Office of Conferences and Special Events was set up in the 1970s to facilitate these (money making) affairs, as well as to handle graduations and the installations of presidents. It has proved invaluable, not least because its presence has relieved faculty wives and departmental secretaries from the need to play hostess, cook, and taxi driver.[7] As with the research institutes, most of the glamour events that have to be handled are in the sciences, but conferences on African literature or Anglo-Saxon England or Latin America Labor History, among many others, have been welcomed and well treated. In addition to conferences run through departments or institutes, many of the one- and two- day galas owe their existence to individual faculty initiative, as when Mike Zweig of Economics put one together on "Religion, the Economy, and Social Justice" (1984) or on class in American society (2002), or Helen Lemay of History on "Homo Carnalis: The Carnal Aspects of Medieval Human Life" (1987).

Faculty research is mainly an "other directed" activity. When they publish research, the faculty of a given discipline are primarily talking to, and seeking brownie points, from others in their specialized fields, and this translates, for the most part, into scholars at other schools. Though the amount of in-house sharing of research findings varies tremendously - depending on the nature of the work and the personalities involved - much of it is conducted by the only person (or one of the very few) at Stony Brook who is sufficiently concerned and knowledgeable (though this statement loses some punch when we think of team projects in physics). For the most part when a faculty member publishes a report on the pros and cons of privatized bus service in Uzbekistan, the work is of more interest to experts on transportation, privatization, and

Uzbekistan - wherever they happen to be - than to colleagues at Stony Brook (who in this case would be in Economics or Harriman College). It is easy to deplore the emphasis on specialization and to conjure up visions of some mythical era when scholarship could be read by all. But the truth, despite lip service about over-specialization, is that detail, and small advances, and highly specialized work, are the essence of research. Within the academy this is readily understood. Selling it to the public, for public relations, and to the government, for funding, can be a good deal more difficult.

Besides research and publication, and teaching, faculty are involved in academic governance and in a wide range of professional activities. Governance is the collective process whereby the faculty voice assumes a role and offers direction in the planning and regulation of the university, even though in the eyes of the State it is the administration that is identified as the university. Furthermore, SUNY faculty, as state employees, have been organized (unionized) since 1970, in accordance with the state's Taylor Law. Unionization touches on some traditional faculty prerogatives of governance, as it does on administrative ones concerning discipline and working conditions. I will come back to union matters in a few pages.

In talking of governance and consultation, we can begin (very quickly) at the top. Over SUNY stands the Chancellor and the Trustees, and the level of faculty governance through which they confer is the (statewide) SUNY Senate, composed of delegates from each campus. This Senate has a state-wide executive committee, three meetings a year, and standing committees on such matters as curriculum, affirmative action, and the status of women. From the SUNY Senate come statements and recommendations about SUNY-wide policies. Though all governance resolutions are but advisory, the SUNY Senate at least gets a hearing with the powers that be, whether this ever affects the administrative mind-set or not.

At the local level each SUNY campus is called upon to have some sort of governance structure, and matters touching the curriculum and degrees need local approval, even if their real point of generation is the administration. In the campus Senate we find representatives of the academic units and others. At Stony Brook a Senate composed of all the faculty gave way in the mid-70s, under the pressures of size and complexity, to one of department senators, senators elected at large, and representatives of the professional staff and student governance. At the time it seemed important to include students, though this "good thing" has failed to hold much interest – a reflection on both the value of senate decisions and of student commitment to policy-formulation. And because Stony Brook is large, some additional sub-division seemed useful; a University Senate, one for issues only pertaining to the College of Arts & Sciences, and a separate executive committee for the Engineering faculty.

As well as its incarnation as a deliberative or legislative body, the senate lives through a committee structure: an executive committee and then sub-groups that advise on such matters as faculty tenure and promotion, the curriculum, budget and planning, and more esoteric matters like the academic calendar. The executive committee of the Senate is the most effective voice of the faculty, though no one with even the most perfunctory knowledge of the academy would place too much weight in this. If no president is really guided or directed by the Senate, the conventions of collegiality do give a fair opportunity for discussions of the Administration's most recent enormities. But by the late 1980s the perennial budget crises and threats of shrinkage, rather than growth, had sapped the faculty of a deep commitment to or interest in deliberative matters. The years of growth, and of high-tension politics had once pushed the Senate into playing a central role that, in the long term, probably was an anomaly, a peculiar feature of peculiar times. Also, while John Toll was willing to discuss many matters with the Senate, and John Marburger listened with great patience, Shirley Kenney's style is more to get on with it and perhaps to wave some business past the Senate as a matter of form. This is not to imply that either Toll or Marburger was ever inclined to change his mind because of the Senate's wishes.

This is a lot about structure, not much about any historical treatment of function. In the 1960s and 1970s – the crucial decades in which the university was shaped and during which strife was a regular feature of campus life, the Faculty Senate was the main lightening rod for debate and deliberation. The Senate (and I mostly refer to the University Senate, rather than to the A&S Senate) was a serious center of and main forum for airing opposition to the administration. In keeping with the small university that had come from Oyster Bay, the senate consisted of all full time faculty; voting was simply that of any and all who chose to attend. When John Toll became president he served as the presiding officer - as the head of the faculty - and only gradually, under the pressure of events and at the urging of the senate executive committee, did he relinquish this position. Since much senate business consisted of attacks upon Toll, with acrimonious debates about his views and policies and a vote of no confidence often just around the corner, the transition to an elected presiding officer, chosen from faculty ranks, seemed a reasonable part of our coming of age.

Though only faculty could vote at these contentious proceedings, meetings were open and students regularly admitted as observers or guests. They came to realize that senate meetings provided a good opportunity to press the administration for news and views about impending decisions and current events. No matter how close-minded Toll's administration was about taking advice, under his leadership it was reasonably forthright about accepting public criticism and explaining, or defending, its policies. One of the first protests at Stony Brook was in 1967, and it was about the quality of campus life, as Karl Hartzell had warned from the start that it pretty surely would be; poor lighting on roads and walkways, complaints about garbage collection from the dorms, building security, and the like. These legitimate grievances sparked lively debate, even before Vietnam and the draft or drug-busts were our main topics of public discourse. When students brought their complaints to the Senate many faculty, like this writer, were happy to support and endorse them. The nature of the issues, if less than cosmic, seemed to sum up where, on the university's list of priorities, student life and the building of a livable community had been placed.

When more serious political controversies engulfed the campus, a year or two after these early signs of dissent, it was in the Senate that faculty debated whether to condemn the police for "gestapo" tactics in the drug bust of 1968, whether to recommend that the University reject research funds from the Department of Defense, whether to allow military recruiters to use campus facilities, and whether to vote no confidence in President Toll (as we did). The woes of our society came home to a suburban university with a vengeance, fueled by student and faculty links with Columbia University and NYC and exacerbated by Toll's desire to conduct business as usual. Also, as well as political issues that I personally found engaging, for many of my younger colleagues (ranging from 18 to about 58) the anti-war movement was linked to a counterculture they found appealing; political poetry, improvisational theater, the right to say "fuck" in public, the freedom to use various drugs that were mostly illegal, the search for a non-hierarchical social and intellectual order (especially in the classroom), and many other forms and manifestations of dissent and generational dissonance.

In an effort to articulate a common voice of opposition to Lyndon Johnson's relentless pursuit of war in Vietnam, many faculty (and students) argued that the University should refuse to accept research money from the Department of Defense (DoD: named, in more candid days, the War Department).[8] The administration argued - with understandable pragmatism but little sensitivity - that such money was only accepted for non-military or non-mission-oriented purposes, anyway. Classified research – closed to public scrutiny, presumably tied to weapons or intelligence, and not publishable for the public eye – was already in violation of SUNY policies. I think Toll was telling the truth here, though he certainly sounded like someone defending the DoD (probably not his intention).[9] In 1971, after a number of earlier debates, the Senate endorsed a resolution that the University accept no further DoD funding, even though the administration had made clear in advance that the motion, as advisory, would be disregarded.

University Senate debate on this difficult issue, protracted over several days, proved to be of exceptional quality - civil, sober, conducted by informed and interested parties. Whether non-mission oriented research, underwritten by DoD funds, helped to legitimate its nefarious projects, or whether a campus was co-opted into the DoD's camp when it took its money, or whether academics were but carrying out the pacific segments of what in sum was very nasty work, or whether civilian peer reviews for funding (as with the NSF) really separated clean from dirty money; all these questions were aired at great length. The sentiment swung heavily against DoD when a number of research scientists– colleagues with heavy credentials and a professional stake in funded research - said that they did not want DoD money to subsidize their inquiries into the natural world. The motion against DoD carried by a lop-sided margin, only to be rejected and ignored by the President.[10] For the faculty to enlighten and persuade each other, over a policy issue of great interest, was as rare as it was exciting (or the other way around, if you wish). However, governance is not just about consciousness raising, and our inability to affect a change in policy was brought home to us in spades. The campus continued to receive and cash Dod checks.[11]

Some individual behavior probably had been affected by our collective exercise in articulating a public and community morality. Some faculty became more aggressive about looking for alternative sources of funding. Others were at least more conscious of the larger implications of what had seemed an individualized research project. In fairness, the DoD only gave research money to people who applied for it; not even John Toll, in his most imperial days, forced a grant upon any of us. Nor was DoD funding ever more than a minor source of all those research dollars whose arrival was so eagerly awaited, as I chronicled above. But in a period of high political consciousness – matched by a great deal of frustration as Nixon succeeded Johnson and things only got worse— symbolic gestures were very important.

Even for less dramatic issues, senate meetings were town meetings writ large. Those that attracted a big crowd often had to be moved, on the spur of the moment, to a larger lecture hall to accommodate the faculty and the (often noisy) crowds of students. The senate might wind up meeting in Old Physics (which holds about 175), or in the old gym on folding chairs, or even (as after the drug bust) on the plaza outside ESS. But the squeeze on space was but one aspect of community that faded as the days of crisis passed.

With the quieter times of the mid- and later 70s, the story was rarely one of confrontation, and a lesser turn-out and a routine agenda were not wholly unwelcome as the Senate mulled over its business.

Furthermore, by the mid-70s the old senate structure was deemed out-dated and cumbersome, and it was time to shift the focus from a general debating society to a representative body with sub-units that paralleled those of a growing administration. And since the faculty was now an organized one, composed (as defined by our contract with the State) of teaching faculty, librarians, and professional staff, it was proper that that the Senate represent these other groups. So change came, and even those who lamented the passing of the town meeting saw that size, complexity, and a union-imposed definition of faculty called for a new order, a new structure of governance. The move to a representative senate had been a priority of both John Toll and of SUNY Central, and they hoped for one that could funnel faculty in-put on administrative matters and be less volatile in its rhetorical identity. The change was accepted, with much faculty in-put, about the same time that the University established four deanships within Arts & Sciences– also in recognition of a need for more structure, more organization, more bureaucracy.

Looking back over the years, the Senate stands out as the most sensitive barometer by which to judge the health and vigor of campus debate and shared decision making. This is one of those "for better or for worse" statements. A vote of no confidence in John Toll, endorsed several times by a heavy majority, probably raised his stature in Albany. In the 80s the Senate backed up its executive committee in support of Ernest Dube's exercise of his academic freedom – the correct decision, but a difficult one for many, and made at a moment of external pressure and much internal mis-giving (about which, see Chapter 8). The Senate authorized the various curriculum changes in the mid- and late-1980s that led to the adoption of the current DEC, as spelled out above. The president of the Senate is the titular head of the faculty: he or she calls the May graduation ceremony to order, and he or she attends Stony Brook Council meetings as an observer.[12]

Beyond its role as a debating society and the legislative

voice of the faculty, a University or Faculty Senate is the source of delegated authority for its brace of committees. These exist to advise the administration and to participate in deliberations regarding student and faculty affairs. The governance machinery oversees new course proposals, has an advisory voice on admissions policies and rules touching student petitions and plagiarism, and participates to at least a nominal extent in discussions of the budget and long range planning. But the most important function of governance, at least from a faculty perspective, lies in the realm of decisions concerning faculty promotion and tenure. The Personnel Policy Committee (PPC) of the College of Arts & Sciences – now called the Promotion and Tenure Committee (PTC) - has been a major player in this area throughout the university's history. In the early years a single committee sufficed for the entire campus, but with the new Senate of the 70s the functions got divided by colleges and units.

That faculty play a critical part in judging their peers and in recommending (or rejecting) them for tenure and/or promotion is the bedrock of governance and decision-making at any serious university. In this area the weight and value of peer reviewing, plus assessments from external referees (faculty at other campuses) carry a great deal of weight. The basic rules governing a junior faculty member's years of probation (running up to five or six years), the balanced procedures designed to assure the candidate a full and fair day in court, and the protection of his or her academic freedom (as spelled out in the canonical statements of the American Association of University Professors: the AAUP) are sacred elements of academic life. Though Stony Brook was always inclined to handled these matters in a reasonable way, the fact that AVP Bentley Glass had been a president of the AAUP helped assure that the university would develop its procedures in conformity with big-time standards.[13]

The Personnel Policy Committee (an elected committee of about seven faculty) receives the personnel file as compiled and evaluated in the candidate's own department. The committee then renders judgement on the department's judgement and transmits the file to the administration (dean, AVP, president), where the final on-campus decision is made. The file contains an elaborate statement by the candidate on teaching goals and research plans - past, present, and future - plus a goodly bundle of external evaluations, mostly concerned with research and publication. In the long haul recommendations of the PPC (or PTC) are good predictors of the final disposition of a case; the committee's collective wisdom and balanced composition make it one of considerable authority - one with whose verdict the administration usually concurs.

Not that the process is always smooth and that personnel cases invariably move forward with cheerful consensus. No university goes through 30 or 40 years of hiring and evaluating without tenure fights, some very bitter and protracted. Sometimes the division of opinion is centered within the candidate's department. In other instances it erupts as the file wends its way forward. In theory, faculty work is assessed for contributions in three realms of endeavor; scholarship and publication, teaching, and service (to the campus and the larger scholarly community). These criteria, set forth in the policies of the SUNY Board of Trustees, are pretty much the norm for any serious school, though a research university places almost all the weight on the first. But cases vary. Though research without service often suffices to get one through, the reverse has almost no chance of hitting the bull's eye. Different fields have their own take on the standards regarding quantity and quality of work. While the publication of a scholarly book is expected from a colleague in the humanities, few young physicists or engineers (or even number crunching economists) see significant scholarship as represented by anything other than an impressive string of articles (though many might have been co-authored as part of a team).

How to balance different criteria and disciplinary norms? In some instances a department declines to support a popular teacher, a student favorite; the case against the candidate usually is that a heavy emphasis on and expertise in teaching fails to make the grade at a university. In other cases departmental support for a candidate gets over-ruled by the PTC and the latter body is upheld, or reversed - in a system much like appellate courts of the judiciary - when the dean or vice president or president renders a final decision. Occasionally both levels of faculty assessment - department and PTC– are overturned and the faculty member gets the boot, though this was rare.[14] Student petitions on behalf of rejected faculty were not uncommon in the days of a small campus and well known student favorites. But in this tough corner of the academy student popularity was a mixed blessing, if not actually a kiss of death, when offered in lieu of publication. The standards at a research university are fairly high, but they are widely known and most faculty who are productive during their probationary years clear the hurdle. Some, of course, decide the game is not for them and they choose to go elsewhere before their final moment of assessment at Stony Brook.

Because it has a different historical genealogy, coming primarily from outside academia, I have held off my account of faculty unionization and separated it from the tale of traditional governance. But the faculty of SUNY have been organized – as organized labor – for over 30 years. This is a significant factor in the history of the University.

In the late 1960s New York State enacted the Taylor Law, which in effect imposed organization or unionization– or the question of whether to choose unionization - upon the many categories of public employees (including the faculty and professional staff of SUNY, except for high level managers and administrators, now deemed to be "management confidential"). The Taylor Law was hardly intended as a bill of rights for the workers, even for white collar ones. Rather, it emanated from an effort to rationalize the growing number of state employees and to lump them into manageable units in the context of labor-management relations. Furthermore, to make matters easier for the state and less politically supple for SUNY faculty, the NY Public Employees Relations Board determined that SUNY would be one big (if not one happy) union; faculty and professional staff and librarians were yoked together across the entire face of SUNY. So a forced marriage between cool partners, from Stony Brook to Plattsburgh to Fredonia, was now the labor picture for the state wide system.[15]

Those in the bargaining unit did have a one-time option of

choosing their representative (with "no representative" as a formal but unrealistic choice on the ballot as well).[16] In the early 1970s faculty unionization was new, unfamiliar, and - to many now called upon to vote – an uncongenial business - more appropriate for blue collar labor than college teachers. From the cluster of groups competing to be the faculty's representative, the voters chose the one that had emerged or split off from the existing SUNY Faculty Senate, the Senate having been asked by the state to set up and run this kind of election. The Senate already had a presence on every campus, and it was exclusively concerned with SUNY - factors that worked strongly in its favor. This new organization (the Senate Professional Association, or SPA), emerged the winner, after a set of run-off elections against such rivals as the CSEA (Civil Service Employees Association), the AAUP, and professional teachers' organizations (NEA, AFT, NYSUT, etc). Mergers became the game plan, and by 1973 SPA had become the UUP (United University Professions) - the representative to this day. Furthermore, in recognition of the realities of being unionized, UUP became a member or component of the AFT and thence of the AFL-CIO. So, like the construction workers who built the campus, Stony Brook faculty and professionals work under a contract that covers basic salary increases, conditions of employment, retrenchment, parking, benefits, discretionary salary increases ("merit money"), discipline and grievances, and other matters that, at first glance, seem far removed from the world of libraries, laboratories, and classrooms.

A contract that covers all of SUNY is very much "one size fits all." It is not designed with great concern for the needs and shapes of individual wearers, and it is deliberately insensitive to distinctions between an up-state, four year college and a university center, as well to Long Island's very high cost of living. Stony Brook never comes away with any special treatment. In addition, the "retrenchment clause" of the UUP contract conceded that the state ("management") had a right to call this particular shot, as it has done several times over the years. In times of "financial exigency," as defined by management, tenured faculty can be and have been fired. Herein lies the sad and short tale of the Department of Education, about which more below.

The other side of the coin is that unionized employees in the United States have had better salary increases in recent decades than those not unionized. Despite the give-away clause on retrenchment, tenure has almost always meant tenure. Also, though there is one UUP for all of SUNY, each campus has a local chapter to stay abreast of local problems and to play a role at ground level. The local voice can be raised against pressure to increase workload ("speed up"), to raise fees for parking, to impose discipline in an arbitrary fashion, and to "contract out" for cheaper services delivered by piece-workers who have neither a union nor benefits. Faculty at Stony Brook also get inexpensive life insurance, a party at Christmas, a dinner-dance in the winter, a chapter newsletter, and some lobbying in Albany. The affiliation with large teachers' unions and large war chests seems to give the faculty some clout at election time, though it is easy to over-estimate what dollars, and even phone calls, do to affect the public voice.

Looking back on a generation of mandatory organization of the academic labor force, the transition from faculty as independent contractors to an identity as unionized employees has been a major change in the world of higher education. This is in keeping with national trends in the public sector, though SUNY was an early participant. When first imposed, most faculty looked askance at unionization. To this day - because of a retrograde Supreme Court decision (in the 1980 Yeshiva College case) - faculty in private colleges and universities cannot demand the right to organize, though the courts have become more sympathetic in the last few years. But for faculty in public higher education the general verdict probably would be that the power and presence of a union has been comforting and supportive, at least in some bread and butter areas. Perhaps the sad part of this great change is not that professors have become part of organized labor, but rather that organized labor no longer has the clout or the friends or the public respect and acceptance it once did.

(Endnotes)

1. To offer undergraduates an opportunity to do research under faculty supervision, URECA (Undergraduate Research and Creative Activity Program) was instituted under Provost Jerry Schubel in the late 1980s. Most of the student work emanates from the sciences, particularly biology, and there is an annual show-and-tell each spring when the work is put on display and justly celebrated. Around 1990 the University also initiated a federally-funded program, Women in Science and Engineering (WISE), in an effort to crack some of the walls of academic stereotyping about science. And in recent years the recognition of undergraduate research has extended to the humanities and soft social sciences.

2. Because serious income is generated by patents - mainly in biology and engineering - there are elaborate state policies that govern the division of royalties between the inventor or principal investigator and the institution. Since the work leading to the patent was conducted on SUNY facilities, and usually with a grant that ran through SUNY, it is accepted that there is both an individual and an institutional interest. By 2000 the University's share was in the neighborhood of $10 million a year.

3. Tom Flanagan (1923-2002) came to Stony Brook from the University of California, Berkeley, in 1978 and he chaired the English Department. *His Year of the French* (1979) was a large historical novel set in Ireland in the 1790s. It won a National Book Award. He followed with *Tenants of Time* (1989) and *The End of the Hunt* (1995), taking Irish History down to the Easter Rising of 1916. All of the books enjoyed critical and popular acclaim, and an Irish movie was made of *The Year of the French*. Flanagan told me he had never seen it but had been told that it was not very good.

4. As well a leave of absence, subsidized by a grant or fellowship, tenured faculty qualify for a sabbatical leave after every 6 years of service. This can be taken as one-semester at full pay or a full year at half pay. At a research-oriented university there are usually other

options: released time from teaching in return for extra duties (director of a graduate program), or UUP awards for minorities and untenured women, or a package-offer designed to meet an outside job offer. Though a sabbatical has to be requested (and granted), virtually no one at Stony Brook ever gets turned down, whereas at some SUNY colleges such leaves are far from guaranteed.

5. When C. N. Yang retired at the end of the 1998-99 academic year the university ran a fancy international conference in his honor and the ITP was renamed the Yang Institute for Theoretical Physics. An honorary doctorate was bestowed upon him at the May, 1999 graduation.

6. A series of "working papers" was published by the Department on such topics as real estate in Harlem, the economics of higher education, and economic development in Brookhaven Town. Working papers are less formal than scholarly articles, though they can have a wide distribution in interested circles.

7. Ann Brody and Ann Forken, who was director until she retired in 2000, have helped with information for this volume – as well as with numerous events I have had a hand in running over the years. They and their staff are among the many stakhanavite offices on the campus.

8. A nice irony is that Stimson College in Roosevelt Quad is named for Henry Stimson. The high point of his long and distinguished public career was as Secretary of War for FDR (1940-45). He had also been Secretary of War for Taft, governor of the Philippines under Coolidge, and Hoover's Secretary of State. He was a lawyer and a semi-local, dying at Huntington, L.I., in 1950.

9. Classified research is standard fare for places like Los Alamos or the Aberdeen testing ground. However, the concept of classified work can now be stretched to cover work done while funded by a corporate sponsor, and it might be for an engineering design or (even) market research for cosmetics. In theory, SUNY does not

permit classified research as a condition of a grant based on a campus, though personnel are presumably free to enter into any agreement they wish for off-campus work.

10. The times were beginning to change and the War was winding down, and Toll pretty much ended the issue with a memo (September 8, 1972) announcing his final rejection of the Senate's advice on this matter. He said that only 4.1% of the campus's $80 million in research money came from the DoD, anyway (with the largest chunk of that going for a project in x-ray scanning in dentistry), though the small size of the DoD component was not the reason for his policy.

11. While it may more properly belong under the discussion of student life, I mention here the long debate over the appearance of armed forces recruiters and those from companies with a high profile in the military-industrial complex (such as Dow Chemical, makers of napalm). Toll's policy was that Stony Brook was "an open campus," making it improper to distinguish between one job recruiter and another. Student protests about their presence led to demonstrations, lock-ins or lock-outs, some violence, and very divided feelings about civil liberties and free speech.

12. The presidents of the Senate, usually serving for one year, were a diverse group: faculty from math, ecology and evolution, history, sociology, French and Italian, economics, physiology, German and Slavic, etc, and by the mid-70s women were often being elected to the position. A woman also was Dean of Social Science in the 1970s (Estelle James of Economics), though she was the only women to reach this level in Arts & Sciences for a long time. Women were assistant and associate deans, and in the late 1980s Aldona Jonaitis served as vice provost of undergraduate students. The glass ceiling was another unlovely aspect of Stony Brook's architecture.

13. The canonical statement on the rationale and value of academic freedom is the 1940 statement of the American Association of University Professors (AAUP), in turn a revision of the 1915 statement, subsequently modified by 1970 interpretive comments and, still more recently, by rewording for gender neutrality. The 1940 Statement has been endorsed by a large number of scholarly organizations and it serves as the beacon in all relevant discussions: *AAUP: Policy Documents and Reports* (1995 edition, Washington), pp. 3-10.

14. This split between faculty endorsement and administrative rejection meant the candidate was entitled to a further assessment by a chancellor's review panel. In such a case the candidate and the administration each choose an advocate, and these two choose a mutually satisfactory third panelist. This panel reviews the case and makes its recommendation, going ultimately to the chancellor. Though the judgement of these panels has usually supported the candidate, no one at Stony Brook has ever been reprieved and tenured by this mechanism. Like the ordinary faculty evaluations, this recommendation is only advisory. Ernest Dube went through this process, as I will describe in Chapter 8. The process is a waste of time – a mere fig leaf.

15. In the hearings before PERB various organizations, vying to become the bargaining agent, argued that SUNY should be cut into several different units. One scheme would have joined the university centers and the two free-standing medical schools. Another was to separate teaching faculty across the state from librarians and/or from the professional staff. PERB decided for the largest possible unit, as was their right, and presumably to the state's convenience.

16. The tale of SUNY unionization is covered in Everett C. Ladd, jr., and Seymour Martin Lipset, *The Divided Academy* (New York, 1975), pp. 243-98 for academic unionization in general, pp. 270-73 on SUNY, and pp. 250-51 on "no representative" as a choice that

was actually the winner in 29 instances out of 367 elections (which I find astounding). Thanks also for valuable reminiscences from Frank Erk, of Stony Brook Biology, who was president of the SUNY Senate in 1969 and helped preside over the creation of the mechanism that ran the first election.

CHAPTER SIX
The Academic Administration: Leadership from the Top

At the start of all this I warned that a chronological narrative was not my style. Though I am willing to deal with "what happened," and to discuss the roles of Stony Brook's founders and leaders, a straight story is clearly not the main thrust of this study. To offer a top-down narrative would be to offer the educational version of the sort of political history that opens with those in power and then trickles downward. I have never written this kind of history in all my years as a medievalist, and I am not about to switch just because I have moved to the 20th century. Of course, this may prove easier to declare than to deliver.

When an historian writes about a topic in which he (or she) has been personally involved, guidelines about distance and objectivity may be hard to follow. By now I hope I have conveyed the idea that there is no single, or final, or definitive history of Stony Brook. No single text can tell all, or be fair to all, or give equal billing to each and every party. Therefore, the best I am likely to do is to be forthright about my choices of inclusion and omission, and to make no pretence that, to me at least, this is merely an intellectual exercise.

So. like or not, in this chapter I accept that, to some considerable extent, the history of a University means a focus on the academic administration. It is the administration that runs the place and that sets much of its tone. The president is the CEO. For SUNY, he or she is the intermediary between the campus and Albany, whether as a hard-nosed guardian of local autonomy, or a running dog of SUNY Central, or – as situations dictate – either or both.[1] And the lesser administrators are but the president's lieutenants, though levels of independence and loyalty may vary. But if they stray very far from the company line they have to go, and they know it.

Albany basically wants little trouble from a campus, and as long as things seem to function – with few questions asked – there is no inclination to intervene, let alone to be swayed by such "events" as student or faculty protest, let alone a vote of no confidence. From the faculty perspective, presidents are judged by how much of the budgetary pie they bring home and by the quality or style of their leadership and vision. Though presidents like to talk about serving the faculty and students, and of being part of the community over which they preside, assessment of their success rest on some combination of personality, dollars, and new initiatives. The time is probably not far off when the success of athletic teams will be added to our criteria for evaluation.

Because Stony Brook is a complex part of state government, much administrative time and energy must be concerned with bureaucracy and the budget, rather than education (teaching and research). There are a million tasks to be handled, many of them far removed from the classroom. Hundreds of men and women labor to keep the wheels turning; employees who devote their careers to the budget, purchasing and travel, business and finance, grounds and maintenance, community and government relations, legal counsel, and fund raising. What most of these people have in common is an almost total lack of contact with classes and labs, though results there rest in good part on their labors. At the annual ceremony to honor long serving employees, people from this other university come forward for their handshake, alongside faculty and librarians, the more visible veterans of the campus. The university was brought to Long Island to provide jobs, among other benefits, and it has lived up to that part of the bargain.

In this chapter I am primarily concerned with the academic side of administration: the president, the AVP (known at times as the provost), deans, the infrastructure that supports them, and their role as spokespersons for and leaders of the university. As there is change in (almost) all things, so this story not only covers a cast of individuals but changes in their titles, in the flow-chart for money and authority, and in the structure of teaching and research. Academic units undergo both fusion and fission, institutes come and go, academic divisions get made, unmade, and remade. Vice presidential areas as well as the VPs themselves go through a revolving door, one that can turn at the blink of the presidential eye.[2]

Stony Brook came through its complicated birth process without benefit of proper parenting; there was no president, in title or power, from 1962 until the selection of John Toll in 1965 (John Lee's short and abortive reign at Oyster Bay being beneath our notice). If building a university from scratch was unusual, doing so without the immediate and strong hand of a father figure was even more so. The pilgrimage from Oyster Bay to Stony Brook was presided over by Karl Hartzell, dispatched from his position as an executive dean at SUNY Central, to keep the place in some order until a proper hierarchy could be found and set in place. Hartzell, originally designated as Dean of Arts and Sciences, wound up as Acting Administrative Officer. He was not a candidate for the presidency, and a genuine replacement was clearly at the top of the long "things to be done" list. The number two man then was Stanley Ross of History; acting dean, and a man with a heavy hand but happy to use the state's open checkbook to hire one (or more) of everything.

John Toll was the final choice of the presidential search committee; the offer was made, he accepted, and he arrived in the spring of 1965. Though he was off campus for a sabbatical semester in the early 1970s, he was the undisputed boss from the 1965-66 academic year until his resignation in 1978. A 10-year span is deemed a good one for a university president, and in lasting beyond that Toll certainly showed resilience. Through a combination of workaholic dedication and glaring insensitivity, he presided over and directed the growth of the university.[3] Whether I talk in terms of numbers of students and faculty (and other employees), or of buildings and construction, or of books in the library, or simply of status and reputation, he largely controlled the many engines that ran, day and night, to turn early promises into red brick reality.

When Toll came to Stony Brook he had before him a virtually boundless horizon of opportunity. In the mid-1960s money for higher education was cascading over the sluice gates; both Nelson Rockefeller in the governor's mansion and the two houses of the state legislature saw SUNY as part of the Empire State's pride and joy. For Rockefeller, support for SUNY was a serious component of his presidential wannabe credentials (though he was also following the lead of Governor Harriman). Toll was given as close to a carte blanche as one gets in life. He inherited just enough structure and momentum from the Hartzell-Ross set up so that not everything had to be built from scratch. On the other hand, there were few set policies or deeply entrenched interests. Toll was able to impose his vision upon the campus – or rather, his vision of research and growth meshed well with the aspirations of state and local leaders, and senior faculty, for the university.

For clarity I divide Toll's era into two roughly equal halves: from his arrival up to the early 1970s (say 1972 or so), and from then up to 1978, when he left (for the University of Maryland, whence he had come in 1965) and when Alec Pond put in a stint as acting president (1978-79). The first portion of this must be, to a great extent, the story of how the problems of the mid- and late-1960s came to Stony Brook, and how the university grew during these years. When John Toll first came for an interview, who could have imagined the length of the war in Vietnam that lay ahead, or the lives and suffering it would entail, or the virulent resistance it would generate, especially on our campuses. In 1965 Lyndon Johnson was largely concerned with civil rights, after the milestone legislation of 1964, and he was proclaiming his "great society" as the progeny of FDR's New Deal.

We were soon to realize that amidst the anticipated turmoil of construction and academic growth, and the quest for recognition and respect, Stony Brook was also to be tested in the fires of such matters as police raids over "drugs" and over the nation's deep divisions touching race and our involvement in southeast Asia. Protests by students and faculty quickly made academia aware of its role in a world under siege, racked by divisions over authority and legitimacy. Where did universities stand when the testing time came and the establishment was under challenge – challenges from college-age youth, the middle class, and the intelligentsia? This, in a nutshell, sums up Stony Brook between 1965 and the early 1970s.

The second half of the Toll years was calmer. By the early 1970s much of the second physical campus was completed - that set of large buildings erected to supplement and supersede those of 1962-63. However, calmer times were also leaner times. After 1970 the state budget was never again to match the heady days just gone by. Though hard times is relative, and we have learned since how much harder they could become, the first touch on the brakes sufficed to send out a shockwave, and by the mid-70s the State was in a serious financial crunch. These years saw the retrenchment of the Department of Education, launching a string of court cases (brought and lost by the retrenched) and a legacy of bad feeling that lasted long after Toll had departed. Lean years, the end of our growth spurt, and the beginnings of the search to make bricks with but little straw. And yet, amidst the leaner times, the academic departments were beginning to turn out PhDs and to bask in the warm light of a growing national reputation. This juxtaposition of contradictions fits the general love-hate/push-pull culture of the university, led as it was by an administration about which most of us were ambivalent, at best.

Looking back to the early years of the Toll presidency, the image is of Stony Brook as a serious, business-like place. Though clearly there was a lot of student social life, and the faculty met for dinner parties and drank cheap wine, the campus had no student union, no proper venue for concerts or theater, little by way of inter-collegiate athletics, no Greek letter organizations. For almost all of us the main business of the university was the university. It was ugly, messy, and fascinating; it engrossed, to an amazing extent, the lives of those who were involved in it.

John Toll had to work out an academic administrative structure that suited his own style. He inherited a strong Dean of Arts and Sciences in Stanley Ross, a Mexicanist from the History Department, but clearly he was entitled to build his own team. He recruited Bentley Glass from Johns Hopkins to become his AVP, the number two man, at least for academic matters. An elder statesman of science, Glass brought an aura of experience and credibility to the campus.[4] Then, because construction and relations with

Albany were so important and time-consuming, Alec Pond became EVP and Toll's right hand man. Pond had chaired and helped build the Physics Department, and he had an old friendship and close working relationship with Toll.[5]

One long-standing administrative problem concerned the College of Arts and Sciences, the academic unit that made up (in both student and faculty numbers) about 80% of the university. If it had its own dean – as it did off and on over the years— what would be the relationship of that dean to the AVP? And if it lacked a single dean— either reporting as a string of departments directly to the AVP or to divisional deans – was A & S so fragmented that it would have trouble claiming its due? The departments were mostly routed through Ross, to Glass, until Ross left for Texas in the late 1960s. Then Sidney Gelber, a professor of philosophy and an active founding father from the faculty ranks, served as VP for Liberal Studies. When Gelber moved up to become AVP, upon Glass's retirement, the University alternated between having a single successor and divisional deans. The tide came in and the tide went out.

Graduate administration, under a graduate dean, also had to be created from scratch. By the late-60s department after department was being authorized to institute graduate training, as we have seen. Within academic ranks this was a major promotion, entry into full adulthood. Because of the rate and scale of growth, with programs springing up like dandelions on a suburban lawn, a centralized authority was needed to keep an eye on standards and procedures. External site visits had to be arranged, with teams of outsiders who were sufficiently astute to be of help but not so snooty as to sneer at us. And, as befits any and every unit in SUNY, there was endless paper work; each graduate program needed a graduate director (and he needed a special-purpose secretary). The position of graduate dean was held, in quick succession, by two physicists and then by two professors from English.[6] The fourth of these - Herb Weisinger, who had come from Michigan State to chair English - held office long enough to preside over most of the growth and the regularization of programs through the 1970s.

One missing link in this chain was a comparable administrator for undergraduate studies as such. Even when Ross and then Gelber were deans of Arts and Sciences or VPs for Liberal Studies – when the University was smaller and less complicated - they had been forced to juggle undergraduate needs against the higher priorities of new graduate programs, and we know who wins this sort of arm-wrestling. Though eventually the University did establish an office of undergraduate affairs, with its own dean or director (Bob Marcus of History, and a student of Sid Gelber's from Columbia days), the weaker sibling always went to the wall. That this appointment was not made until 1974-75 says a lot about priorities. Furthermore, Marcus was junior in rank to the other administrators, and this seemed to symbolize a position with fewer resources and less authority. Where the others had dollars, his office took over undergraduate advising.

The structure of the academic administration, along with the people chosen to fill key positions, tells a good deal about priorities and the preference for a top-down over a more populist or democratic model. The people involved were representative of the political and demographic world of their day; almost all male, almost all white. If Stony Brook never took a lead in breaking down walls of social, racial, and gender inequity and neglect, it was probably about on par with comparable institutions. While Toll had one administrative assistant who was African American, another, the most rule-bound and inflexible flunky on his fairly rigid staff, was an elected officer of the American Civil Liberties Union.

My narrative may convey the idea that I – along with virtually all my friends on the faculty and many of the students— found little to like in the Toll-style of doing business. This is correct. However, I am not sure what would have satisfied most of us in those hectic times. The tensions within a university - generated by the clash of agendas and personalities— meant that no particular resolution of conflict, no mediation between alternatives, was going to be universally accepted. Furthermore, in terms of personnel no management team is going to be in place for more than a few years; people, like the crises they deal with, come and go. It is easy to fault Toll's style, as well as to fault many of those whom he entrusted with its implementation. But we were all engaged in an on-going and collective learning process, usually being conducted with limited control of the larger factors. Building a university from the ground up is an almost unique experience.

The internal difficulties were greatly compounded by location. Stony Brook was predestined to be an academic island in the midst of a conservative ex-urban area undergoing its own growth crises. Though the first large protests about campus life did not have ties to the anti-war movement, there had been a teach-in about Vietnam as early as 1965. Student pressure was beginning to build, and early skirmishes over the quality of campus life are easily read, and not just by hindsight, as harbingers of what lay ahead.[7] The new university, if still thin on women faculty and men and women of color, was full of Jews, radicals, and hippies. It was not the old Stony Brook, which was surely one of its saving graces and a source of pride to those of us who had been plunked down in a community that found us so alien.

Publicity, or infamy, or an un-wanted limelight, shone suddenly on the night of January 17, 1968. This was the "great drug bust," an event that was to shape much of Stony Brook's public image for years. The massive, middle-of-the-night raid by about 200 Suffolk County police, and the waves of sensational publicity it generated, frightened parents well into the 70s (though it probably excited their children). The bust served to bring all sorts of local and academic divisions to the fore, and "it was no accident" that it came at the very time that campuses were being fingered as hot beds of opposition to the escalating war effort. Suffolk county voters were to give Richard Nixon a gigantic plurality at the polls. It was eminently logical that the university was held up as a breeding ground for the counter culture and political dissent. And by local standards this indeed was the case; Stony Brook was indeed a center of protest. No reason to wonder that local sentiment was very much in support of the police swoop on dormitories where, supposedly, drug dealing and drug using students were tucked up in bed (and not always alone, or in the room for which they had paid). The information about who was involved in the drug world (marijuana and pep pills; no hard stuff in those innocent days) had come from campus snoopers - undercover agents and pseudo-students with police connections-plus the too-casual world of rumor and gossip. Students were hauled from their beds, handcuffed, and led off to jail, while armed police stood by lest these dangerous perps, and their unkempt and sleepy friends, threaten the law and order on which the Republic rested.

Some three decades later this idiocy on the part of local politicians and police officials is hard to take seriously. But there was little humor in such nocturnal excitement at the time. The media had a field day; sensational and local were the two best keys to selling papers (and TV news).[8] Furthermore, who was willing, in troubled times, to speak on behalf of these hardened young offenders? The county police commissioner, Commissioner Barry, was taken by the tough-cop image that had swept J. Edgar Hoover to FBI fame and fortune. Barry talked incessantly to the press about nipping drugs, sex outside marriage, communist subversion, intellectual dissent, and the Bill of Rights, all in one fell swoop. President Toll - to the dismay of many faculty and students – said that the forces of law and order were entitled to our support. He urged the campus to comply with authority; the police were only doing their duty. He had little choice, given that Stony Brook is a state university and that marijuana is (still) illegal. But he might have kept his mouth shut. Neither, alas, did he express much compensatory sympathy for the students arrested for what was usually a street-misdemeanor, not the object of a major raid. Neither did he show much indignation about the publicity-oriented invasion of the dorms.

Nor was this unseemly business allowed to remain a Suffolk County matter. The New York State Senate Committee on Crime decided to hold hearings – eager to cash in on the publicity and to hear titillating tales of undergraduates who partied and smoked pot with TAs and even faculty. As in most witch-hunting investigations, the senators wanted the faculty and staff witnesses to "name names"– from whom did you buy, to whom did you sell, with whom did you . . ., etc. Activities that many of the participants had thought to be part of a private world – whether one of foolish behavior or not - now became someone else's publicity ballpark. And through it all, there was sympathy and a good deal of fund raising from the faculty (mostly for legal counsel), but nary a sympathetic or supportive word from on high.

The drug bust and the consequent debates and hearings and court proceedings were still another in a series of major disruptions of the university's normal agenda. The whole mess certainly gave the lie to the old cliche of "any publicity is good publicity." The administration had to deal with its internal troubles, while newspapers and public officials of Long Island made much of their self-appointed duty to supervise the internal clean-up. A professional counselor, hired by Alec Pond, was brought in so he could dispense his self-proclaimed expertise on cleaning up the campus. This hire, along with the counselor, were met by derision from most of the academic community. But subpoenas to faculty and staff, mandating an appearance on Vescy Street in New York City, were hardly a matter of amusement. When university personnel - faculty, students, staff of the dean of students' office - had their names blazed across the papers, they correctly said that the intention was to smear them, not to deal with "crime." At least one jail sentence for a refusal to name names was served (by Michael Zweig of the Economics Department, in Riverhead - one of the few faculty caught up in this mess who remained to become a tenured professor). There were jail sentences for students who had sold or actively distributed pot; the local courts were eager to capitalize on community hostility and to talk tough about minor offenses. Dave Tilley, a popular dean of students, looked to be the fall guy the administration was going to offer the wolves; campus support helped save him, and some of his staff, from this fate.

Protests against the US involvement in Vietnam erupted at Stony Brook - as they did at most U.S. campuses - at virtually the same time as the drug busts. To many caught up by and participating in political protests and involved in the counter culture, the two forms of activity were clearly linked. Counter-culture (drugs, sex, very loud music as played by disreputable performers of dubious patriotism) and opposition to authority went hand-in-hand. Some who demonstrated may actually have thought that the unending dissent and disruption heralded the dawn of democratic involvement in society. Many others, from the other side of the fence, thought the raucous and vulgar students to be the first wave of a new nazism. Fairly or not, the Stony Brook administration became identified with authority - and, by extension - with Lyndon Johnson and his war. The war in Asia - a long way from the Brookhaven town hall in Patchogue - came home with frightening force and immediacy (helped by graphic and ubiquitous tv coverage). If few middle class students were actually drafted out of college and sent off to Nam, the mere specter of the draft was frightening. It symbolized government intervention in our lives and the power of the state to use us. As the lies of Johnson and Nixon were exposed, respect for authority crumbled at every level, from the White House to Toll's pronouncements about the need to triple up dorm rooms designed for two. Universities were being reviled as complicitous or co-opted partners in the war: classified research, mission-related research, running dogs of the DoD, recruiting for the armed services and the CIA, jobs with Dow Chemical, and the like. Conspiratorial theories and hard-nosed analysis converged; Stony Brook students often found intellectual, political, and social protest their most compelling educational experience. If "relevance" was the benchmark against which ideas were being tested, a rethinking of academic priorities was part of a new agenda of discourse and participation.

Many studies have looked at the waves of revolutionary sentiment and action that swept across our colleges and universities in these troubled, if exciting, years. Stony Brook is but one chapter, or even a few pages in a chapter, though on Long Island it was the story, off and on, for about four or five years. But while classes were being canceled (as for three days in October, 1968, for a dialogue of healing and reform), and buildings occupied, and students arrested, the work of building the university proceeded apace. We have looked at the rate of construction for the "second campus:" the late-60s and early 70s saw the completion of seven-story buildings, of more dormitories, and of the expanded Melville library. By now Stony Brook was the major single-site employer of Suffolk County, with over 3000 employees, and it was on its way to achieving recognition in the world of research and graduate education.

The second half of the Toll era was calmer; almost anything would have been, given the confusion of growth and the intrusion of the outside world that marked its first half. The one great exception was the retrenchment of the Department of Education, and in this instance things were not nearly as disruptive, or as disrupted, as they should have been. Between the early 1970s and Toll's resignation in 1978 the University's growth rate slowed markedly and sober reality replaced boundless optimism (as well as protests and activism). Some of this was natural; our adolescent growth spurt was over. But some of it was external; a new political order in Albany and Washington meant that the gusher had been capped. By the early 1970s the state of New York was reining back on its great commitment to SUNY.[9] There would be growth and support, but not at the exponential rate of the previous decade. Stony Brook would have to move ahead slowly, especially as it was now called upon to strike a balance between the vast needs of the Health Sciences Center and University Hospital and the main campus.

Tighter budgets and the changing priorities of Toll's later years meant that Master Plan projections of 25,000-plus students were never to be realized. Toll complained as early as his 1971 report to the chancellor about the cut-backs. They had come sooner, and were deeper, than anyone had anticipated.[10] They meant a commensurate reduction of hiring and construction, of admissions and enrollment. But these years did see the virtual completion or maturation of graduate programs across Arts and Sciences and Engineering, as well as the creation of more research institutes. However, new ventures were fewer and less ambitious. We can take Harriman College is a case in point. It was set up in the early 1970s as an applied policy program, preparing undergraduates for work in government and policy-oriented ngo's. It had a foot in policy studies and in quantitative social science, with faculty from engineering and physics as well as from softer fields. But the mission wavered, and by the 1980s it was moving toward a reincarnation as a business program, with an eye on small business development. Harriman is an example of an interesting idea, or a series of semi-related ideas, that never quite found a home or a role. It still dreams of a serious (graduate) program in business, though it now lives its life as a department within the College of Engineering.

A major sea-change in the history of Stony Brook, and a major affair of Toll's later years, was the decision to retrench the Department of Education. When Toll determined in 1975-76 to eliminate Education, the decision was made in response to orders from Albany to formulate a plan for fairly deep cuts, necessitated (supposedly) by impending budgetary disaster. But whatever the larger obligation Toll had to meet, the response he chose sent out a number of significant messages. One was to other Long Island colleges; you could have Education, a field that draws students and tuition money – a message that can be seen as fitting into SUNY's historic policy of "no war on the privates." Toll was also indicating that a large unit in A&S - but one without a graduate program or eye-catching and externally funded research - failed to make the cut when the chips were down. The decision to retrench was taken despite the Department's service to the community, or its vast number of majors, and with no regard for its high proportion of women and minorities (students and faculty) - areas in which it was a campus leader. SUNY policy and the UUP contract both dictated that a single unit should take the hit, rather than spreading the damage around. But the specific decision on whom to hit was a local one. It came down to our President, in action, earning his salary and implementing his vision.

Just as the building of the hospital gave Stony Brook a new niche in Suffolk county, so the termination of Education sent out a powerful counter-signal; no training of teachers for K-7. Education is a popular major, especially for students of limited means. It is a straight path to a white collar job, and on Long Island one that is quite well-paid. In so far as there was a social message encoded in the decision to retrench, it was, if this is your road into middle-class life, Tough Luck - Go Elsewhere - Pay More. Though the faculty of the Department fought their retrenchment (and retrenchment means FIRED, regardless of tenure), they were destined to lose. The UUP contract said that if the State retrenched in accordance with Article 35 of the contract, it was ok, if unwelcome. The decision was a management prerogative, not negotiable when put into operation. Nor could the courts save the effected faculty, given the contract. An immediate outcome of the termination of several dozen faculty lines was to free resources for other priorities, particularly for new hires in areas with graduate programs. In 1974-75, when its demise was being debated behind closed administrative doors, the Department of Education numbered eight professors, five associate professors, 13 assistant professors, 19 lecturers (fulltime but not on tenure-track lines), and three adjunct faculty. This was a large department: 26 "permanent" faculty and a huge number of part-time and year-by-year staff.[11]

What soon became clear in the debates in the faculty Senate, at chair's meetings, and elsewhere, was that while other departments and faculty might deplore the decision, they would not utilize their own resources to rescue retrenched faculty. And since the contract stipulated that the same tasks could not be done elsewhere on campus by other faculty (including any new hires), this in effect ended K-7 teacher training, as well as the Stony Brook career of most of the affected faculty. A few Education faculty were picked up by other units on an individual basis, and they were able to remain at Stony Brook. But for most of the Education faculty, it was a bitter end to jobs and even careers. Retrenchment is a serious psychological assault; no one goes through the experience without being severely wounded, and the awareness of their subsequent rejection by colleagues, after being professionally liquidated by the administration, did not help the healing process.

Stony Brook did continue to train secondary school teachers (for 8-12 or thereabouts). This was permitted under the contract and acceptable by the administration. Secondary ed programs are run through the disciplines and departments: secondary school teachers in math, English, social studies and history, etc. In fact, such programs flourished, and have continued to do so - popular majors and a good avenue to employment. But in the retrenchments of the mid-70s the university made a clear statement about who carried weight and who did not. Neither the huge enrollments nor their low per capita cost counted for much when Toll decided whose blood should be shed to meet a budgetary squeeze, though the administration did do a lot of agonizing over the summer before it dropped the ax. And if there was little public applause for

President Toll, few faculty or departments went out on a limb for their fallen comrades. The hard line agenda, with little regard for the student community and/or a diversified faculty, was imposed by the administration, endorsed by much of the academy.[12]

By the late 1970s the days of big growth were long over. Toll has presided over tumultuous times and he had seen the campus go from a small red brick to a serious research university; prize winning faculty, a hospital and medical school, the looming presence of big science, millions of dollars in grants, a productive faculty, and more of the like. He was still a young man, as the gray beards of higher education are counted, and when he received an offer to return to Maryland as president, it seemed reasonable that he accept. His resignation was announced during the 1977-78 school year. It was the end of an era; assessments of that era were mixed, then, and have remained so ever since.

The transition that would eventually end with the selection of Jack Marburger opened with the appointment of Alec Pond, the executive VP, as acting president for 1978-79. Though the AVP outranked the EVP on the flow chart, and Bentley Glass had a national stature beyond anyone else in the administration, there was no question but that Pond was Toll's right hand man. They were an effective team, and Pond had filled in when Toll had been on administrative leave. An acting president is appointed by the chancellor, and an on-campus person of experience is often the designee (though now days they look outside). The acting president serves until a new president is chosen; a one year interval is the customary hiatus between the old and the new. Choosing a president, however, is apt to be a power struggle. The process begins with a search committee, under the aegis of the Council. Such committees tend to be large; many constituencies (including students and alumni, along with faculty) push for inclusion. Candidates are screened and interviewed, and a few finally make it to the short list presented to the Council, whose members are appointed by the governor in a frank process of political recognition of local eminence.[13] The council in turn recommends to the chancellor and trustees for the formal offer. No participant in this chain is bound by the recommendations from below, though the search committee's choice (or from among its choices) usually gets the garland.[14]

When Alec Pond became acting president his first reflections were that he had no presidential ambitions. During the course of his year in office two vocal factions - pro-Pond and anti-Pond - emerged. Many powers in the science community (led by C. N. Yang) felt that our future would be safe and the Toll legacy of growth and research best preserved by the elevation of his loyal lieutenant. Others thought we had come to a logical point for a new direction; the budgets and the growth-waves that Toll (and Pond) had ridden had flattened out; a gentler, more student-oriented campus might be a good idea. Debate within the faculty grew heated, and finally Chancellor Wharton made a campus visit in the spring to see if the deadlock could be resolved. His decision was to thank Pond and to appoint, as acting president, Richard Schmidt, head of SUNY medical center at Syracuse, for a year.[15]

Schmidt was a complete outsider, and his year in office brought an air of calm. He was not interested in becoming president, and his presence guaranteed that Alec Pond would not be. A new search committee was constituted, and in the spring of 1980 it announced its recommendation: John H. Marburger. The selection of Marburger, dean of the College of Arts and Letters at the University of Southern California, was approved by the off-campus powers and he took up the reins in the autumn, 1980.

Jack Marburger wound up serving as president of Stony Brook for 14 years; he only stepped down (to join Physics and Electrical Engineering) at the end of the 1993-94 academic year. Because state budgets were always difficult during his long administration, and because the campus had reached full growth by the time John Toll left, it is easy to characterize the Marburger years as years of consolidation and internal development rather than of growth. Though it is hard to say how much it was a matter of contrasting styles and how much a matter of a different and more difficult era, Marburger concentrated less on new initiatives and turned rather to matters like the quality of student (and faculty) life. Life was calmer, at least most of the time. In the 1980s there was little sustained strife on U.S. campuses, and the major issues generally were budgetary. The anti-intellectual assaults of the Reagan government made their inroads, but in ways that aroused less passion and little protest. The status quo seemed a good stand-off in a difficult world. Governor Cuomo, though a liberal by national standards, was never a friend of SUNY, and while the legislature usually sweetened his mean-spirited budgets, no great leap forward was ever on the cards.

Much of the energy of Marburger's years went to organizing the operations of the campus and rationalizing pedestrian and non-academic areas like purchasing, finance, personnel (human resources), campus operations, and the office of the dean of students (where many functions over-lapped those of undergraduate studies). At the same time, these were years of major curriculum revision. Marburger spent a lot of time talking with those involved in student and faculty governance. Most of his plans for change (upgrading athletics, arming campus police, revising the undergraduate core curriculum, pushing affirmative action) were widely discussed before implementation. He had good "people skills" and he enjoyed using them, as even faculty who found him lacking in focus were willing to admit. The softer, gentler approach to running Stony Brook came through in such events as the authors-and-editors reception. Attention went to teaching awards, and faculty were nominated for life honors and fancier titles (like SUNY distinguished professorships). Student prizes became a regular part of the yearly cycle; dinners at the president's house, recognition for contributions to diversity and the LI community, for being scholars and scholar athletes, and the like. Staff and civil service employees were also singled out for meritorious as well as for long service.

Though there was a good deal of turn over in the higher ranks of the academic administration under Marburger, the formal organization remained basically the same: an AVP or provost, deans for the four academic divisions and for graduate and undergraduate affairs, and for Engineering and Harriman, and then the department chairs. Shortly after Marburger arrived Sid Gelber resigned as AVP, after years of working to soften the Toll-Pond style, and Homer Neal, also a physicist, came to Stony Brook from Indiana to become Marburger's first mate. The University now had an unusually young team, with the energy and enthusiasm that seemed appropriate for their years; Marburger was 40 when he took office, Homer Neal of couple of years younger.[16]

The Marburger years seemed cursed by a high turnover rate at the upper levels of the academic administration. The impression was that Toll had enjoyed and profited from more stability. This may be erroneous, and the turnover under Shirley Kenny has been even higher (or faster) than it was under her immediate predecessor. Is this a new way of academia; a reliance on administrators who come in from elsewhere and are always ready to move on, in contrast to faculty recruited from the ranks and usually ready to return to their more humble station after they have served a term? Or is it the effect of more difficult working conditions: stress, modest salaries, endless budget crises and hiring freezes? There have certainly been some high level administrative hires that are hard to defend. A prevailing faculty view is to assume hostility from and mediocrity by a new administrator – always accepting that there is a chance of a pleasant surprise. Whatever the reasons, turnover of his administrators seemed to be a regular part of Jack Marburger's life in high office. If we begin with Sid Gelber (whom Marburger inherited and who was quite ready to step down, once the transition had been made) there were five men as AVPs between 1980 and 1994. The office of graduate dean was a comparable revolving door: seven deans, plus an acting dean, in those years. Since each administrator wants to make her or his own mark, rather than carrying out plans already on the drawing board, or on the ground, turnover means discontinuity and disruption. Trying to develop new initiatives in a world of declining budgets invariably turned the job into 70-hour-a-week holding action with little scope for innovation. SUNY administrators earn a fraction of what those who run the privates on Long Island take home, even without factoring in the scandalous case of the former president of Adelphi. And though replacing a provost or a dean is less complicated than a president, here too we have an elaborate search and the chancy chemistry between the new bureaucrat and his or her bosses. Transitions are always risky, and my wife likes to remind me that the devil you know is probably better than the one you don't.[17]

One area that received a good deal of attention in the Marburger years was affirmative action and what we once referred to as "race relations," mostly on campus, a bit in the community. The Marburger administration made efforts to diversify the university, in terms of the color and ethnicity of its population, and to alert the campus to the problems of sexual harassment and date rape, as well as to those resulting from the growing diversity of the student body. But consciousness raising is a tricky business, and enjoinders for tolerance and empathy often get stuck in a bin marked "easier said than done." Furthermore, the Dube affair, which I treat in Chapter 8, muddied the waters and strained relations between people who otherwise might have been supportive allies in the cause. It detracted, sadly and seriously, from the record of the Marburger administration in this area.

The office of Affirmative Action and Equal Opportunity is the campus watchdog over matters touching racial and ethnic demography, facilities for the disabled, and the general status of all groups and categories covered by civil rights legislation. One key role of the Office is legal, as a compliance or enforcement officer. As a recipient of federal money Stony Brook must be in accord with guidelines regarding hiring, job postings, and the use of funds available for targeted groups. A great deal of data must be collected and submitted to the appropriate federal agencies. The other key role of the Office is to scrutinize specific procedures and hires (and to grant waivers for a huge number of cases that always seem to be exceptions to the rules). Though it rarely comes to outright opposition, the Affirmative Action Office has a potentially adversarial role when set against campus units that have an eye on a specific recruit for a position. And to complicate the matter a bit more, the Affirmative Action Officer is on the president's own staff, serving at her or his will and passing judgement on issues that ultimately go to the president's desk. Not the best position for an overseer and/or whistle blower, especially for one who works without tenure.

Affirmative action guidelines, and the university's first affirmative action officer, go back to the late 1960s. A committee report from 1970 was already indicating that greater efforts were needed, were we to accomplish anything in the realm of Equal Opportunity hiring.[18] The Director was the pressure point or voice for better practices, and she tried to point out that consciousness raising, at the very least, was within our powers. Though the Toll-Pond administration favored diversity and minority hiring, like so many other worthy goals that had to be juggled, it seemed to be one that we never quite got around to dealing with, at least not as a very high priority.

Nor is the task as easy as it might sound. The pools of minority PhDs, particularly of African Americans, are small, and Stony Brook departments were often prone to fall back on the idea that such candidates would be hard pressed to produce first rate scholarship while simultaneously providing a role model, especially for students. That this rationale against diversification served as a self-fulfilling prophecy, or a cop-out, needs little elaboration. Not surprisingly, most African American faculty at Stony Brook have been in friendly or pertinent fields; Africana Studies, Nursing, Social Welfare (and the last two are in HSC). Nor was the local neighborhood climate much inducement to take a position were it to be offered; conservative, heavily white, slow to accept Blacks (and then Latinos and Asian-Americans), occasionally openly racist and hostile. Academics may be liberals and even radicals in their individual political choices, but the structure of discipline-oriented academia is conservative and change comes – if at all – but slowly and often with some pain.

In an effort to give more visibility to Affirmative Action and Equal Opportunity, if not too much independence, Marburger set up a grid of AA/EEO committees to cover the entire campus, with an umbrella committee at the top. While a veto on any given hire (by not "signing off" on the paperwork) was not within the power of these committees, they did provide a forum for discussions of policy and for lobbying for the cause. To a limited extent affirmative action issues worked their way forward on the hiring agenda. But here too, the turn-over of officers, coupled with legal and administrative restraints, and the complications of compliance and oversight, and conservatism if not latent racism, meant the University had limited success in terms of hiring. When we compare the ethnic composition of the faculty in 1990 or 1994 with that of 1979 or 1980 we see that, for all the talk, there had been little change.[19] It was a very static situation – rather remarkable, given the number of hires over the years and the supposed commitment to change. The percentage of African-American and Hispanic faculty went from 10% in 1975 to 15% in 1990 (and then it had declined to 13% by 1994).[20]

There was considerably more progress when it came to redressing the gender balance of the faculty, though here too the gains came early and then leveled off. "Progress" was uneven across the campus, of course, with many more women in the Humanities (and in History) than in most of the sciences - and here Engineering's tale was especially sorry until very recent years. But by the early 1990s there had been a genuine change, if we make a comparison with the early days of the University (other than foreign languages and English, where women were always prominent). Problems of equal pay, or of equal respect, or of equal opportunity for promotion and advancement - in faculty or in administrative ranks – lasted for years, and even a partial victory by the plaintiffs in Coser vs. Moore (for which, see the Appendix) hardly leveled the playing field. Women stand at around 20% of the full time faculty, and on hold at that level for some years now seems to be the tale. As newer hires, women still tend to be more represented in lower faculty ranks than do men, and as the primary carriers of domestic obligations their rate of publication is slower than that of men of their age (including, in numerous cases, their own partners).

By way of contrast, the (undergraduate) student body really has changed in the last several decades. Some credit for this to the university, but much more to the changing demography of the Northeast. At the beginning of this new century state universities are well on the way to a time - predicted as coming within the next decade or two - when a combination of various "minorities" - Asian American, Hispanic, and African American - will comprise over half the undergraduate student body. At least Stony Brook seems to have welcomed this trend, which means a diversity of cultures, colors, of first- or home-languages, and of student interests and identities. The academic and social development of ethnic studies and consciousness raising activities is comparable to what it was in the 1960s, when Stony Brook played the game but often fell short when it came to a serious commitment of resources or priorities.[21]

Graduate student ranks have been extremely diverse, in terms of ethnicity and passports and visas and green cards, from the start. The common wisdom is that doctoral programs in the sciences, especially in engineering, run heavily on students from abroad – largely from Asia (India, and more recently the Peoples' Republic of China, Japan, and Korea), since U.S. industry siphons off much of the domestic crop prior to the PhD. A particular point that made Stony Brook a familiar name in China was the role of C. N. Yang as an advisor on scientific education to the Peoples' Republic. This made us a drawing card even before Nixon normalized relations with China in 1971, and students came here in fields far removed from theoretical physics. By the 80s the internationalization of graduate students had gone from the sciences to most of the social sciences and was making itself known (even) in the humanities. In turn, these students would eventually carry Stony Brook's colors around the world, which in turn means that their own students are apt to follow in their steps – or so the argument goes.[22]

This look at affirmative action and diversity is but a dip into the issues that preoccupied the University during the long stretch of the Marburger years. I have already discussed the imposition of a more rigid set of liberal arts requirements upon undergraduates – the DEC— as a major "reform" of the late 80s and early 90s. Another– also covered under student life - concerns the up-grading of intercollegiate athletics. Athletics was an under-developed area, perhaps by design, perhaps simply because of the immense list of projects that always seemed more important. By the late 1980s Marburger became receptive to a call for up-grading athletics, especially football and basketball. Toward the end of his years he gave a green light for the climb from Division III of the NCAA (National Collegiate Athletic Association) to Division I, class AA. This was a controversial decision, touching resources and personnel and also the basic identity or tilt of the university. Marburger claimed he was but heeding the voice of the campus, which is always an easy way out of a tight corner. To me it was clearly a case of his hearing what he wished; many of us heard voices that said NO.

A final comment on Marburger's administration. It (or he, if we wish) was extremely tolerant of protest and activism, both from students and faculty. I think it fair to end with some compliments, a balance to my criticisms about the upgrading of athletics and the arming of campus security (The Police). Under Marburger's lead there was a willingness to look for a middle ground– more than under Toll before or Kenny after. He tried, most of the time, to adhere to the virtues of civil society. A graduate student strike in 1986-87 was not treated fairly or wisely, and some students were eventually hauled off by the Suffolk County police when they refused to fold up their "tent city" on the central mall. But generally there was an absence of chest thumping. In 1985 students - led by but not limited to African American undergraduates - conducted a long symbolic sit-in in the Ad Building, protesting corporate support for apartheid in South Africa. Marburger met frequently with them; he allowed them a good deal of lobby space, he tried to make clear he was on their side, and he gave them a few minutes on the podium at the spring graduation ceremony. In sum, Jack Marburger could be less than the aggressive leader many felt the University needed, and he was inclined to delegate decisions to lesser subordinates and then to stand back. However, in a run of 14 years he was usually a nice man. He did not go home and compile enemy lists, and - as was said of Beowulf in the Old English poem I have assigned to thousands of students over the years - he slew not his hearth companions while drunk.[23]

The resignation of Marburger - announced during the summer of 1993 - and the search that brought Shirley Strum Kenny to Stony Brook, as third president on this site, is the proper place to end the bulk of my tale, though miscellaneous reflections keep popping up about things since 1994. As Marburger said, turnover in the presidency is the time for the university to take stock of where it has been and where it would like to go.

In talking both about the faculty and the administration I have painted a picture of a university that offers a reasonable academic challenge to its students, but one that does most of this within the confines of traditional bread-and-butter teaching. I have not given much credit to the various attempts to present alternatives, variations on the main theme. Every serious school has some of these – something to brag about, something to attract and hold unusually dedicated students, something to allow special talents to be spotted and nurtured. These alternatives are for the few, however they are chosen, and they cost a good deal, however the accounting is done, at least when compared to stand-up lectures and lab sessions run by a team of TAs. But they have become a regular part of the total package, just like those fancy dishes on a menu that are billed at "market price."

By the 1990s Stony Brook could offer a fair assortment of these off-the-beaten-track alternatives. Though costly, the University made certain that they had a high visibility and could serve as bragging points for public relations and recruiting. Such side routes as the Honors College, the Federated Learning Community, WISE (Women in Science and Engineering), URECA (Undergraduate Research and Creative Activity), the coordinated freshman program, and the Living-Learning dorm programs had to be given more attention and money, on a per capita basis, if they were to have any chance of success. We all need something for the highlight film.

The oldest of the experiments is the Federated Learning Community, devised in the mid-70s as the brain child of Pat Hill of the Philosophy Department, with strong support from Sid Gelber. A group of about 20-25 motivated students and an interdisciplinary group of about 3 or 4 or 5 faculty would participate in seminars around a theme (e.g., The Environment), as well as take some regular courses that touched the theme. One of the faculty, that year's master learner, would attend everything and also devise a special seminar, for students and the other faculty, on the theme. In that most of the students and faculty involved gave their year in the FLC a high rating, the experiment or variation can be considered a success. But, of course, in keeping with the other variations on the learning format, small groups that are given special privileges have enough common sense to say that it was a wonderful experience.

By definition, the FLC must be small, and in so far as the faculty are relieved of some of their other duties in return for their participation, it has to be considered an expensive alternative. The Honors College, by contrast, has followed a model that permits of considerable growth, going from a freshman group of 20-25 to a group for each of the four years of that size (or more). But again, special classes, tiny seminars, and other extra prizes make this kind of program an elite and costly one. One major problem at Stony Brook is that faculty are not hired for an interest in such ventures, and the programs have a constant fight to find dedicated people whose departmental chairs are willing to spare them from the regular discipline-oriented curriculum they are expected to deliver. The Administration tends to encourage the development of alternatives, though it is often hard pressed to maintain the original level of special funding without which the project never could have left the ground. Once in a while there is some help from a source like the Carnegie Endowment or the Lillie Foundation, but such funding tends to come with term limits and provides rather shaky planks on which to build the edifice.

The lesson here – both for the alternatives to bread-and-butter education and for a survey of the Administration over the long haul - is that a University lives by juggling its commitment to long-range plans and the future with a need to meet the crises and problems of the day. To say this about Stony Brook is only to indicate that within a few decades we too have managed to join the gang; the new kid on the block now looks, for better or for worse, pretty much like everyone else.

(Endnotes)

1. The first woman to preside over a SUNY campus was Virginia L. Radley, President of Oswego: acting president, 1976-78, and fully invested president, 1978-88. Women have presided over SUNY Binghamton, the College at Old Westbury, and elsewhere. When Shirley Kenny was chosen president of Stony Brook in 1994 she was already president of Queens College, CUNY.

2. A big university is a complex corporation with many vice-presidential areas. In the 1971 organizational chart there was an executive VP, a VP for academic affairs, a VP for finance and management, a VP for the health sciences center, a VP for liberal studies, and a VP for student affairs (plus numerous associate and assistant VPs). But against this seeming proliferation of equals, Bentley Glass used to say, "There are vice presidents and there are vice presidents."

3. A "John S. Toll Society" has been established through the Stony Brook Foundation to honor the first president. Membership is to be a magnet for serious fund raising, with a focus on the planned giving of estates, real estate, life insurance, jewels, stocks and bonds, and any other goodies worth $25,000 or more. Membership in the Society carries various privileges, including the invaluable one of free campus parking.

4. Bentley Glass (1906-) served as president of Phi Beta Kappa, the American Association of University Professors, the American Association for the Advancement of Science and other learned societies, many of them in the field of genetics. He was a fellow of the National Academy of Science and of the American Philosophical Society, and an early leader in the science community in his emphasis on the social history of science. After C. N. Yang he was the most distinguished figure on the early faculty.

5. T. Alexander Pond (1924-) had his PhD in physics from Princeton. He came to Stony Brook in 1962, the year the campus opened, and he served as chair of Physics before becoming Toll's EVP. He served as acting president when Toll was on leave in 1970 and 1975, as well as after his departure in 1978, and he left Stony Brook to become executive VP of Rutgers, the prestigious state university of New Jersey, in 1982.

6. The first graduate deans were David Fox (physics), Robert Jordan (English), and then Herb Weisinger (English). Arnold Feingold, a physicist, had served in this role during the last year at Oyster Bay to expedite the move and the creation of the graduate programs.

7. Student protest was not invented (or discovered) in 1968. There had been a student strike at Oyster Bay when Al Austil was (temporarily) fired as dean of students. Also, student protests over civil rights had racked many campuses in the early 1960s, and though Stony Brook had little involvement with the early days of the Civil Rights movement, there were already currents blowing in the wind.

8. The main Long Island papers were *Newsday* and *The Suffolk Sun*, though the former was more widely read in the western part of the Island in those days. Each local community had a weekly and they were usually unfriendly to the University's growth, interests, and personnel (especially its students), seeing themselves as guardians of local mores against the SUNY Visigoths who were trying to climb the walls.

9. Donald Axelrod, "Higher Education," in Robert H. Connery and Gerald Benjamin, *Governing New York State: The Rockefeller Years, Proceedings, Academy of Political Science* 31, 3 (May, 1974), pp. 131-45: 138-45, on Rockefeller's response to the need to trim the budget, and 135-38 on his policy of providing direct aid to private colleges and universities.

10. The early catch-word, in days of great optimism, was that the

University was striving for "comprehensive excellence" - that is, quality programs across the board. Then, as the belt had to be cinched in, Toll switched to "selective excellence" which meant "yes" to growth and development for favored areas, "no" or "not now" for those that did not rate so highly.

11. The Education Department probably taught more students per dollar than any other unit on campus, with a range of 5 introductory courses, 10 at the 200- or intermediate level, and 26 at upper levels (including the "practice teaching" placements in the local schools). Its regular faculty of 26 included 10 women, and there were another 14 women among the 19 lecturers and the 3 adjuncts.

12. Though I obviously tell the tale in terms of a view hostile to the decision to eliminate education, it is that of a faculty member who opposed and publicly deplored the retrenchment from the time it was announced (via pink slips in the mail). Toll had been instructed to make a major cut that would not harm the University's research mission; nor was he to make one across the board (that is, a little here, a little there). His administrators and the SB Council went over this decision with him, through the summer, 1975, and they all came to accept the retrenchment as necessary, though they lent their support with varying degrees of reluctance. Administrators and members of the Council did go to the chair of the trustees to see if there could be an alternative; none was forthcoming. Virtually every SUNY campus retrenched; Stony Brook was about in the middle in terms of numbers of people and programs. The issue is reviewed, from a faculty perspective, in *AAUP Bulletin*, August, 1977, pp. 237-60, with Stony Brook treated, pp. 252-53. Because the retrenchment was carried out without meeting the AAUP's standards for consultation and/or an adequate demonstration of financial exigency, the AAUP's national meeting voted to place the entire SUNY system on its list of censured administrations - where it still remains. The UUP was not sympathetic to the AAUP censure, given that its contract was one of the major fault

lines in the AAUP evaluation. In the four SUNY university centers a total of 27 tenured faculty were retrenched; another 55, on tenure-track lines but still on term or probationary contracts, were also dismissed.

13. The College Council is the local body, appointed by the governor, with authority to oversee certain aspects of the University: choice of a president, supervision of student rules of conduct, naming of buildings, being among them. It is both a watchdog over the campus and a champion of its interests and needs. Harriman's first Stony Brook council had Judge William Sullivan of Rockville Center as chair, Ward Melville of Stony Brook as Honorary Chair, and such members as David Sarnoff, chair of RCA in New York, a labor representative from West Hempstead (Paul Jennings of the Electrical and Radio Workers), William Coe (grandson of the estate owner), and Norman Newhouse, editor of the Long Island Daily Press. Soon the council's members came down a notch in fame and wealth as terms ended and new appointments were made. The campus president meets monthly with the council and fills it in on events and problems.

14. In the selection of Shirley Kenny in 1994 there was a split between the search committee and the Council over the two finalists. In such a case the voice of Albany (Chancellor and trustees) is decisive.

15. Both Toll and Pond returned to Stony Brook to receive honorary degrees; Toll in 1990, Pond in 1998. As well as the "John Toll Society," there is a large oil portrait of Toll, beside one of Marburger, in the galleria of the main library.

16. John H. Marburger (1940-) received his PhD in Physics from Stanford and climbed the academic ladder - professor, chair, and dean - at the University of Southern California. After he came to Stony Brook he served on various committees appointed by the governor: an advisory one on public power and the nuclear gener-

ating plant on L.I., that on the stream-lining of SUNY, etc. He went on to become director of Brookhaven National Lab, and - at this writing - has been serving as President Bush's science advisor (about which the least said the better). Homer Neal (1942-) received his PhD in Physics from the University of Michigan. He came to Stony Brook from Indiana University, where he had been Dean of Research and Graduate Development. He served as Provost (AVP) at Stony Brook, 1981-86, and went to Michigan in 1987 to become vice president for research (and he also served as acting president and as chair of Physics). He served on the Advanced Award Panel of the NSF, 1976-79, and the National Science Board, 1980-86.

17. After Neal resigned Marburger chose Jerry Schubel, long-time dean of the Marine Sciences Research Center, and then Tilden Edelstein (an historian), who came from Rutgers, and finally Bryce Hool, an economist who was Dean of Social and Behavioral Science. So of the four provosts or AVPs of the Marburger years (not counting Gelber), two were new comers to Stony Brook, two veterans of the local administrative drill.

18. Vera Rony, the University's first affirmative action officer, came with a background in civil rights and labor: the League for Industrial Democracy, organizing in North Carolina, Committee for Racial Equality. She found the administration's assurances of support for the cause easier to enlist while being interviewed than to gain when she was on the ground and had problems to remedy. She concluded her Stony Brook career as a faculty member is the Social Sciences program, trying to develop a Labor Education program for the adult education constituency.

19. When Beverley Harrison was affirmative action officer in 1982 she published a newsletter, covering personal profiles and statistics. She gave coverage to women and their problems and progress, as well as to the situation of the disabled on campus. I assume this was a wise and deliberate effort to move affirmative action away from a single focus on race.

20. In 1975, out of a main campus (i.e., excluding the Health Science Center) faculty of 679, 19 were African American, 14 Hispanic, with a "total minority" number of 67. Ten years later the 1985 figures were 745 faculty, 20 African American, 15 Hispanic, and 95 in the "total minority" category.

21 This too is contested ground. The Administration can point to a long record of efforts to diversify the employee pool (at all levels) as well as to offer mentoring programs, special initiatives (including special grants, fellowships, etc) for minority students in science and engineering, special orientation programs, and more of the like, much of it supported by external government funding. From the perspective of many of the faculty in Africana Studies or of students, as expressed in *Blackworld* or other campus channels, the University is located in a racist area and has never been willing to make the kind of effort that would lead to real change, whether the concern is faculty numbers or student problems.

22. Turner Fellowships, explicitly designed for minority graduate students (African American, Hispanic American, and Native American) were created in 1987 with special state funding. They were named, locally, in honor of W. Burghardt Turner, a retired member of the History faculty and a civil rights activist on Long Island for many years, long before he came to Stony Brook in the late 1960s. The Fellowships guaranteed their recipients five years' of funding (assuming satisfactory progress and good standing); they pay about 20% above the regular TA lines. They have helped attract and retain minority students and by the mid-90s were showing results – in the form of students receiving MAs and PhDs.

CHAPTER SEVEN
Student Life and the Student Community

A look at student life will obviously entail attention to topics like athletic teams, clubs and publications, concerts and talks, and the problem of integrating day-commuters into the campus community. Though these are matters of interest and importance, were they to be our sole focus they would make students and student life peripheral to the university's main functions - something we only turn to after the serious adult business of Toll and Marburger and building the campus. Rather, as both active agents and as consumers or receivers, students and their concerns are and have always been an integral part of the whole business. Their presence, needs, and voice (at times) had a major role in shaping the university - in helping to determine its expenditures, priorities, and public face or image. Extra-curricular and residential activities are but part of the tale, and they will be presented here, but as blended with rather than detached from curricular ones.

Though Stony Brook – created to be a comprehensive research university - has never been known as especially student-friendly (certainly not when compared to its other priorities or to many older SUNY schools) students are of some passing importance. Much of the campus, in terms of space, is devoted to non-classroom student use, and students and their problems, both academic and personal, claim a great deal of administrative attention and money. Some of this is a logical extension of the educational enterprise, while other aspects - like dorm judiciaries and the counseling service— are the infrastructure than any community generates as part of its own social dynamic. Students and student life have figured in all the topics and themes I have talked about.

However, because students sometimes take a back seat, or have allowed themselves to be directed to a back seat, they can get overlooked in a discussion of constituencies and interests.

In so far as undergraduates have a collective academic identity or presence, they are served by the office of Undergraduate Studies. This office, created in the mid-70s, always had to make do with few resources and alongside, rather than in place of, the departments that house the majors. At various times much of the undergraduate advising has been housed in Undergraduate Studies, to the relief of the departments, and support (financial and emotional) for various minority programs, pre-professional advising, the academic side of student judiciary matters, and the coordination of courses (through the Curriculum Committee) runs through this office. But in the mid-90s the office lost its dean-level standing, and President Kenny has allowed it to function under a collection of lieutenants but without a captain. Alongside Undergraduate Studies, in either a complementary or competitive fashion, is the office of the Vice President for Student Affairs. This office, succeeding the old and traditional dean of students, supervised extracurricular student life, though where to place new-student orientation, or admissions, has often been still one more contested bit of terrain. The vast world of dormitory administration is part of the University's business network – another administrative world, and one about which I have little to say. So the upshot is that undergraduates are under the umbrella or two or three administrative areas, though when functions are shifted or personnel hired, fired, or demoted, one certainty is that student in-put is not a major factor in the decision. And of course the students' own governance (Polity) has some authority in those carefully delimited areas in which it is are allowed to operate.

Student life at Stony Brook was predestined to be difficult. The campus was built in the middle of nowhere, surrounded by an unfriendly community. We would always have problems trying to mesh a student body that was 50% dorm residents, 50% locals who left every evening for parental homes or some off-campus equivalent. These sober considerations meant that the quality of student life would always be problematic. Nor did the ugly, sprawling campus help. Because most of the dorm residents were really but a few hours (or less) from home, the chances were that many of them would leave on Thursday or Friday for a long weekend, which in turn compounded the problems of weekend anomie and boredom for those who did stay– whether from choice or necessity. The classic statement is that there was little social and cultural life because so few students were around on the weekend, and if so few students were around where was the incentive to develop the cultural and social life. This circular thinking may have become a self-fulfilling prophecy, and true or not it has always haunted Stony Brook. I personally think it has been grossly overestimated as a factor in shaping student life, but this may be another case of an adult with a different perspective passing himself off as an expert on the social life of a (much) younger generation.

A few more thoughts at the start, reverting to an earlier theme, the political economy of SUNY. When SUNY was on the drawing board the idea was that there would be no tuition – as was the case at the City University. By the time Oyster Bay was opened the fees were $200 for the year, with a remission for those in the education stream. But gradually higher tuition, raised by the Legislature as part of the state budget package, became a regular feature of the SUNY system (which generally has a uniform tuition across the state, though local fees could vary). A differential between NY State residents and out-of-state students is pretty standard, as is a higher rate for graduate students than undergraduates (though most full-time PhD candidates were likely to be on TA lines which covered tuition plus).

We get an insight into the world SUNY was created to serve when we realize that even the low tuition was difficult for many students (and/or their families). If we look at 1965-66, the year in which John Toll took over, we go back to a time when undergraduate tuition for a state resident was $200 per semester: $300 for those few from elsewhere. Fees and deposits added about $150 (some returnable, if you didn't break anything); double occupancy in the dorms was an additional $365 for the full year, plus $440 for a plan of 21 meals per week. Ten years later the basic tuition had risen to $650 per year for a state resident in the first two years, $800 for "upper division" students (and non-NY residents paid $1075 and $1300 per annum). Double rooms in the dorms were up to $650, and learning from bitter experience, the University was now levying a $5.00 bad check fee.[1] Amidst much political controversy, the state passed a share of rising costs directly back to those being served; by 1989-91 undergraduate tuition was up to $1350 a year, single dorm rooms per semester now went for $1110 (and a shared double was but a bit less: $1035). Mandatory meal plans were no longer the norm, and there was a cooking fee of $374 (or $242 if one lived in a suite).

Compared to what the privates ask of their students (or their families), this is small money indeed. But for the SUNY constituency, many found these costs, along with incidental fees and the price of commuting by car, a serious financial hurdle. By way of assistance, the state and the federal government had a range of financial assistance programs. Many were need-based, and some were either specifically for or steered toward minority students. Many financial aid programs rest on a variety of student loans, to be paid back at low interest rates after graduation. Scholarship and fellowship programs might give some money outright to students of merit, and often money was earmarked for students of specific racial or ethnic or academic categories. A list of such scholarships in the undergraduate bulletin served as a come-on to prospective students and a lifeline for some already at Stony Brook. From the federal government there were Pell Grants (that once covered 60% of costs), and a federally funded work-study program, allowing those who could demonstrate need to find jobs on campus. The State put most of its help into TAP (Tuition Assistance Program) - a sine qua non for thousands of undergraduates, though the late arrival of the checks was a given. Regents' scholarships and Equal Opportunity money (for minority students, largely dispensed through AIM: Advancement on Individual Merit), all helped, at least a bit. In addition the University had scholarships of its own, based mainly on money donated in honor or memory of an individual: in memory of Ashley Schiff or Elizabeth Couey, or given by the Class of 1970, or for outstanding work in Latin American Studies (a Simon Bolivar scholarship), and many more. But Stony

Brook's own funds were always very limited– a top-up, at best, to state and federal programs, and Stony Brook's students come from a world where some sort of help is essential.[2]

Graduate student tuition is always higher; more specialized training is deemed to be worth more - and it costs more to provide. In 1968-69, as many of the graduate programs were moving toward maturity, the tuition was $300 per semester (for a full-time student) or $20 per credit (for the many part-time students). Health insurance ran to $32 for a 12 month year; $69 for a student and spouse; $117 for student, spouse, and child. But inflation is the law of life, and by 1986-88 graduate students were confronted with a tuition bill of $2150 (and $3735 if from out of state). A double room in a graduate dorm was $1750 per annum, plus $200-300 in cooking fees. But the real squeeze on graduate students was such that even with a TAship of $3000, as it had been around 1970, or of $6-8000 around 1990, life at Stony Brook always cost more than the state could provide. Many, if not most graduate students, had to borrow money, work at other jobs during the school year and the summer, and learn to live austerely. This is not to present graduate school just in terms of a financial squeeze, but somewhere on the horizon there was pretty sure to be a pile of bills and dollar signs. Though SUNY remained inexpensive when compared to the private sector, the dreams of the 1940s were shattered by inflation, Cold War military budgets, and the withering of a populist ideology.[3]

But students, unlike faculty, do not live by bread alone, and we turn now to some of the less mundane aspects of the college experience. Whatever individual problems - financial, psychological, intellectual - a student copes with in college, the ordinary depiction of student life does seem to center on extra-curricular activities and social life. Over this, in the administrative framework, presides the Dean of Students, or since the mid-70s, the VP for Student Affairs. In the nostalgic if hardly idyllic days at Oyster Bay the dean was expected to oversee most aspects of student life beyond the classroom. At such a tiny place he was a familiar figure, and he too was in the firing line that engulfed so many faculty and staff in that world. Students went on strike in support of Al Austil when President Lee fired him - which means that they boycotted classes. And though Austil chose to leave at the time of the move to Stony Brook, he was the dedicatee of the first yearbook, the (1957-)1961 Specula. In a mix of sentiment and mawkish humor, he was hailed: "He has been our Father Zossima, our Socrates, and our Santa Claus. He has been our opponent, our protector, our champion and our friend."

But life on the new campus was not all grim problems and the challenge of half-built buildings. An early Stony Brook yearbook offers a welcome respite from the tedious litany about the lack of campus life. In fact, if we had not been told of a school spirit problem we might think that some people actually enjoyed their time at the University. For a campus of several thousand students, the 1966 yearbook depicted what seems like a lively scenario. There were numerous academically-oriented clubs: biology, chemistry, math, education, pre-law, pre-medicine, among others. These sound a bit nerdy, but their popularity says something about student interests as well, perhaps, as about the absence of sexier alternatives. There were student theater productions: T. S. Eliot's "Sweeney Agonistes" and plays by Shaw, Lorca, Dylan Thomas, and Sean O'Casey. Such roving minstrels as the Charles River Boys, Dave Brubeck, the Clancy Brothers, Simon and Garfunkel, the Fugs, and Paul Butterfield had done their thing at Stony Brook that year. There were student publications, plus organizations and clubs devoted to chess, rifle practice (not yet politically incorrect), WUSB (the student radio station), religious identities, a chorus, Young Democrats, and dormitory councils, as well as Polity (the student government).

Nor was it only for the mind; clubs or teams had carried the Patriot colors (red and gray) in basketball (5-14 record), judo (2-3), cross country (9-6), track and field (7-4), plus bowling, swimming, gymnastics, tennis, and crew. And long before there was a call for equal faculties for women, there were women's teams in swimming and volleyball. It is embarrassing to note that there was also a cheerleading squad. Given the size of the campus, and the strong presence of intra-murals in addition to inter-collegiate sports, we hardly seem to be falling into a black hole of tedium, neither for athletics (in the old gym, the pool, and the adjacent fields) nor for social and cultural events. Those students involved in organized activities may not have realized how bad things were supposed to be. Institutions become more complex over time. In student affairs rising expectations and compliance regulations have added to the burden, welcome though their payoff might be. Since the days when David Tilley was dean of Students (and a "good guy" during the 1968 drug bust and subsequent investigations), little has become simpler. By the early 1970s the world of student affairs had reached a level of size and complexity that called for a VP, and Elizabeth Wadsworth, with a background in international education, was appointed by John Toll to this new level of command. Her world was complex; the 1974-75 catalogue tells of a staff with two acting assistant VPs, a director of international student affairs, a director of university housing, and a dean for student administrative services. Nor did the waterfront become less crowded; by 1983-85 the bulletin listed 11 divisions of the student service universe, covering disabled students, minority students (in numerous programs), day care, etc. By now this world was under the sway of Fred Preston, who came from the University of Massachusetts to become VPSA in 1981 (and is still in place).

An aspect of student life, always with us but less pressing and omnipresent than it was in 1962, concerns rules and regulations of conduct and behavior. There are still - and always will be - codes defining acceptable conduct in such matters as academic honesty, a dorm's permissible boundaries of autonomy, drink and drugs, sex and sexual harassment, and related niceties of civil society. Student judiciary bodies oversee rules defined as within their purview, while quasi-academic bodies hear about cheating and plagiarism, classroom misbehavior, and (for balance) the misuse of professorial authority or discretion. In the early days a university was expected to stand in loco parentis (in the place of parents), especially regarding sexual activity and related matters like dorm visiting hours and alcohol. This world, perhaps more than most others, has changed beyond recognition.

The varieties of student activities and interests are too numerous and diverse to cover except in the most summary fashion, as we saw from the yearbook. For a different wide angle view, I turn to student publications (where students offer other students bits of information and opinion), to athletics (where some participate and others watch), to interest groups (where participation is a basic ingredient), and to public events (where people are brought to campus to offer wisdom, humor, or noise). Student government (Polity) gets passing mention; countless other engaging and commendable forms of social and cultural life get slighted through no fault of their own. In the memory of alumni - looking back to youthful vision and follies - student activities loom large. They conjure up a world of escape from academic pressures and one of socialization and friendship, of idealism and optimism - whether sustained in later life or put on the shelf with t-shirts and beer mugs.

The funding and regulation (or recognition) of student activities and organizations is an issue every university has to deal with. Some official approval - whether for a concert or for the French club - is to be expected. The traditional solution rests on some shared involvement of the VP or dean and the elected student government. Early in Stony Brook's history it was determined (in keeping with state policies) that the basic apportioning of student fees for activities would be determined by Polity, the elected student government. Obviously, this gave Polity a lot of power, a major say in the distribution of a large kitty. It also dictated the direction of much of Polity's energy and focus, perhaps making it more supervisory and less political than it might have been had the money run through other channels. But Polity's decisions were usually exercised within accepted boundaries; recognized groups were entitled to a share of each year's fees, and allocations were not to fluctuate too capriciously as groups were in or out of favor with the current executive board. But for all the facade of participatory democracy, students are not likely to exert control over critical areas of campus life, much though they might be affected by them. The large student-oriented businesses, like the bookstore and the meal plans and cafeteria contracts, are handled by a special corporation, The FSA (Faculty-Student Association), with student members but not student control. Really big bucks are too serious to be left to the kids, and student opinion about the quality and quantity of the food served by the vendors is rarely the key factor in awarding the contract. This should not come as a shock.

Student publications are a good starting point. They tell us about freedom of speech and the level of student analysis, a tale of impressive diversity. They are a feature of virtually every university - including those in countries under repressive regimes where the student press can be a powerful magnet of resistance. Stony Brook (or Oyster Bay before that) hardly qualified as a repressive regime; a relatively open field for all sorts of publications has always been the pattern, and it is a Stony Brook tradition worth bragging about. Some publications enjoy semi-official status, like *The Statesman* (the student newspaper – successor to the *Sucolian* - as in "State University College on Long Island" from Oyster Bay), or the yearbook, *Specula*. Others have had varying life spans, some lasting over several decades, others appearing but once or twice. Some publications are mainly intended as the voice of a particular interest - academic, or religious or racial/ethnic – while others have more ambitious reach. All of them seem to have trouble reaching the whole Stony Brook audience: irregular distribution, the indifference of would-be readers, a dislike of the message. It is hard to say there ever has been such a thing as the voice that everyone reads or that covers the entire waterfront.

My high regard for the number and range of student publications is reinforced by the fact that Stony Brook has never offered much training in journalism and that virtually no student involved in writing or editing gets paid. A few may get some academic credit for their efforts (via internships or independent projects, plus a handful of journalism courses housed in the English Department), but most student writing is just a labor of love. Furthermore, whatever their shortcomings and deficiencies, these publications are distributed gratis (except for the yearbook). In so far as there is a common culture on the campus, it is probably set and fueled more by the student papers than by any other factor. Often they have been outrageous and provocative; nothing produces a common bond, albeit a short-lived one, like an inflammatory article or a column on abortion or race or the holocaust or Mother Theresa. Neither good investigative journalism nor bad taste is treasonable, and the discomfort that freedom of the press causes the administration - or particular groups, or individuals - is but the cherry on the cake of student journalism. That these vulgar and/or muck-raking items are often racist, or reactionary, or sexist, or anti-intellectual, or personally offensive, goes with the territory. And - to give credit - there have been few efforts by the University at censorship; more flack, and more calls for restraint, come from offended students than from those in official positions.

The *Statesman* has been the regular campus newspaper since the beginning. It conforms to the expected model of a voluntary student newspaper. Its strength is regularity of publication and a standardized if limited format: campus news, a weekly calendar (that catches about half of events), ads that steer students to local businesses and services, sports (both on- and off-campus), and odd snatches of collegiate news from elsewhere. As a cultural artifact through which to recreate Stony Brook's history in the year 3003, the *Statesman* would leave us well informed about current music and movies, up-to-date on local restaurants and bars, and alerted to social and cultural change through the presence of ads and columns on abortion, birth control, and sex - topics once taboo in this open guise. At the same time we would be left pretty much in the dark about the curriculum and the faculty, and poorly informed about state government, SUNY, and the political economy of the university.[4] However, it should be said that the *Statesman* does the best it can. Student interest in faculty matters, let alone in the administration, is not a high priority - except when scandal raises its lovely head or when a boost in state tuition is proposed in Albany.[5]

In keeping with my random dip into Stony Brook's history, we can take a closer look at some issues *Statesman* over the years. What changes in style can we pick up? Are there clear distinctions between the small and still-new campus of 1965 and the fully mature and busy one of two decades later? Though such changes are a logical inference, what actually emerges from issues of the paper is that there has been surprisingly little change, at least in style or format. In fairness, a student paper, like a college athletic team, runs in short-term cycles; rich and lean years, depending on editorial skill and the break of events. Fruits of experience and maturation evaporate quickly as editors graduate and new hands hit the keyboard.

Given these reflections, the conclusion is that any issue is probably a typical one; the law of large numbers and random sampling. If we turn to the *Statesman* of February 13, 1980 – a rough mid-way point in our journey - we find a modest ration of campus news, more than compensated for by a lively culture and feature section. A bonus of this particular issue is the personals, the day before Valentines Day; "Dearest Charlie. I love you now and always! Be my Valentine Forever, your baby, Dianne," and so on for 4 1/2 romantic pages. News articles warned that the State wanted to close a SUNY campus (a standard scare item from Albany in tough times); Amman College, a dorm in G quad, had voted to house the Federated Learning Community; the Health Science student organization was seceding from Polity's control. Professor Zweig had been to and now returned from Iran, and editorials attacked Governor Carey's budget as well as a decision about the academic calendar (fewer class meetings, more minutes per class). At this time there was an impressive culture-feature section, some 12 pages of "Statesman Alternates," with reviews of films, new disks and records, and live music in NYC and on the Island. Sports coverage revealed that the bowling team's loss to Suffolk Community College was "heartbreaking," which may argue the need for dispassionate journalism. One likes to think this was in irony. That the women's swim team came in fourth in a meet - of an unspecified number of competitors - shows greater circumspection. Nor should we neglect the opportunity to go to Bermuda for spring break for $289, or to get a pair of contact lenses for $59, or a hair cut in the Union basement for a mere $4.00.

Along with the Statesman, as a venerable institution, comes *Specula*, the fairly standard college yearbook, produced each spring with an eye on a summary of the year just navigated, especially attuned to revisiting the experiences of the graduating class. The yearbook is a corrective or foil to the newspaper; *Specula's* overview of the year, presented in the editor's introduction, balancing the newspaper's ephemeral but on-the-spot coverage. In a similar fashion, medieval monasteries often appointed a monk as the in-house chronicler: this year it snowed at Easter, this year we got the bones of St Kenelm, this year the new latrine was finally completed, etc. A college yearbook serves a comparable purpose, with better photographs.

Over the years there were changes in the yearbook, one being the transition from black-and-white to color pictures, and in the late 1960s and early 1970s there often was a mix of the styles. The 1970 yearbook came in two volumes, one being wholly devoted to "photo-journalism" shots of the campus. Some editors added shots of world events and personalities, a touch that sets their year in context when the alumni thumb through their volume. That for 1976, to mark the bicentennial of the Republic, had a long section on the early history of Long Island. This was adorned with sepia pictures, designed no doubt for their pseudo-antique air. Occasionally an editor is moved to write extensive prose, but in most cases the photos are identified with little by way of explanation or comment. Sometimes there are local ads, congratulating the class and reminding them of the local watering holes where their money will always be welcome.

If the regular student paper, once or twice or thrice a week (at various times), plus the yearbook, are the bookends of student journalism at Stony Brook, there is a long shelf of stuff in between. Some, like the *Stony Brook Press* or *Blackworld*, have lasted for years – the–*Press* since 1979 - though their appearance may be sporadic and their history likely to reveal wide swings of quality and editorial focus. Many other publications appeared, perhaps for an issue or two, perhaps for five years of more; eventually most of them went the way of all flesh. Like faculty conferences and institutes, many of these initiatives rested on the enthusiasm of one or two people - perhaps inspired by events or by a perceived hiatus in the local scene - and their departure, or loss of zeal, or lack of funds, eventually brought the curtain down.

Blackworld has lasted the course pretty well as the voice of the African-American community, with a strong focus on undergraduate programs and cultural events. By 1975 it was publishing its second volume (i.e., year 2), and it has worked to raise racial consciousness. It carries a mix of Stony Brook news and items of particular concern to the campus's African American community touching the rest of the world, with a regular eye on the national and international scene. A typical issue (November, 1979: VIII/2) covered a campus performance by Alvin Ailey's dance group, a report on a university committee on "minority concerns," an interview with Professor Leslie Owens on whether he would remain as chair of Africana Studies, and news of border fighting between Zambia and Zimbabwe. This last probably got little mention in the *NY Times*, let alone in other campus publications, important though it has proved to be. In addition *Blackworld* frequently prints poetry by Stony Brook students, and there often are so many features that a given issue is about half-way between a newspaper and a magazine.[6]

The *Stony Brook Press* is "the other" newspaper, a would-be rival and/or a brash and highly opinionated complement to the *Statesman* and a running critic of the latter's more conventional coverage of the campus. *The Press* sees its role as bringing satire, biting political commentary, a harsh look at the administration, and a huge ration of foul language with an "in your face" discussion of sex and the sex organs into the public discourse. It often raises issues barely touched elsewhere, and its self-styled mission of vulgarity and finger pointing is generally welcome – if a little tedious, issue after issue. That of July 1983 carried a list of campus salaries. Though this is open information, as we are all public employees, *The Press* played on the distinction between access and publicity. But of some interest; C. N. Yang made $101,000, Marburger $69,600, the dean of Engineering $58,200, and the majority of the cleaning staff in the neighborhood of $9344.

Other student publications have made a mark. *Fortnight* was a feature magazine, appearing every other week (hence the name) through the 1970s and into the 1980s. It carried poetry and creative writing, interviews, news and feature articles about campus developments and personnel, in-depth discussions of campus safety, student sexual practices (what, how often, with whom), and such serious news as the plight of Kofi Awooner (who had taught in English and was in jail in Ghana for political reasons). Because it had no specific mission or obligations, *Fortnight* was often an interesting extra with insights and critical comments that could be developed without the pressure of tight deadlines. The list of the publications that went through the revolving doors is much longer, and had I not collected many such items on my messy shelves they might have had no history at all. No one has ever done a market survey to determine how many people on campus, let alone from which constituencies, read which publications. Nor does the hit-or-miss distribution help, since the bins in some buildings rarely get emptied and re-filled. Among publications with a short life, there was the *Stony Brook Times: A Lampoon Magazine* (around 1978-79): it spotted a vacuum that needed filling, though it could not sustain the effort. *Showcase* (also of the late 1970s) was "The Stony Brook Magazine of Fiction and Humor," with an erudite insert, "Victorian" which made fun of Jane Austin, Matthew Arnold, and other figures usually well beyond the reach of student humor. A short-lived *Brain Food: Everybody's Humor Magazine* made a small splash in 1991. The title tends to indicate that many of the best ideas, probably hatched by a boozy group in the wee hours, were exhausted by effort of picking the title.

    For an issue or two in the days of political turmoil, radical students connected with SDS (Students for a Democratic Society) tried their hand at an explicitly political newspaper, *Vanguard: A Journal of Radical Thought* (begun and pretty much ended in January, 1969). The Haitian Students Organization made a number of runs at having a publication *(HSO Voice)*, and the religious organizations (especially Hillel) can be counted upon to speak to their own followers (and to as many others as choose to read). Hillel, in fact, has a fairly ambitious publications program, running to news, newsletters, and information on holiday services. Chinese American students, long before Asian-American studies and the Wang Center, published *Harmony*. Volume V, no. 3 (March 1977) carried interviews with C. N. Yang and Shi-Ming Hu (who taught Chinese). The editorial talked, even then, of the need to enlarge the

Chinese Studies Curriculum - a perennial gap in the offerings - and ended with ads from Chinese restaurants and an additional five pages in characters. Other fleeting efforts included *Macondo, Latin America Speaks, The Patriot, Stony Brook's Only Free Press,* and *Introspect* (May, 1968), with a radical but unaffiliated perspective. In a burst of intellectual euphoria or hubris undergraduates from Sociology published a journal, *Verstehen – A Forum for Sociological Perspectives.* Its brief life (around the spring 1984) was probably not a major blow to the campus, though its mere appearance indicates a seriousness (on most pages) that seems hard to imagine today.

Like most colleges, Stony Brook had a literary annual, *Soundings,* from early in its short history. If few Stony Brook alumni have gone on to fame and fortune as writers, dozens of students did publish prose and poetry in this semi-official magazine. For several years in the early and mid-70s *Anonymous* appeared, as a complementary publication, devoted to feminist issues and published with the help of the Women's Center and supportive faculty. *Ascent* had a brief existence, but its billing as a "forum for discourse" may have sounded pretentious and too serious for long-term success.

Graduate students turned out their own sizeable list of publications, in keeping with the idea that they had their own issues, their own dialogue. Some of their efforts were intended to give their perspective on areas of university life dealt with, though differently, in official publications; grad student orientation manuals and advice on how to adjust to life in the boonies. These survival booklets were mainly for newly arriving students, which meant that each version had to be replaced in a few years, as neighborhood bars, along with graduate deans and INS regulations, came and went. These booklets were written by veteran graduate students who now knew how to work their department and the administration. New students found it comforting to hear of such matters from their peers, as these efforts often made more sense than the official line given them at a hectic orientation run by a well-meaning Graduate School.

Some graduate student efforts at publication focused on

academic areas and issues. Certainly, in the days of numerous TA lines and lavish money, departments encouraged all sorts of ventures. In the humanities and social sciences students might link with peers in adjacent disciplines, in what we can think of as horizontal connections (whereas science students are more tied to vertical links, directly into their mentor's research). This encourages common efforts, and student-run conferences (such as "Crosscurrents: Theory, Praxis, and Culture," October, 1991) attracted graduate student participants from other schools, even beyond the metropolitan area. Sessions on "the postmodern sublime" and "transgressing textual boundaries" caught the edge of current interest and research, though a good deal of traditional research was actually being done and now getting spun and reworded so it appeared to fit the new speech molds. But political awareness was usually a good part of graduate student interest, as reflected in such a publication as *Voice of the 3rd World*, produced by the 3rd World Graduate Student Organization in 1980-81.

Athletics are the aspect of student life that generates the widest interest among those not personally involved. The activities of the decades can be divided into intra-murals, club sports (games played on a non-league basis), and inter-collegiate competition. Another distinction grew in importance by the 1980s: men's teams and women's teams. The growth in the number of sports, and the rise in level of competition from club level to Division III of the NCAA to Division I AA (by 1999) are ways of marking the shift from the casual, let-everyone play approach of the 1960s to the standard U.S. college model with (specially treated) athletes in high profile sports as the new campus icons. The likelihood of a drift toward athletic scholarships seems strong, though direct aid from state funds is not allowed. But much of this, as I write, lies in the future and therefore is not grist for an historian's mill. It is not a reassuring prospect.

The pages of *Specula* offer an easy guide to team fortunes, and I have given a survey of organized sports and team success for 1966. Intra-murals, organized largely through dormitories, as well as for commuters and groups such as departmental graduate students, have always been popular - as marked by the trail of custom designed t-shirts and celebratory beer parties - and a source of great pride for participants. The original campus did come with a gym and playing fields, though the gym was not ready until 1963. It housed basketball and squash (played with great success under Coach Snyder's eye, albeit on odd sized courts) and the swimming pool, and the fields were just outside for (touch) football, track, and softball. Gradually, in keeping with new trends, new sports have been added; soccer, volley ball, lacrosse, hockey, etc - all done, more or less, with an eye on women's equal access to the sport and to equivalent facilities and support.

A friendly and low level inter-collegiate face was a part of Stony Brook, even in the Oyster Bay days. With no recruiting and no scholarships, and pretty basic facilities, and a coaching staff that either doubled as the physical education faculty (some with academic tenure) or served as part-timers, expectations were realistic, which means not usually very high. Some teams produced a star or two - like Stuart Goldstein who became a squash all-American and then a successful professional - and winning seasons were not unknown. But to a considerable extent the joys of competition and companionship, as the old sayings go, were the main reward.

We can follow the tale of growth by looking at the scene late in the Marburger years (1991-92). We now have an impressive number of teams or sports, and something close to parity between women and men, at least in this sort of tally. Women's sports often did well; the volleyball team was 36-7 and had post-season success, and the tennis team went 8-1. Not so fortunate, or skilled, were the women's teams in basketball, soccer, or swimming, but there were opportunities for many participants, and I also note that the University fielded teams in cross country, softball, and track and field. Men's teams competed in these sports, as well as in lacrosse, baseball (not softball), and football (a 6-4 record for the season – soon to decline as we moved upwards into tougher competition). Anyone who follows sports, or higher education through *The Chronicle of Higher Education*, or even the daily paper, knows how complicated and controversial is the area of inter-collegiate athletics. As I have editorialized above, it suffices to say that through its first three decades Stony Brook had the good fortune to spare itself most of these pitfalls. In fairness, it may be the case that the university for many years turned its back – out of indifference, disdain, or other priorities - on an opportunity to pick up some name-recognition on Long Island that might have helped with undergraduate recruiting, and perhaps bigger sports will cover some of the lost ground. And if the alumni, or community philanthropists, take vicarious pride in such matters, they can be pretty certain that any checks they write will be cashed as quickly as possible.

Another area of student life is that of speakers invited to campus: beat poets, nobel laureates, acrobats, tv comedians, rock groups, and others brought (and paid) for a live performance. This kind of list is not a gauge of the creativity or active involvement of Stony Brook students, but rather one that enables us to see the student body as hungry consumers (with some 10-18,000 wallets and appetites) and the campus as a concentrated and lucrative base for consumption. The list of the invited indicates that students (and the rest of the university community) constituted a respectable stop on the circuit, and student organizations could raise enough money from a local audience to meet the going prices for some big-names. Skimming the issues of *Specula* shows the high Stony Brook profile in the 60s and 70s as a venue for concerts. Before MTV and the miniaturized cd and the vcr, touring groups playing live music were a major part of the music world; traveling evangelists of the new culture, albeit mostly playing to the already-converted. On the scene, to give but a partial list for 1970-72, Stony Brook was host to James Taylor, Joe Cocker (who came twice), the Grateful Dead, the Allman Brothers (in 1970 and 1971), the James Cotton Blues Band, and the Beach Boys. Big time stuff without even the need to leave the campus.

In terms of mere numbers, most of a university's guest speakers in any given year are likely to be visiting faculty, talking before disciplinary colleagues on fairly esoteric matters. But Stony Brook, like all other schools, makes some effort to bring men and women with somewhat greater public renown. So in addition to rock concerts, there are lectures, readings, and presentations, given by public intellectuals or public figures. Some events bridge or even unite the worlds of faculty, students, and the community, and those invited to campus run from the erudite and highly cerebral to popular and familiar names in the media, arts, entertainment and politics. The same years that brought those familiar bands and combos I have just named (though not heard) also saw good crowds turn out for Dr. Benjamin Spock, Dave Dillinger, William Kunstler, Maier Kahane, Dick Gregory, Alan Ginsburg, and Jules Feiffer, among the many. Such names take us back to a world of student activism and a strong interest in the anti-war movement, the counter culture, race, and a free show.

In the 1980s, with support from *Newsday*, the Long Island daily paper, the provost (AVP) launched an ambitious series of speakers. The idea was to attract students and a general public from beyond the campus, as well as the usual suspects of faculty and staff. Admiral Rickover (atomic submarine fame), Jonathan Kozol *(Death at an Early Age)*, Carlos Fuentes (Nobel Prize in literature), and Mark Mathabane *(Kaffir Boy*, a tale of growing up black under apartheid) were but some of the famous people to appear. When a speaker did catch campus attention, his or her talk became part of the common dialogue; one could ask in class "did you like what he or she had to say" and "would you go again?" We are always short of cultural links that jump the barriers of age and rank, just as the political views of faculty and students seem to have diverged steadily for the last 20 years.

It is reasonable, though with a generous margin of error or inexactitude, to talk of high brow or high culture events, staged for the tastes of faculty and (older) members of the local community, in contrast to those that fall in the realm of what we term pop(ular) culture, designed mostly for a student audience. Classical music has been played by Music Department students and faculty, as well as by guest artists, from the earliest days, though the move from recitals in odd classrooms to the Staller Center did not come until the mid-70s.[7] The audience at classical music usually has a small contingent of undergraduates, and many of those students are music majors. On the other hand, a late night show by Joe Piscopo seems to draw few of my colleagues, and if they do attend they seem reluctant to talk about it in my department's coffee room.

In the academic calendar, graduation comes at the end. Though to the faculty and administration the commencement is their show, students likewise have a proprietarial view of the day. And given that most undergraduates live but a few hours from home, and that a large proportion of them are the first of their immediate families to earn a B.A., the turnout of relatives and friends is high. When the University was small a single graduation ceremony sufficed, covering all units and sorts of degrees. There was a basic menu; a visiting speaker, the class valedictorian or president, and university officials, all enjoying their moments in the sun (literally; the ceremony was outdoors). But after 1970, when an open mike drew a whole queue of students awaiting a turn to denounce Richard Nixon, John Toll, and the Suffolk County police, the decision to have departmental ceremonies, with a common ceremony for graduate and honorary degrees, was announced as the new policy.

Graduation ceremonies for or by each academic unit proved to be extremely popular; student academic identity focuses on one's departmental major and faculty, in so far as there is much focus at all. Certainly, few students have strong feelings for the central academic administrators, and their words of parting wisdom are dead spots in a day tilted towards celebrations with one's own circle. Departmental ceremonies specialize in low-key speakers, individualized recognition for achievements, and a lot of photo opportunities. They have proved a satisfactory closure to the years of college, a comfortable finale to the long grind. The main ceremony - moved to the indoor sports complex as a guard against inclement weather and boisterous behavior - focuses mostly on graduate and honorary degrees. As a state university Stony Brook is expected to avoid high-profile political figures as speakers, and the main show has few surprises and not many people who get us much space in the newspapers of the metropolitan area.[8]

From the perspective of university history, publications and athletic teams and student organizations are relatively fixed stars. Editors and players and officers come and go; the *Statesman*, the yearbook, the basic student clubs and groups remain in place. But there are changes, new games in town. We can follow some new patterns of student life, reflections of changing demographics as well as shifts of emphasis from protest politics to opportunities for undergraduate research and for credentialing in a heterogeneous and complex world. As the University reached full size and its student body became less white and more diverse, a greater emphasis on racial and cultural differences (as in Asian-American activities and the Islamic Students' Organization) began to show. And in many ways, as the late 1960s gave way to what are generally thought of as more conservative times, the emergence and development of fraternities and sororities and religious organizations seem in keeping with the change.

It is easy to look back on the old days at Stony Brook as a golden age – a small campus, students and faculty in some sort of quasi-familial community, and a preference for intellectual over social and athletic forms of recreation. This is fantasy. The campus was always diverse, its students always inclined to go off in many directions, its faculty divided and at loggerheads over all sorts of issues. What about the problem of integrating day commuters into the campus's daily life– one of the original and perennial issues that Stony Brook has wrestled with. In 1976 two enterprising undergraduates (Marsha Small and Wayne Smith) were authorized to produce a booklet for the benefit of those who arrived anew each day: *Welcome to the Life of a Stony Brook Commuter.* The authors recognized that feeling separate and unequal was a fact of commuter life. They gave advice on adjusting to going to college while living at home – whereas most of the literature focuses on the problem of no longer living at home. How to find a room or to share a house, when it was time to make the break. And then, once away from home, how and where to park, or not to park, and how to use the campus bus system. This was helpful for those forced to face such problems on their own. The general tenor of the booklet was that living at home is inconvenient and tends to keep the student - socially, if not academically – in the world of high school and high school friends. Whatever the problems of dorm life, that there is usually a waiting list for rooms indicates that neither life with parents nor in a rented room is the choice of the many.

Student life, needless to say, cannot be neatly summarized

by looking at activities and won-lost records. When the nation's students were deeply enmeshed in politics, as in the 1960s and early 1970s, Stony Brook students tried to hold their own against the activism of Berkeley or Columbia. Nor was the Stony Brook administration alone in its persistent inability to project much sympathy for student problems.[9] Radical (left-wing) student organizations like SDS (Students for a Democratic Society) and PL (Progressive Labor) led sit-ins and demonstrations, as well as activities best not spoken of. For how much of the campus did these students actually speak? Many, from student and faculty ranks, lent support, both moral and material. However, it is easy to lose sight of a conservative middle, of the many who chose to stand on the sidelines, or even on the right. Some agreed with the radical assessment of the war in Asia but did not view the University as an enemy, nor the campus an appropriate field on which to wage the struggle. And farther over on the political spectrum, radical students were openly opposed by such groups as Easy Company, composed largely of engineering majors eager for a punch-up as their preferred alternative to protests and sit-ins. While the campus did remain relatively free of violence, voices were strident. Some who actually supported the US military must have felt cowed - citizens of a country they now saw as being trashed by its own brightest and best. These were angry, not romantic times.

But not everything was invariably grim and serious. The raw buildings of 1962-63 weathered, ivy did grow. Student culture and tradition can spring up like weeds on the lawns that Stony Brook parents were working to mow and trim. We need not go as far afield as a protest march to the draft board in Smithtown to find students shaping their own world, nor need we go to Harvard or Yale for customs in place when Jefferson kept slaves. The murky pond at Roth Quad quickly became the home of an invented tradition. At first this instant culture centered on a duck (or a number of look-alike ducks), christened Leon, who swam in those mysterious waters; this filthy creature took on mythic status. By the 1970s The Roth Regatta was an annual spring event, with rubber dinghies (later replaced by paper mache and duct tape), gliding across the stagnant waters. No one has contracted typhoid, and there is strong rooting for sponsored boats that bear the banner of clubs, dorms, and even academic departments. While Oxford and Cambridge have to go to London for their annual boat race, Stony Brook students need not even leave campus.[10]

Other forms of organization and student culture put down roots and grew as they could. Fraternities and sororities were not an official part of the original profile of student activities. By the 1970s they were beginning to appear. In an era with serious worries about hazing and discrimination, Greek letter organizations never approached the prominent role they play at many campuses, where they were established in a more sedate era and boast of those fancy houses that dominate much of the social and athletic scene. At Stony Brook they are just another set of interest groups, though pledges sometimes march around the campus in military drill. Some of the most active Greek activity has been among African-American and Latin undergraduates, where their involvement serves as a bonding mechanism to counter an enduring element of de facto segregation.

Another component of traditional campus life that became more visible over the years was the religious and denominational groups. In the 1960s worries about the separation of state and church may have been taken more seriously, and private matters like religion were farther back on the public agenda than they have become. Stony Brook always had to wrestle with its proper stance: whether to close on the Jewish holy days (not for many years, but doing so since the 1980s), to hold school on Good Friday, concessions to religions other than Christianity and Judaism? None of the denominations have ever had a special building, though some (Hillel for Jewish students, the Newman Club for Catholics) have resorted to off-campus sites at various times. By the 1990s all the organizations were brought together in the Humanities Building; a common site raised their collective visibility and, perhaps, contributed to an ecumenical perspective. A move, in 2001, to rehabilitated space in the Union moved them a bit away from the center of student life but did offer them something close to a genuine home.

To some students the presence of faith-based organizations offers a hand of personal comfort; to others their value may lie in their liturgical and social side. As the University demographics have changed, the religious "check a box" identity of the students has shifted. Between 1973 and 1982 the proportion of entering students who were Jewish declined from 38% to 19%: Roman Catholic numbers climbed from 29% to 46%: Protestants held steady at 13%. More recent figures would show the continuation of these lines on the graph, and Islam has made a real impact in the 1990s and Eastern Religions (and perhaps some "new age religions?) would also come in for mention. The University has complied with requests for kosher food, in a dining hall, and more recently for hallal cooking as well.

In some ways the pastors and chaplains can be compared to the part-time athletic coaches, though they operate with less official support and no one has rushed to build them the devotional equivalent of the indoor sports complex. A priest or reverend or rabbi usually has a role at the main graduation; the tradition of an invocation and valediction is accepted, and those on whom this honor falls usually are astute enough to offer something so general that not even I can take much exception. The professional cleric (and many have been women) takes the lead in encouraging students of appropriate background to keep that identity, and marriages (and formal ceremonies and rites de passage) can be arranged through the chaplaincy. Religious prejudice – whether intended or vented from sheer ignorance— does seem to burst upon the scene; bigotry and/or ignorance in student publications, anti-semitic statements, slurs on Islam, and the like. At such times the pertinent chaplain is expected to stand as a semi-official spokesperson - and sometimes to be in the middle between off-campus denominational pressure and the campus's need for a teacher and counselor, not a paid lobbyist. Generally the campus has been well served by its clerics; they have been cool-headed, ecumenical in outlook, and voices against an unseemly commitment to parochial entrenchment.

Speakers and performers from outside were but one part of the cultural scene. We can turn to a vast array of student contributions, in both high and popular culture: theater, music, art, dance, etc. Though the Theatre (sic) Department has always had to suffer from a limited graduate program, a steady stream of students with some talent and a lot of dedication can be counted on. Each year's run of plays, resting on student actors, is ambitious and well attended. While the level of performance varies, commitment is a strong plus, and there usually is a schedule of about half a dozen productions; a mix of new plays (some written to premier at Stony Brook) and classics, and dance also gets woven into the schedule. The program for 1992 was typical; Sheridan's 18th century "The Rivals," some new or lesser known works like "M. Butterfly" and "Burn This," the Stony Brook Dance Ensemble in "A New Peace" (an original offering of dance and acting, from two faculty members, Amy Sullivan and William Bruehl), and two "No Plays" from Japan, booked for a campus appearance as they toured the country.

Student music, with a doctoral program in performance atop the undergraduate major, is a more serious enterprise. The proximity of New York, for both students and faculty, has always been a selling point, though the special-purpose SUNY College at Purchase, for the performing arts, may have been a serious rival over the years. The Music Department prepares graduate students in both theory (which includes the history of music) and performance. Music students, along with faculty and a huge number of outside performers, present something, at some level and of some scope, during most weeks of the school year. As well as the Stony Brook Symphony - primarily a graduate student effort - there are scores of recitals by candidates for graduate degrees, plus a student involvement in Sunday afternoon baroque concerts, and serious performances by faculty and alumni. In addition, the Gospel Choir can be counted upon for a lively concert or two each year. Even beyond all this, many from Stony Brook are in local choral groups, in chamber groups, and the annual "Messiah sing-along" in December.

Nor is the Art Department to be omitted from this appraisal of home grown high culture. The main highlights of each year are the faculty show and the MFA (Masters in Fine Arts) show, displayed in the large gallery of the Staller Center. Art is also displayed in a smaller gallery in the Student Union, and in the library's gallery, some of it being the work of the undergraduates whose demand for studio courses always runs far beyond the supply. What the University lacks is a museum, as well as a major collection to display therein. Though the curator of the Staller Gallery does bring small exhibitions and shows from the larger world, Stony Brook has a way to go before it gives Yale's Mellon Center of British Art a run for its money.

In looking at student life, that of graduate students stands a world apart. They interact with undergraduates, both in the academic setting, as their TAs, and socially, but they are primarily integrated into the culture of their disciplines and departments, and they generally hang around with others from their own academic fields. Their social life spins from this setting of shared work, housing, and student politics (the Graduate Student Organization and, by the 1990s, the Graduate Student Employees Union: GSO and GSEU). Though many who come from afar begin by living in the dorms, most graduate students look to move off campus as money, new roommates and friends, and knowledge of the locale come their way.

The world of graduate students is also a world of older students, many of whom come with partners and children. Furthermore, the bulk of the full-time PhD candidates receive TA money and are thereby tied into their department's teaching and research life. In this setting the politically charged discussion of whether a graduate student is an apprentice– learning his or her craft from the masters – or a serf, doing menial labor for a minimal return, is a perennial one. I have talked about how seriously the TA funding fell behind, almost year by year, while the cost of living on Long Island invariably ran above the national levels of inflation. Furthermore, the gulf opened at an early date between graduate student funding in science fields, where grant money can be used to top-up state lines and provide summer stipends, and students in fields with no additional source of funds (such as History). The differential can be as high as 50% between students who are all considered as being fully funded.

Beyond the TA money, the university did not exactly rush to provide additional services and amenities such as reasonable health care for the entire family, day care for pre-school children, and a pool of on-campus jobs for partners. In fairness, these are quality of life matters, often poorly covered at schools far older and richer than Stony Brook. But when graduate students threatened a job action in the late 80s they wanted the "extras" as much as or more than a simple across-the-board increase in TA money. As far back as 1970 the Toll administration had been unmoved by requests that day-care be considered as a service or obligation that went with running graduate programs. A reasonably good day care service – with a means test for those on very limited incomes— did come into existence, but it did so mostly through a combination of faculty pressure, deeply committed graduate students, oodles of voluntary labor, and the use of unpaid undergraduate interns. Not much thanks to the Administration for all those diapers changed, noses wiped, and parents given a few minutes escape from their eternal rounds.

Given these disparities, and the likelihood of exploitation and speed-up, it is no wonder that graduate students looked to organize. The GSO, with representatives of each program, functioned as a graduate student government - pressuring the Graduate School for better treatment and for even treatment across the board, for legal help regarding the INS and the IRS, etc. The GSO also had an interest in social life; a graduate student pub, intra-mural teams, plus a grad student ombudsman (of either gender) attached to the graduate school. These measures helped, but the structure of academia makes full realization of graduate student demands unlikely. Job actions and threats of go-slow, in various departments, might elicit a good deal of faculty sympathy, but such measures (whether threatened or actually carried out) could do little beyond tinkering with internal workloads and getting some clarification of departmental policies behind awarding and renewing TA lines.

A more militant route for graduate students lay in organizing as labor: a graduate student union (GSEU) seemed a reasonable way to approach problems, given that the SUNY faculty had been organized for years while their apprentices could not join that union. To be organized meant coming to grips with an identity as poorly paid employees, rather than as dignified apprentices in an ancient and noble craft, but this distinction can be of little significance in the treatment of graduate students within a department, where personal relations often count for more than do labor-management negotiations in setting the tone. The impact of unionization is, rather, in the power to negotiate uniform or at least (maximum) standards for work load, along with benefits. However, if a formal labor-management discourse is recognized in law, it has had a hard fight to be accepted as part of academia, and the prolonged, nasty, and so-far unsuccessful struggle by Yale graduate students in the early 1990s was a sobering defeat. At the turn of this century the courts, to my great surprise, seem to have become more sympathetic to efforts on the part of graduate students, as they have to part-time and adjunct faculty, and faculty at private universities. This is a peculiar if welcome trend in a nation turning more and more to non- and anti-union labor in the service and industrial sector.

It is hard not to sympathize with graduate students at Stony Brook. Their morale and comraderie largely revolve around living off campus, which means the expenses of a car and rent, in a part of the world that may not welcome the university but happy to over-charge students for rooms, houses, and apartments. For years now the academic job market has been bleak, so the hard and underpaid work while in a graduate program has at best a problematic payoff in academia, still the principle career choice of most who go the whole course. The life of the mind, as we like to say, is a comforting one, and if the pay is never going to be great, there is a good deal of free time and choice on how to spend it. One further bonus is that, as an academic, you mostly have colleagues who agree with your politics. This alone, in Bush's America, is a not inconsiderable plus.

One final aspect of student life. This is one that trails one through life. It is being an alumnus (to use the male of the Latin: or an alumna, for women graduates) of the University. Such creatures are to be tracked down and, these days, solicited by their

Alumni Association. Virtually every school in the world, from pre-kindergarten through the Institute of Advanced Study at Princeton, has some sort of alumni organization. They keep alumni informed and in touch with each other, and basically they are the war room of fund raising - that golden calf at whose base we all worship.

Stony Brook, in keeping with its general insouciance regarding students, did not get into this game very seriously until the Marburger years. At first, the University had very few alumni, to belabor the obvious. Furthermore, Stony Brook graduates of the 60s and 70s were mostly young, as the life cycle runs, and very few had spare cash, let alone an inclination to turn their thoughts to wills, bequests, and estate planning. Many of these alumni – or so they tell me on occasion, if they can be believed - left Stony Brook with warm feelings about the quality of education and memories touching protests, construction, and the general scruffiness of a school where a student once threw a pie at John Toll. But such memories do not pave a wide trail toward contributions, and the sort of money that builds a stadium, or a dorm wing, or even a urinal in a men's room, has rarely been forthcoming.

By the 1980s there were now thousands of alumni, plus a growing feeling that the university should cultivate some traditional traditions, just as it had a growing need for other-than-state money. In keeping with these developments, Alumni homecoming weekend became an autumn fixture of sorts, though a fairly feeble one, while the Alumni Association did grow in terms of contacts and fund raising. In a world of venerable institutions with deep fund drives (netting, for instance, $4 billion for Harvard) and graduates of immense wealth who leave property and old master paintings, Stony Brook seems condemned to a second place for many years to come. The spirit may be willing, but so far the flesh has been on the weak side.[11]

(Endnotes)

1. In 1975-76 graduate student tuition was $1200, while professional school tuition $1600, a reflection of the truth that students with professional degrees (medicine, dental medicine, etc) were likely to make more money than PhDs. This meant they could also be asked to go into debt to fund their training, since the ultimate payoff would more than cover their student loans.

2. As I write this in the summer, 2003, the state is about to impose a tuition hike of $950 a year (the first such raise since 1995). This goodly sum is less than our own trustees and chancellor asked for in the winter/spring; they thought a jump of $1400 would be of help to the system. They did not factor in a drop in enrollments with the consequent drop in revenues. The new tuition hike will mean a level of $4350 for in-state residents, up from $3400 (with out-of-state students paying over $10,000 a year. The 2003 session of the Legislature, following the governor's lead, slashed $184 million of state support from the current SUNY operating budget of $1.9 billion. Even with the higher tuition in place for 2003-04, New York undergraduates will be asked to pay less than half of what the nearby University of Massachusetts is planning to charge its own citizens.

3. With a sensitivity to student financial problems, as defined and articulated in the quaint language of a bygone era, the 1971 bulletin, listing various campus services, said: "Through the Financial Aid Office, baby sitting services of Stony Brook coeds may be obtained at going rates."

4. Not meant to make fun of the Administration and its official publications, but rather in recognition of the fact that different constituencies are happiest when relying on their own mouthpieces.

The Administration has put out a huge range of different items - some being fairly general (like *Campus Currents*) and others reflecting the special interests and doings of the Research Foundation, the Stony Brook Foundation (the fund-raising organ of big brother), the office of the provost, the Affirmative Action Office, and so forth. Needless to say, in-house publications place a heavy emphasis on good news" (such as, an award to the Hospital; little about a special team of state auditors over there, checking the books).

5. Even then, undergraduate interest is surprisingly slight, even for matters that make the courts and the newspapers. In one such case the University showed more compassion to a high ranking employee who stole a six-figure sum from research accounts than it did to students caught passing joints, gratis, to their peers. John Toll gave a character testimonial on behalf of his crooked staff member - who did not go to jail.

6. To alight, again, at random: *Black World* in September 1981 looked at the plight of the Palestinians, at Grenada, and at a party on campus sponsored by a united front of minority-focused groups: African American Students Organization, the African Students Organization, the Caribbean Students Organization, and the Haitian Students Organization.

7. Sid Gelber, as dean and then AVP, had much to do with building the strength of the music department and the road shows that came to the campus. He left Stony Brook for a few years to serve as president of Mannes College of Music in Manhattan and his commitment to and lobbying for high quality classical music deserves a special vote of thanks, at least from those of us who go to the concerts.

8. The fire wall that was meant to hold controversial speakers at bay did have some cracks, and the University bestowed honorary degrees (though it did not always turn over the podium) to such public luminaries as Bayard Rustin (1983: Civil Rights leader and

a socialist), Lee Krasner (1984: artist), Betty Friedan (1985: feminist author and activist), Isabel Allende (1991: author and vocal public conscience against the Nixon-backed coup in Chile in 1973), Nina Totenberg (1992: NPR commentator and broadcaster), and Jocelyn Elders (1994: Surgeon General of the U.S. and advocate of masturbation). Academic figures of distinction – of considerably less concern to graduates and their loved ones – were people like Joan Scot, Carl Schorske, and Lipman Bers (two distinguished historians and a mathematician).

9. At times it was even hinted that students were being crowded together so the university could admit more minority students, the obvious conclusion being that it was "their" fault that "we" were being squeezed. Students saw through this and were able to separate the problems of dorm life from those of making Stony Brook more diverse and more receptive to minority undergraduates.

10. The Roth Regatta boasts an admiral, a vice-admiral, an honorary commodore, and various other nautical ratings - all presumably needed to keep the lesser ranks in line and to give the proper touch of dignity to those who aspire to the footsteps of Horatio Nelson. In recent years my History colleague, Bill Miller, has served as the on-land commodore of our boat.

11. Gradually this will change. A 1991 Alumni Association booklet listed 60,000 alumni, broken down by states and by graduating classes. Money raised by the Alumni Association is distinct from money raised by the Stony Brook Foundation - the corporation within the University that raises and then administers gifts and donations. The Foundation presides over money for specific purposes and for the permanent endowment (which did grow from $1 million in 1982 to $5.5 million by 1989). The history of the Foundation is a tale with more episodes of turn-over and start-again than of great financial coups. A new state university– seemingly built and supported by the state – has trouble selling itself to donors in the metropolitan area.

CHAPTER EIGHT
Town and Gown

The story of town-gown relations is - once more, and like so many other aspects of Stony Brook, and now for the final time - a story of a difficult relationship. Parties in an arranged marriage who only met at the church door, SUNY Stony Brook and its nearby community began as strangers. It had all been arranged by hardhearted marriage brokers (in Albany and New York City) and the partners were told, when they came face-to-face, that they should learn to live with it. They gradually came to accept this, though there were many years of little sympathy and, at times, of open hostility. Loggerheads rather than harmony was the theme, perhaps well into the 1980s (and beyond). But the bond was clearly an indissoluble one, and by now we can say that reasonable accommodation and some understanding - if well short of a love match – usually is the modus vivendi.[1]

Two qualifications or further considerations. One concerns what is virtually a universal constant - that universities frequently have strained relations with their local communities. The other has to do with what we mean by community or town in this context. When we refer to "town-gown" we tend to accept a very parochial definition; Stony Brook Village (along with Setauket and other very near neighbors in north Brookhaven) as the "community" that comes to mind.[2] It is easy, and perhaps only natural, to accept the immediate neighborhood, as defined by geography or proximity, as that to which we refer, and under whose gaze - friendly, indifferent, or hostile - academic growth and development have taken place. But, as I argue below, this is myopic. The "town" in "town-gown" has moveable and expandable boundaries, depending on what is at stake; anything from the deli by the train station to the state of New

York and well beyond.

We can begin with the oppositional stance of town and gown – an important polarity in Stony Brook's history. The standard treatment of town-gown relations easily comes to rest on a tale of neighborhood resentments, campus insensitivities, and economic and demographic inter-relationships between the two worlds - unwelcome students cluttering stores but spending welcome dollars, etc. A broader perspective adds to this, just as it reminds us that the tale of SUNY Stony Brook is here too another case study in the analysis of higher education. A University gives an identity, if not always a welcome one, and it offers jobs to and in the local community. But it also is the 600 gorilla in terms of land use, traffic, and local clout.

Colleges and universities far older and richer than Stony Brook, and with much higher name-recognition, are also fated to go through cycles of up-and-down town-gown relations, with "down" the predominant mode. Cambridge, Massachusetts, is the home of middle income families and of those below the poverty line and even of the homeless, just as it is the home of a famous and obscenely rich university. Stony Brook's revered academic neighbor right across LI Sound in New Haven is also set in a depressed and run-down city. Many who live in these famous university towns might suggest that academic renown is poor compensation for privileges enjoyed. And this ambivalence is compounded by the ubiquitous presence of those young men (and now, women) whose student lifestyle bespeaks a world well insulated from the cruelties of the job market in the rust belt. Adversarial feelings sometimes get acted out in bars and pizza joints. The universities suffer from various categories and levels of local hostility, and town government is often caught in the middle.

Nor are Stony Brook's famous academic neighbors alone in this, though there is a tendency - from the perspective of a new public university– have limited sympathy for Harvard and Yale. The student and community uprisings that convulsed Columbia in 1968 began when Columbia decided to build a gym - and on its own land, though touching the Harlem-edge of its ivy-clad precincts. The University of Chicago dealt with the question of how to survive in a deteriorating and dangerous neighborhood by getting the city fathers to have most of the neighborhood torn down.[3] More such tales about other schools and their town-gown relations could be told, mostly to the same tunes; misunderstanding and mistrust, conflicting and diverging views of who contributes to whose welfare, etc.

At least SUNY Stony Brook never alienated its neighbors because they envied us the charming buildings and opulent lawns that signal a manicured escape from reality. The area immediately surrounding the campus was far from impoverished; quite affluent, in fact, when compared to those decaying industrial towns of the New England. In fact, the university's original buildings were closer in style to low security prisons than to the country club grounds of Wellesley College near Boston or the California state campuses that overlook blue Pacific breakers. The original Stony Brook campus is still held up as an example of the "neo-penal" era of public design and construction.

To offer a less-than generous interpretation of early town-gown friction, we can say that one of the grudges of the Stony Brook-Setuaket-Oldfield community and its mostly-white, middle and upper-middle class residents was that the students (and many of the faculty) lowered the tone of what had been a rather classy and insular Christian community. Though Ward Melville, as the founding donor and original philanthropist, may have envisioned some sort of public version of Williams College, set in postcard-pretty Williamstown, Massachusetts, what actually arrived were beards, a very occasional Black, a lot of Jews (faculty and students), protests and noise, and a range of alcoholic and chemical substances unlikely to win local favor. That these people, phenomena, and activities were making their presence felt on virtually every other campus in the nation as well was little consolation to those already living out here, let alone to those about to move from the City to escape these very problems. Suffolk County's political structure was conservative-Republican, and its life style was cut to match this popular cloth.

If we look at the sociology of up-state SUNY campuses and college towns, we get an edifying comparison. Though there are local variations, in general these campuses, and to some extent even the university centers at Albany and Binghamton, offer a very different model of town-gown relations. In this comforting model the college is recognized by townsfolk as constituting the main industry, the cultural and social focal point, and the local pride and joy. It is the educational equivalent of the GE or IBM plant that kept many of these same towns alive and prosperous through much of the 20th century. The factory was there because of a pool of available labor, and the SUNY campus was so located because local legislators had taken care of their own when it came to distributing the public largesse. A reciprocal relationship between town and gown lies at the heart of this friendly paradigm; the colleges at Brockport or Oneonta are too vital to the community for any division of interests to lead to a serious rift. A local might throw a Saturday night punch (though no SUNY student would think of retaliating), but town fathers and mothers know whence comes the butter for the local bread.

SUNY Stony Brook never had a college town to go alongside it, and Stony Brook, New York, never was a college town. The university came too late; it was plunked down in the middle of nowhere, miles from any useful aggregation of retail shops. Nor was it particularly wanted by the local residents, with their snooty view of self and community. Nor did the relentless growth of the campus do much to right matters. Despite University promises about open hearings in advance of expansion - hearings designed to allay misgivings about space and size and sewage - and despite a token buffer zone - the campus grew to more than double the Melville gift of 480 acres in less than a decade, and this saga of growth pertains to acreage, human numbers, paving, traffic, and BIG buildings. And even worse - though not relevant to my story – there came the HSC, and the south campus, and the south P lot for parking, and finally the Veterans' Home – and in the 21st century, a stadium with flood lights and perhaps a land grab in near-by St. James. Growth pushed the university farther and farther to the south and east - into land that god had surely intended for private development. If the seven-story Math-Physics Tower was unwelcome, what can we say about the looming 18 stories of the HSC?

That the HSC building won an architectural award cut little ice with those who watched its rise, floor by floor and phase by phase, until it dominated the horizon from Middle Island to the Connecticut shore. The local weekly papers of the Stony Brook-Setauket and Port Jefferson communities showed little support for the beleaguered University in the days of drug busts and legislative hearings, and both sides of the town-gown divide nurtured their own version of those dramatic times. Local papers tend to side with "old timers" and local business interests, as their news articles are by and for such people, their gossip columns concerned with local comings and goings, their editorial policies and advice designed to cater more to existing views and prejudices than to enlighten or enlarge the local perspective. The arrival of the University – both cause and effect of the expansion of population – was tied to the pressures of growth, as well as to dissidence. Before 1960 the only north shore high school between Smithtown and Riverhead was that in Port Jefferson, to which students were bused from both east and west. By 1980 the Three Village School District (of Stony Brook, Setauket, East Setauket, and Old Field) had built and was supporting a huge system, topped off by two junior high schools and a high school the size of Amherst College. Mount Sinai, immediately east of Port Jefferson, was about to go the same route; Port Jeff Station already had built its own (costly) system. Surely, the University had to be blamed, in some fashion or other, for school taxes, the troubled lives of local teenagers, and the growing congestion on an inadequate system of roads and highways. The picture of public higher education as socio-political scapegoat is not an elevating one. Unfortunately, it sold pretty well for some years in Suffolk County.

This highly localized definition of community that I have been using is the one we generally have in mind when talking of town and gown. But SUNY Stony Brook is located in Brookhaven town, in Suffolk County, on Long Island, at the outer edges of the metropolitan region, in New York State, and in the tri-state area. This childish recitation - stopping just short of the world and the universe - reminds us that, in some senses, local is as local does.

We have choice when it comes to defining community, as we have options when we choose the criteria and the contexts that will govern the discussion. Nor, needless to say, is a state university about to pick up and move out of the line of fire. Loved or unloved, it is pretty easy to find.

When we think of local opposition to the university's growth it is prosperous homeowners and conservatives voices that come to mind. But there are other frames for our picture. As a focal point for large-scale employment, Stony Brook provided a major source of jobs – at first in construction, and then on a more permanent basis. And this needle points to the hundreds and hundreds of blue collar and lower-middle class men and women who were either already in the area, or who made the treck eastward from NYC in search of new homes and employment opportunities. Many of the Stony Brook jobs were state civil service, obtained by passing an exam and then, once hired, being relatively immune to considerations of race, class, and color (and the boss's temper, to some extent). Civil service positions carried decent benefits (health, vacations, sick leave, personal days, etc) as pluses to set against low salaries. Secretarial jobs were pretty much understood to be women's work, which is both sexist and a statistical reality. In any case, these positions were the source of a regular paycheck for huge numbers of local residents, including many men working in traditional "men's" areas like grounds, maintenance, and the physical plant, and as bus and snow plow drivers.

If few of these blue collar employees were on track for faculty or administrative ranks, and if few lived north of mid-Island, they too paid taxes and constituted a significance component of the community. Their voices usually go unheeded in establishing a framework of town-gown. Few of the many histories of American colleges and universities worry much about how the infra-structural community of service and non-academic labor comes into existence, let alone how it helps carry the university – at least, unless or until there is a strike or a class-action suit. The class system is as American as apple pie. [4]

What I present as this "the other" community was not always totally without voice. Though nothing really came of the effort, there was a multi-racial push in the mid-1980s for low-cost housing in Brookhaven, built with federal funds. At a number of public hearings administrators and faculty were among those who spoke in favor of the idea, along with community advocates and voices from the minority communities. But the specter of low-cost housing ran too strongly against the credo that holds class and race divisions (de facto segregation) in residential patterns to be god's way and good for real estate values.

Local resistance always proved to be too hard a nut to crack. In the late 1960s, at the height of the Civil Rights Movement, there had been local pressure – from the non-white, non-affluent community and from many faculty and students – to have open housing ordinances adopted by various units of local government. When such legislation is on the books, court orders and injunctions in probable cases of discriminatory renting and selling can be dealt with more expeditiously; federal and state laws are remote and only invoked in a slower, more cumbersome, and more costly process. Many of us marched in Patchogue, where the Town legislature met, and in the face of national unrest after Martin Luther King's death in April, 1968, Brookhaven Town passed such an ordinance– for what it is worth. But the high water mark had been reached; the incorporated Village of Port Jefferson proved adamant against such localized legislation, though some on the Village Board did avow that "Negroes" had been among their best friends in high school. If the University's record on behalf of a more equitable community is not its strongest point, it is not without some plusses in the grade book. In fields like community health care in Brookhaven Town, crusaders like Elsie Owens, a graduate of the school of social welfare and a tireless worker for good causes, was able to ignite sufficient fire to get a community clinic built in Coram, about 10 miles south of campus. Appropriately, this County facility is named in her honor, and though the push for the facility came from the non-academic community, it would have been much harder, if not impossible, without supportive faculty from the med school and social welfare.

One way universities work to mollify local sentiment is by churning out data on how much the university (as an institution and through its vast work force) contributes to the community. This is usually expressed in terms of the numbers of employees and families (that is, of jobs provided), the dollars they spend, the kudos achieved and the skills offered, and the amenities now available (such as music at the Staller center). Stony Brook does its share of this with information about the impact of its employees. As most of these live locally, their salaries are pumped directly into the local economy, where they support businesses and mortgage banks, and they both necessitate and help fund the infrastructure that accommodates them. The University said, in 1981, that it was the employer of 7000 people, and by the early 1990s the number was up to about 9000 (where it has remained) – and of these, about half lived in Brookhaven Town.

Nor is the university's economic impact its only form of out-reach. For example, the role and use of the Staller Center, as a magnet for community cultural and recreational interests, has grown in a slow but steady fashion. And this has been matched by moves to open the gym and the sports complex (not to be called a field house) for high school basketball tournaments and track and field championships, as the campus tried to mesh with the external world. The audience at chamber music in the Staller Center, at about $25 a ticket, seems to be split about 50-50 between those with a direct university connection and those without. Of course, as our culture has been transmitted, baroque trios seem mostly for the white-collar, middle class (and elderly) world. Names listed in Staller programs as donors and patrons reflect this, as they do the town-gown break down of the audience. In the high-donation brackets we find a good sprinkling of local corporations: Key Bank, Prudential Real Estate, Roslyn Savings, Newsday, Fleet Bank, and others with a sense of local identity and a view of culture as good public relations and a tax deduction.[5] Many others in the local community, who neither know nor care about the Emerson Quartet, are happy to come to the campus for a wrestling tournament, a computer fair, or a Christmas presentation of The Nutcracker in which their kids, from local ballet schools, pirouette around the stage.[6]

Though the presence of the University assures us of a concentration of many hundreds of highly skilled, relatively affluent, and articulate women and men - many of whom have a fair amount of free time– only a few from faculty ranks have looked to make an impact through local politics and organized community activities. Neither faculty nor staff have rushed to run for elected positions on local school boards, nor to chair civic committees in local fund drives or preservation crusades (though the University President is often an honorary board member). The exceptions to this assertion might actually run to fairly reasonable numbers, over the course of three or four decades, but it seems this sort of reticence or avoidance is common through much of academia. Exceptions, as in places like Berkeley (University of California), where veterans of student politics from the 60s have run for and even been elected to local offices and the school board, are noteworthy. The social and cultural divide that separates the academy in focus and orientation from the local community generally keeps the worlds apart. Mind you, this is not always to the credit of faculty members who can think of themselves as too lofty to dip in local waters. But mostly, the prevailing idea is that of separate spheres.[7]

Students, as citizens of the state and the nation, were especially unpopular off campus because of community perceptions about what was occurring on the campus, rather than because of any role they actually played in the neighborhood. But when the voting age was lowered to 18 (in time for the 1972 election - so they could join their parents in endorsing Richard Nixon) the possibility of a new area of conflict arose. Students wanted to vote in local polling places - not to tilt local races (which were of little interest to most of them) but to have a say for or against presidential and perhaps senatorial candidates, and to do so without the need to obtain an absentee ballot or of making a trip home (election day not being a university holiday). They were confronted with a series of obstacles reminiscent of the Old South before the Civil Rights movement, and here the issue centered around their identity as local residents.[8] Ah yes - if they registered and voted in Stony Brook village (at schools and church halls) they might clutter the polling places. And if they voted locally, they might tip the balance toward Democrats – and thereby help open local floodgates for cranks, reformers, and liberals.[9]

Thanks to Polity and such organizations as NYPIRG (New York Public Interest Research Group) and SASU (Student Association of the State University) there was a serious effort to mobilize the student vote, and eventually a polling booth on campus proved to be the best answer. But at least students do not vote in the local school board elections (or library board elections) - as they do not pay local taxes - and a considerable degree of separation will always exist. That half the undergraduates are commuters, mostly from Suffolk County to begin with, certainly softens the potential divide of electoral politics; they can go home to Hauppauge or Patchogue to exercise their citizenship rights in favor of Right-to-Life candidates. That young people vote to the left of their elders is probably a myth fostered by those elders when it is useful to demonize the student voice.

This look at town-gown relations has been cast so as to widen the issue - to turn it from the parochial foundation on which it usually rests, even without nostalgia about a Hendrix concert or a punch-up between students and locals in the Union. To drive home the idea that town-gown relations are also a case study in a wider tale of society and politics, I now turn, at considerable length, to one of the most complicated and troublesome episodes in the history of the University. This is the "the Dube affair," which began in 1983 and which ran for some years. This case study takes us far from the relatively friendly confines of the campus - that familiar stretch running from the South P parking lot to the LIRR tracks. The Dube affair touches the politics of distant nations and the agenda of international affairs. It is also the University's most dramatic and traumatic test of academic freedom and of the ability of the academy to control its own agenda.

The case study - the ultimate town-gown problem that I sum up as the Dube affair or controversy - began in the summer, 1983, and took three or four years to play itself out (as much as such matters ever have an end). I go over these events in the context of town-gown relations to emphasize that such matters can and sometimes do transcend local elbow rubbing, and on occasion get turned into the local stage of wider issues.[10] This episode, along with the retrenchment of Education in the mid-70s and the class action suit of Coser versus Moore (for which, see the appendix), seem to stand as the major intellectual, moral, and professional crises in the history of Stony Brook. And in each case, the volcano blew up when local issues intersected with or were absorbed into larger ones.[11] Regardless of how I assess the winners and losers, all these controversies left victims, a great deal of post-traumatic stress and hostility, and an enduring memory of the University's vulnerability in moments of crisis. In some respects the Dube affair vindicates the values of the academy. In a different light, it reminds us of the thin wall between the protected world of academic freedom and the power and reach of those, with other agendas, who see the campus as a legitimate extension of the battleground, when push comes to shove, and who move onto the attack on "our" ground..

As we are often reminded, no one is an island, no sparrow falls without consequence. In 1983 Ernest Dube was an assistant professor in the Africana Studies Program, still without tenure. He had come to Stony Brook a few years before, having entered academia fairly late, and he came with a Cornell Ph.D. in psychology. Before he had entered academia he had spent many years in his native South Africa, working for the African National Congress (The ANC: Nelson Mandela's party). His experiences at home - fighting apartheid at a time when its ultimate fall seemed but a distant dream - included a term in jail on Robben Island. Leaving South Africa was a condition of his release from prison, though he continued to work for the cause. At Stony Brook, in a small academic unit (AFS had but two tenured faculty in 1983), Ernest ("Fred") Dube taught a number of courses, mostly in race, cognitive psychology and cross-cultural analysis, often with an eye on their political implications. Since his arrival in 1977 he had never been in any controversy; neither did he (before, during, or after the "affair") seek the limelight that, unfortunately, came his way. Except that his personal history was unique among the 700-800 faculty on the main campus, he was just another hard working, untenured faculty member - though one of the few black ones and one of the very few Africans.

In 1983, in the large (and profitable) summer school program, he offered one of his regular undergraduate courses, Africana Studies (AFS) 319: The Politics of Race. In the context of this course, and indicated in his syllabus and clearly figuring among the assigned books and topics, there would be an examination of Zionism as a possible form of "reactive racism," meaning that Israel, founded on Zionist ideology and as a refuge against persecution and genocide, might have gone down that very road and turned upon others over whom it now had control. Zionism as an ideology– and not Israel as a political entity - was not his only example of this phenomenon; he looked at examples from Europe (especially Germany) and Africa ("his own" South Africa), among others. And in his course this particular aspect of racism would be a focal point for reading and lecture/discussion for a week or two. The topic or issue was a significant part of the course, but hardly its main concentration.

The books assigned for the course were serious ones; the question about the nature of Zionism was always treated in the context of sober and comparative discussion. There were never any allegations of venting or preaching by Dube, who had a very laid back style as a teacher. No student in the course was pressured to choose the "is Zionism racism?" as his or her topic for the prescribed paper. There were alternative questions and topics; each student was free to choose. The issue that was to blow up had just been tucked in, one of a number of open-ended and controversial questions. Furthermore, Dube had taught the course before, and always without incident; it was cross-listed with Political Science (though Political Science later cut this tie and disavowed a course that actually dealt with politics). AFS 319 seemed to be just another course - and perhaps one of the few in the College with topical and arguable subject matter— at least as far as the instructor and most of the students were concerned.

A student in the summer school course, puzzled by what to him was an unfamiliar slant on Israel and Zionism, took his query to an Israeli academic who was winding up a stint as a visiting faculty member in Political Science and who was about to return home.[12] The departing guest found Dube's approach and assertions objectionable. Asking no questions of the instructor, or of anyone in the chain of command, our visitor went directly to the newspapers (*Newsday*) and the Jewish organizations of Long Island and NYC. The response from beyond the campus was as one might expect in a troubled world; an immediate outcry against the issue that Dube had raised, and particularly against the context in which he had placed it - and very soon, by the logic of witch hunting - against Dube himself. The organized Jewish community is invariably and understandably sensitive to analogies between the Holocaust and other horrors, apart from this instance of linking Zionism (and by extension, Israel) with castigated behavior. That Dube was a Black African - probably unaware of the sensitivity of the American Jewish community - hardly helped. Moreover, matters were especially touchy in 1983; Israel's military ventures against Lebanon and its general swing to the right had now made American Jewry, or at least its more liberal elements, ambivalent about an Israel they had long supported with few reservations or criticism. Dube was an outsider and a convenient scapegoat for troubled consciences, and his color and his larger political perspective were not likely to be calming factors. The legions rallied against a man who could be portrayed as using a public university classroom to say that which could not be said. Nor, unfortunately, in terms of moderate if not supportive voices, was the Black-Jewish alliance as firm in 1983 as it had been in the high water days of the Civil Rights Movement.

As the Dube affair hit the media the campus was quickly brought under the gun of public criticism for "not doing anything" about Dube's exercise of academic freedom and of the way in which he chose to exercise his professional and pedagogical responsibilities. Governor Cuomo was quick to join the chorus; in fact, he came forward to lead it. His comments were in the form of the BUTS - as in, "I'm all in favor of academic freedom . . . BUT" - and each of us is free to fill in the rest of the line. It might be "he went too far," or "there are things you can't say," or "academic freedom has its limits," or "academic freedom must be balanced against responsibility." The Dean of Social Sciences at Stony

Brook, to whom AFS reported in the chain of command, asked the University Senate's executive committee for counsel. Their reply, after serious but brief deliberation, was that this was an academic freedom issue, which translates to mean that Dube had acted correctly and responsibly in his classroom. The voice of the Senate meant, as far as the faculty were concerned, that we would just have to live with the criticism and maybe even raise our own voice in defense of our values and integrity.

The Executive Committee of the Senate had looked into the matter before giving the Dean the benefit of its wisdom, and the inquiry had quickly exonerated Dube. The questions were whether any student had felt pressured to accept Dube's view (if, indeed, he really believed that Zionism was racism; classroom opinions are not necessarily those of the instructor espousing them). It became apparent that no student had been pushed to choose "Zionism as racism" for his or her paper. Nor had Dube down-graded or harassed any one who disagreed with him and who chose to defend Zionism, either in class or in written work. Grading was fair and even, regarding topics chosen and points of view espoused. Case closed, at least as far as peer-investigation was concerned; academic freedom covered the Dube waterfront. And though there were personal misgiving by some colleagues over what Dube had assigned and taught, there was virtually unanimous agreement that he should be supported. Early in the autumn the entire University Senate endorsed the summer judgement of its Executive Committee. With few dissenting votes it was once more affirmed that nothing improper had gone on in the class; Dube should be left alone.

Easier said than done. Or, as I said above, this was ok for the gown but hardly for the town – as defined here by a large, intrusive, and hostile definition of town. There were two problems. One was that the Stony Brook administration had to continue dealing with an outraged public, on up to state legislators who mumbled about the mis-use of university funding and the need for more intrusion and control. Meanwhile, the news service that feeds Jewish community newspapers across the country issued a steady stream of hostile news releases, one-sided quotes, and racially-tinged warnings about anti-semitism in the Black, leftist, and Jewish-academic world. "Self-hating" Jew was a charge leveled against some of Dube's on-campus supporters. Jewish organizations demanded an apology, presumably from President Marburger, as well as a wider investigation and a protracted dialogue on Black-Jewish relations (when they really wanted Dube's head). Jack Marburger and AVP Homer Neal had to spend much time and energy trying – with quite limited success – to smooth the troubled waters. There were public panels and forums, in-house dialogues with a racial and religious balance, meetings with liberal rabbis to relieve some of the pressure from conservative rabbis, and the creation of a vague if safe-sounding body, a Committee on Faculty Rights and Responsibilities – a fig leaf that seemed to promise more in-house scrutiny in the future. Marburger was unhappy about the way the hot potato had been passed to him, perhaps rather casually, by the Senate. The faculty, mostly shunted aside by these off-campus pressures, were dismayed that they could do almost nothing to cool the issue. Marburger and Neal - often with gritted teeth - did the right thing and defended academic freedom, though with some fairly open misgivings.[13] So the year passed, if painfully.

There was still another aspect of the issue, waiting to rear its head. Dube, as an assistant professor, was nearing the time when his tenure would normally be deliberated. Because of the flack over the affair, and the mistrust and suspicion it had generated on all sides, AFS had been temporarily moved from the Social Sciences to the Humanities, reporting to a different dean, one largely unscathed by the heat of the first assault. And because AFS was such a small unit, the normal procedure in a personnel case was to constitute an ad hoc committee with faculty from other units brought in to help assemble and evaluate the file, alongside the tenured AFS faculty. This procedure was followed; the committee was put together by the Dean (of Humanities) to build a brief for (or against) Dube's promotion and tenure. The file would climb the rungs of the ladder, regardless of the judgement rendered at each preceding stage. In this case the unusual option of postponing the "mandatory" decision for a year had been adopted in the hope that time would exert a calming influence.

So, in 1985-86 (rather than in 1984-85) the procedure for a personnel decision was put in place. Finding faculty for the ad hoc committee had been a delicate task. Usually those chosen to assemble a file are sympathetic to the candidate, though their formal decision awaits the external and in-house evaluations that they have worked to assemble. The committee weighed Dube's contributions, which included his position as a role model in light of his background and experience; I think he was the only black South African on the faculty, and certainly the only person with personal knowledge of the ANC's great crusade. The ad hoc committee, including the tenured members of AFS, recommended that he be granted tenure (with a split on promotion). The College personnel committee was divided, though the general thrust was again for tenure (as an assistant professor). This was a faculty voice on his behalf, but not a resounding one. However, it would have been adequate to enable him to remain at Stony Brook.[14]

Despite the faculty's qualified endorsement, every level of academic administrator successively voted against Dube, rung by rung, man by man. Though the administrators made much of their soul searching, Dean Neville, the Dean of Humanities, and then the AVP, and finally Jack Marburger, all overcame their unease and voted against tenure, whether as an assistant or associate professor. They held that the lack of published scholarship outweighed the factors in Dube's favor. In deference to clauses in the union contract, this split between the faculty and the administration opened the door for still further appeals and reviews; another faculty committee, which in turn confirmed the original vote in favor of Dube, for what it was worth. This complicated procedural reassessment then went to the SUNY Chancellor, and this process also turned out to be tortuous and to consume still one more year. But in terms of Dube's future at Stony Brook, it was all to no avail. As Chancellor Wharton prepared to leave SUNY, in February 1987, he rejected Dube's case, virtually as his last action in office (and one he put off as long as possible). His rejection said that it was all very unfortunate, that Dube was indeed a likely victim of prejudice, and that his tenure case had been poisoned from the start. Perhaps, Wharton suggested (naïve or disingenuous?) Dube might inquire elsewhere in SUNY for a position. But beneath these ambiguities, for all the public agonizing, this was termination.

After the chancellor's rejection of Dube there was still a lot of smoke, though most of the shooting was effectively at an end. Dube brought suit against SUNY - using Wharton's final words about victimization as proof of prejudice by Stony Brook and by the system - and eventually he gained some satisfaction (in the form of a monetary settlement) and a job at Evergreen College in the State of Washington system. The AAUP sent a team to investigate whether Dube's academic freedom had been violated - and if so, whether this had contributed to the decision to terminate. Though the AAUP report was well short of a ringing endorsement of Stony Brook and of SUNY, they said there had been sufficient due process and sufficient peer review so they did not recommend calling for (a second) censure of Stony Brook– on top of the SUNY-wide censure for the retrenchments of the mid-70s. On the Stony Brook campus bad feeling lingered; AFS faculty and students felt strongly that Dube had been a victim of racism - a potato too hot for an indecisive administration to hang on to. Some who thought this assessment harsh still thought the Administration painfully narrow and rigid in its standards, given Dube's unusual background and that AFS's focus was on undergraduate teaching, rather than on research and publication. Others thought that, controversy aside, it was just another case of perishing because of not publishing.

In this narrative I have tried to be dispassionate – not an easy path, as I was deeply involved from the first. It always seemed likely that it might be one of those instances where the system would work, in terms of procedure and due process, but that we would, nevertheless, wind up with the wrong result. The Administration— not particularly anxious to buck further criticism by awarding tenure on a border-line case to a faculty member whose mere presence would continue to generate hostile publicity - presented a common front, though whether by collusion or the confluence of separate deliberations is open to question. In any case, Dube got a tough decision, and a mean one – from Dean Neville, from the AVP, from the president, and finally from the chancellor. The operation was a success but the patient died.

The Dube case affected fewer people directly than did the

retrenchment of Education. However, in a strict sense this affair was supposedly an in-house matter, while the retrenchment of the 1970s – though a dreadful answer to a genuine budget crisis— was a response to a state-wide dilemma. The University lives with many tenured faculty whose cases were also border-line ones, and if Dube's scholarly publications were thin, there were extenuating circumstances (including the age at which he had come to academia). For some reason I had hoped that Marburger would decide that this was the occasion for the gown to tell the town that it would handle its own business, in its own way. But, alas, as with John Toll after the drug bust, presidents of state universities do not have the luxury of giving the community the raspberry so they can demonstrate to their faculty that they share faculty values and the faculty's supposed high priority for academic freedom and the wayward spirit of intellectual inquiry.

This whole issue may seem a strange note on which to conclude a chapter on Stony Brook's fit with the community. The case was of little note or interest to most of the students (and perhaps to most faculty), even while it raged with such heat. The campus's African American community, at all levels, followed it with close attention, and years later it remained a litmus test in terms of gauging activism and commitment. Moreover, as I have said, it brought home to many of us the extent to which public higher education is a process carried out in public space. The institution's nakedness and vulnerability were cruelly exposed for all to see. We may talk of ivy walls and ivory towers (at least as figures of speech); in reality the University has but limited control of its budget, its boundaries, and its agenda. In some ways we in the academy have a say in running our world; in others ways, we learn on painful occasions how limited we are. A phone call from a state senator cannot be fended off because the president is trying to catch up on his paperwork.

On the other hand I do not want to conclude with a plea that the academy is or should be sacred space, a temple precinct amidst a crass and materialistic world. A public university is paid for, at least to a considerable extent, by public funds. While academic freedom and classroom autonomy and faculty tenure are basics -

not open for debate and supposedly not in need of vindication - when they come under fire they are not always easy to sell, even on and to the campus. Faculty hold that freedom to enquire entails a freedom to discuss sex, politics, abortion, racism, poverty, corruption, the stupidity of SUNY trustees, pot-shots at the governor, and the tunnel vision of the voting public. This is the academic way of serving the public interest and promoting the public good, at least as academics see it. Sometimes this is unpopular, and it is frequently misunderstood. A last and rather sorry lesson of the Dube affair was that almost no one in a position of public authority supported him. Governor Cuomo knew better, but he could not resist the cheap shot. The Anti-Defamation League of the Bnai Brith knew better; they were founded to combat religious, racial, and ethnic attacks– not to engage in them. It was a tough matter; taking sides in "the good fight" can be distressing.

Let me end this sober tale on a note of more cheer. It is safe to say that the University's immediate neighbors had trouble adjusting when a research university, with big science and very big buildings, was dumped in their lap. The parties in this arranged union learned to live with each other-even to enjoy a bit of the interaction and to profit from each other's strengths-though it was far from an overnight process. Perhaps the most ringing endorsement of the improved nature of this relationship can be found - not in a university publication or pronouncement (which no one believes anyway)-but rather in the voice of one of the old locals. John McKinney, editor and publisher of local newspapers since the 1960s, ran a retrospective editorial in the first issue of *The Three Village Herald* to hit the newsstands in the new millennium (January 5, 2000). In it, he summarized the changes in the Three Village Area during the second half of the 20th century:

> "But what is principally different is the presence of Stony Brook University. Influenced by the University, a conformist white Anglo-Saxon Protestant community gradually became multi-ethnic, and more tolerant of differences than in its hidebound past. Taking a long look back. life here fifty years ago was placid, serene, and dull. The University brought art, ideas, intellectual resources, even ethnic restau-

rants. It gets my vote as the greatest influence for good on the Three Villages in the last century. Melville performed esthetic wonders in a run-down community, but it was the University that provided the economic driver for a prosperous economy, and a renaissance of spirit."

This is heady stuff for a Stony Brook faculty member to read from the pen (word processor) of a local and vocal skeptic, one who had to be won over to such a sympathetic view by the perspective of the longue durée. I hope it was not just the euphoria of a holiday season and the excitement of 12/31/99. All in all, it's not a bad report card for the University to show to those who ask how it has fared in those 35 or 40 years that we can measure from the ground up.

(Endnotes)

1. Though a new football stadium, named for State Senator Ken Lavalle and holding about 8000 seats, opened in 2002, and with floodlights that are often on in the evening, has not exactly reassured the local community that its interests regarding congestion and traffic are of great concern when they clash with (funded) university priorities. After the completion of HSC most University construction has been within the inner boundaries and loop roads of the campus, though the State Veterans Home – imposed on the University rather than chosen - came very close to community housing. A fight is brewing– summer 2003— over land in nearby St. James, coveted by the University as well as by local developers who are thinking of such vital social amenities as ugly mini-mansions and another golf course.

2. A guidebook to the area from a few years back devoted almost no space to the University: Howard Klein, *Three Village Guidebook* (Three Village Historical Society, editions of 1976 and 1986). The University figures on pages 168-69, getting as much attention as the Robert Cushman Murphy Junior High School.

3. Students at the University of Chicago, not in sympathy with the university's plan for neighborhood "renovation" in the late 1950s and early 1960s, said that "Urban Renewal was Negro Removal." Riots and town-gown violence almost caused the students and faculty of Oxford to leave, at various times in the 13th and 14th centuries, though the charms of nearby Stamford, in rural Lincolnshire, proved even less enticing.

4. University employees honored at the annual service awards ceremony (for longevity) bear this out. At the service ceremony that covered 1999, the 3 people honored for 40 years were all faculty, as were 10 of the 11 honored for 35 years. But when we come to (a mere) 30 years of service we can count 18 faculty, 5 librarians, and 11 from staff and administrative positions. For the 25 year men and women, it was 16 faculty, 1 librarian, and 24 staff and administra-

tors.

5. The more modest patrons of the Staller Center - listed in the program as "benefactors," "patrons," "donors," and lesser ranks - represent a mix of university (faculty, staff, administration) and non-academic friends. The big money - as with all centers of high culture - comes from corporations and the really wealthy, those able to give in the thousands.

6. The Long Island Symphony Orchestra's main concert site is the Tilles Center at C. W. Post, in Nassau. However, they often play 2 or 3 concerts a year at the Staller Center.

7. Aaron W. Godfrey (Latin, in European Languages) ran for the state assembly, as a Democrat, from nearby St. James. He lost. John Pratt (History) was elected to a term on the Port Jefferson School Board (a non-partisan village matter). Many faculty (and staff, and students) have been active in local reform politics, the campaign against LILCO's nuclear power plant at Shoreham (which was successful, in that the plant never opened), civil rights activities, greening local highways and parks, and the sort of civic projects the League of Women Voters and such groups devote themselves to (harbor pollution and the use and misuse of natural resources such as the quality of Long Island's underground water level). In the local elections, autumn 2003, a number of Stony Brook alumni were on the ballot, and several of them won their races.

8. Ironically, when Stony Brook had a large Jewish student contingent the high holy days were not an official university holiday; faculty were asked to avoid assigning work that could not be made up and to avoid giving exams. In the 1980s, perhaps to counter a reputation for institutional anti-semitism that came with the Dube affair, school was officially closed for Rosh Hashanah and Yom Kippur. No other religious holidays receive official acknowledgement - at least not so far. Passover can sometimes be folded into a mid-term spring vacation, but in some years it comes too early or too late; the University has closed for the Sedar days, but only after

1994. Good Friday is obviously on a Friday, when the academic university is near stand-still in any case. And Ramadan, whatever is restrictions and rules, does not ask the faithful to take a day off work.

9. Steven Englebright, with an M.A. from Earth and Space Sciences, has been the NY assemblyman from the University's district since 1992. He has pushed a pro-environment and liberal line as a Democrat. He served in the Suffolk County legislator for several terms before he moved up the ladder, and SASU (Student Association of the State University) named him their legislator of the year in the late 1990s.

10. The best concise account of this complicated business is in the AAUP's journal, *Academe*, Jan/Feb 1990, pp. 55-66, being the report of the ad hoc committee that came to Stony Brook in May, 1987 to evaluate whether there had been a violation of Dube's academic freedom and due process rights. The recommendation (made to the Academic Freedom & Tenure Committee of the AAUP) was NO, though it was a near thing, and Committee on Academic Freedom and Tenure and then the entire Association concurred in this. The ad hoc committee that came to Stony Brook to investigate was composed of Ted Finman (University of Wisconsin), Pheobe Haddon (Temple), and Donald Koster (Adelphi). They received no help from the Stony Brook administration.

11. I do not count the drug bust of January, 1968, because there was little internal dynamic - except in terms of how to address the matter after the fact. I have tried to show that much though I deplored (then, and now) the response of John Toll to the drug bust, he had little room in which to maneuver once it had been staged. Also, being primarily a student matter (in terms of victims) the whole business was of a different nature from the retrenchment of Education, the Dube affair, or Coser vs. Moore.

12. To name a few names, though in my text I want to preserve

some figment of disinterest; the visiting Israeli professor was Selwyn Troen, a dean at Ben Gurion University. The Dean of Social & Behavioral Science was Egon Neuberger, a long-time veteran of the Economics Department and academic administration. The president of the University Senate was Ron Douglas, of Math (later to serve as Dean of Physical Sciences and as Dean of Undergraduate Studies), though he was away when this business broke in the summer. His chair was taken by the president-elect of the Senate - this author. So it was I who presided over the summer deliberations and who reported to the full Senate in the autumn, when Douglas was in the chair.

13. As an example of the attempts to air, and thereby to defuse the controversy, the University held a symposium (in May, 1984), "Academic Freedom, Academic Responsibility, and Society," and invited Ralph Brown (Yale Law School, former president of the AAUP), Rabbi Arthur Seltzer (the local Anti-Defamation League chair and the most aggressive voice of the Jewish community against Dube and the University), and Sidney Hook (political philosopher and, by 1984, an aggressive conservative), among others, to say their set pieces. Campus committees were formed so people of different views, colors, and politics could waste each other's time.

APPENDIX
Coser vs. Moore

Coser versus Moore was a class action law suit, filed in 1976 on behalf of over two dozen Stony Brook women against the University (SUNY in generic terms, Stony Brook as a specific defendant). The women came from the teaching faculty (both on the main campus and in the Health Sciences Center), the library, and the administrative or non-teaching professional staff. Though they did not receive much satisfaction in the decisions eventually handed down by the courts, by the time the case wound down (in 1984) the climate and culture of the academic work place had changed a good deal and women at Stony Brook, as elsewhere, were more likely to get a reasonably fair shake regarding salaries, terms of employment, and opportunities for promotion (and tenure) than they had been at the start. Rose Coser, the first named among the plaintiffs, was an eminent sociologist with a primary appointment in Community Medicine in HSC, while Elizabeth Moore was chair of the SUNY Board of Trustees.

Well into the 1960s and the era of federal civil rights legislation there were still rules on the books, as well as a long tradition of sexism, discrimination, and condescension, that worked against women in academia. When I came to Stony Brook in 1964 the state had an official nepotism policy, forbidding the employment of close relatives (at least in the same branch of state government). This legislation, intended as a progressive measure in the 19th century when cronyism was the bedrock of public office, functioned now to block the hiring of faculty wives from full-time and regular positions on the campus. And beyond the statuatory hurdles which were soon to fall before civil rights laws and judicial and administrative interpretations of what constituted discrimination, much of the culture of the workplace, including that of most universities, was deeply sexist. It was often assumed, and with truth if with little justice or decency, that women could be hired for less money than men with comparable credentials, that they would tolerate being placed on a slower road to advancement, and that they would shoulder many of the "domestic" burdens of institutional life – ranging from making coffee in the department lounge to carrying an inordinate share of undergraduate advising. That they were often called upon to stand as role models for their students but further complicated their lives and often drew them away from the straight and narrow path of professional advancement that many of their male colleagues stuck to with little distraction or deviation.

What was true of the academic world in general was very much the case at Stony Brook. The need for quick growth and quick recognition meant, as I have argued above, a good deal of unquestioning acceptance of traditional and conservative practices. Though women were on the faculty, and in respectable numbers by national standards, they generally tended to be clustered at lower ranks; lower salaries, heavier duties given their junior status, apt to be passed over for both formal promotions and for in-house perquisites (such as teaching summer school or travel money), and – given the customary division of domestic duties for those with children— seemingly slower to establish themselves as publishing scholars with a professional presence in their discipline.

The University was not unaware of these problems, and in a formal sense it took steps to cover itself against complaints, if not to right the ship of sexist bias or individual inequities. We have seen that by the late 1960s the Administration had created an office of Affirmative Action, and many memos and directives from the office of the President and the AVP stressed the need to hire a diversified faculty (both in terms of race and gender). But words from on high, even if sincere and well meant, may have but little effect on the policies and practices that actually determine personnel and professional decisions as they are made at the departmental or unit level. And if those words from on high were but a smoke screen to cover the Administration – as many perceived them to be – the likelihood of their having an effect on the realities of the hiring and treatment of women was even more remote.

A class action suit allows a group of people with individual problems that share some common legal ground to merge their grievances into a unified or collective complaint. In May, 1976 Rose Coser (perhaps the most eminent of Stony Brook's women faculty), along with 26 co-complainants, brought a suit against the SUNY Board of Trustees, John Toll of Stony Brook, and SUNY Chancellor Ernest Boyer. I have already covered the general tenor of the common complaints; individuals from the various campus constituencies and work forces who entered the case each offering their own version of how they had been passed over and held back. The women had filed a complaint with the Office of Equal Opportunity in 1974, under Title VII of the Civil Rights Act of 1964, and now they were determined to press forward – and to win redress – through the courts. They employed a sympathetic New York law firm headed by Judith Vladeck, and they were ready to fight for their cause.

SUNY was very disputatious and litigious about such matters – perhaps more so then than in later years. A successful class action suit against a branch of state government was seen as likely to open the floodgates for many others that would follow. Hence, the State's policy of opposition, rather than of conciliation or of compromise. A suit against the State of New York is handled by the Attorney General (then Robert Abrams), and his office, with the eager compliance of the Stony Brook Administration, began to dig through the mountains of paper that academia generates in order to convince the court that the University had not been deficient in fighting discrimination and that virtually all of the individual cases were without merit. The status, credibility, and campus and professional contributions of the plaintiffs were going to be trashed so the Administration's policies would not be found wanting, across the board, and so that individual settlements could be held to a minimum (if they had to be paid at all). If the filing of a class action suit was a declaration of war, the ammunition with which it would be fought would be, to a great extent, statistics– sociological, economic, and historical statistics about comparable salaries, the evaluation of service and years in rank before and after promotion, the number of women hired and retained, the way in which candidates for positions were chosen, how jobs were advertised, etc. National as well as New York and Stony Brook comparisons were critical to the arguments of both parties. Needless to say, "Coser" and "Moore" reached different conclusions about these matters, whether they were squeezing the same data or whether they were reaching in different directions for material supportive of their side of the case.

The decision of George C. Pratt, of the U.S. District Court, was delivered in August, 1983, after a bench trial (which means hearings before the judge) of 12 days. His decision was basically in favor of the defendants, that is, for the State and against the Stony Brook women. The plaintiffs appealed the decision to the 2nd Circuit of the federal court system, and on July 3, 1984 the new decision, issued by a team of three federal judges, basically affirmed the original judgement of Judge Pratt. In a class action suit the burden of proof rests with the plaintiffs (Coser et al.), and neither Court held that they had been able to present a case that over-rode the University's responses and defenses. The essence of the matter seemed to be that the University had indeed covered itself sufficiently so that no deliberate pattern of systematic discrimination existed, or at least no pattern that could be demonstrated to the extent that it met the legal standards. As well as the University Affirmative Action Office, the Salary Equity Task Force (1973) and a special presidential directive of October, 1974 about Toll's concern for future hiring to diversify the campus's profile gave sufficient substance to Stony Brook's claim that it was opposed to discriminatory treatment and that it had moved – strongly and from an early date— to counter any unhappy or unfortunate situation that existed.

If the Courts did not quite buy all these claims at face value, the burden of proof was just too high a hurdle for the plaintiffs to clear. Though there clearly had been disparate treatment of women (and of numerous men), it was deemed necessary to produce compelling evidence of "a discriminatory motive," which was hard to do. So with the issue of "sex-stratified employment," the existence or proof of which by itself did not carry the legal weight needed to prove a discriminatory policy. The inequities in hiring numbers, in salaries, and in treatment regarding working conditions and promotions were accepted by the Courts, but not to the extent or level that constituted clear signs of a discriminatory policy. The great batteries of statistics never brought down the walls; there was "no statistically significant disadvantage of women faculty in initial placement," as well as "no class-wide pattern or practice of discrimination." The law required demonstration of "gross statistical disparity," and this proved to be beyond what the plaintiffs were able to offer. In the court of law, the State of New York, SUNY, and Stony Brook had beaten off the challenge. Moore triumphed over Coser.

A few individuals from the 30 or so plaintiffs did pursue their complaints and received some satisfaction in the form of a monetary settlement from the State. Since the original suit had sought "monetary, declarative, injunctive and any other appropriate relief," these settlements were some vindication of the original charges. But otherwise a great deal of effort and money went for naught, in a legal sense, though it counted for a great deal in consciousness raising, morale and solidarity, and a warning to the Administration of the power of the public gaze. Judith Vladeck and her associates (especially Joe Garcia, who handled much of the court work) worked at well below the going rate of a first class law firm, and the plaintiffs, their friends, and the state-wide union (UUP) contributed many dollars. Much of the money went to hire experts to build the statistical case, which by hindsight may have been a weak reed or a mis-direction. But if the original charge of "pervasive, system-wide discrimination on the basis of sex" did not get the endorsement of the Courts, it was something about which the University would concern itself. In recent years President Kenny and Provost (AVP) Robert McGrath created another task force on salary inequity, with a special eye to women's salaries, and this time they heeded the advice to award significant pay raises based on service, scholarship, and teaching. If not many things in our world seem to improve, it is likely that the old legacy of Coser vs. Moore, along with changing times and more sympathy about equality and opportunity, contributed to change for the better.

This appendix had been written to explore an episode of

Stony Brook's history that, in my eyes, shows the University at its worst. Though a class action suit is admittedly a dangerous threat to an institution, the University's rush to litigation – rather than to mediation or conciliation – seems contrary to the proper culture of the academy. Whether charges of discriminatory treatment – be they financial, professional, or racial – are merited or not, the federal court systems is a harsh setting in which to assess them, and plaintiffs generally only look in that direction when all other doors have been slammed in their faces (and locked tight).

When I looked above at the retrenchment of the Department of Education I certainly acknowledged that the state's budget crisis was real, whatever I thought of John Toll's response. And when I looked at the protracted and what was ultimately the short-sighted treatment of Ernest Dube, I did acknowledge that the external forces were overwhelming and rather frightening. But in the case of Coser vs. Moore, it was more a case of bloody mindedness within our own precincts, rather than of larger necessity or external forces and powers. Individual salaries and promotions are a local matter. The University could have acknowledged the justice of the complaints and moved, perhaps over the course of a couple of years, to rectify most of them and to level the playing field – as well as to indicate that the lessons learned would be applied in the future. I would like to say that the plaintiffs in Coser vs. Moore lost the battle but that they helped win the war. Maybe they did; maybe it's too early, or too optimistic, to say.

Some Pictures: Some General Comments

In keeping with my general approach in this history of SUNY Stony Brook, I have not looked for pictures that catch the drama of "special events," such as students in handcuffs after the drug bust of January, 1968, or a pie in John Toll's face. If construction is the main memory-beyond personal experiences and thoughts of old friends, when one looks back on the earlier days of the campus-so it is appropriately the main theme here. Beyond that, a few pictures of the appointed leaders of the University (with John Toll's looming presence being an appropriate tribute to his leadership), some miscellaneous shots of the campus, and finally a "find the author" photo that somehow became the university's poster shot for various official publications in the early years of this new century. The maps or diagrams have been taken from the Undergraduate or Graduate Bulletin for the appropriate year(s). Otherwise, with a few exceptions, the photos are from the university's collection, as found in Special Collections in the Melville Library. Once again, I offer thanks for help so cheerfully and generously given by Kristen Nyitray and Jason Torre in this regard. I acknowledge the generosity of the University for the use of this material. Needless to say, the captions are my own and reflect neither the views of those who took the pictures nor of those therein depicted.

Coe Estate-
This mansion was the main building of the idyllic campus in Oyster Bay. The realities involved in creating a new college, let alone the tension caused by the decision to become a research university upon the 1962 move to Stony Brook, made life on the Coe Estate more complicated, and more exciting, than SUNY Central had envisioned.

Dorms Under Construction-These were the G and H dorm complexes, being thrown up to accommodate the first students. When completed, each unit would hold about 1,000 residents.

Dorms in Blizzard of 1978-School was officially closed for some days after the heaviest snowfall in a quarter century. Stony Brook's snow removal facilities were better than those to be found at Florida State.

Hartzell & Toll-Karl Hartzell was the Chief Administrative Oficer at the new campus, and he is depicted here with his successor, the officially appointed and fully empowered new President, John S. Toll.

Marburger & Schubel-Jerry Schubel had been the long-term chair of Marine Sciences before serving as graduate dean and then, for a short period, as provost-the number two person in the academic chain.

Toll and Pond-Alex Pond (T. Alexander Pond) was John Toll's first lieutenant, moving up from the chair of the Physics Department to become Executive Vice President, the stand-in for Toll when he was on leave, and Acting President for the year after Toll's departure for the University of Maryland.

Library, 1962-The central building of the original campus, though the incarnation depicted here was completely swallowed by the additional building that was wrapped around it in 1971. This building housed most of the administration in the very early years. As such, it was the site of various student sit-ins, demonstrations, and arrests in the difficultdays of the late 1960s and early 1970s.

Library-Humanitites Construction, 1971-Heavy construction, in the very midst of all other activities, was the name of the game for many years.

Marburger, Neal, & Preston-John Marburger is shown here with two members of "his" team: Homer Neal, his first AVP, and Fred Preston, the VPSA who has lasted through the time of publication.

Toll & Ross-John Toll inherited Stanley Ross as Dean of the College of Arts and Sciences. They both were aggressive builders, though Ross, a Latin American historian by training, left after a few years for an administrative position at the University of Texas.

Social Science, construction-This building was built to hold all the Social Science Departments, though by 1978 it had become the exclusive preserve of the Psychology Department (though like everything else on the crowded campus, it continues to serve as a multi-purpose classroom building). This building was an early deviation from the rectangular, red brick model, though it was not well built and full of inconvenient surprises (including a semi-enclosed garden).

Aerial Photo, 1983-compared with photo 16: the campus encroaches on any and all.

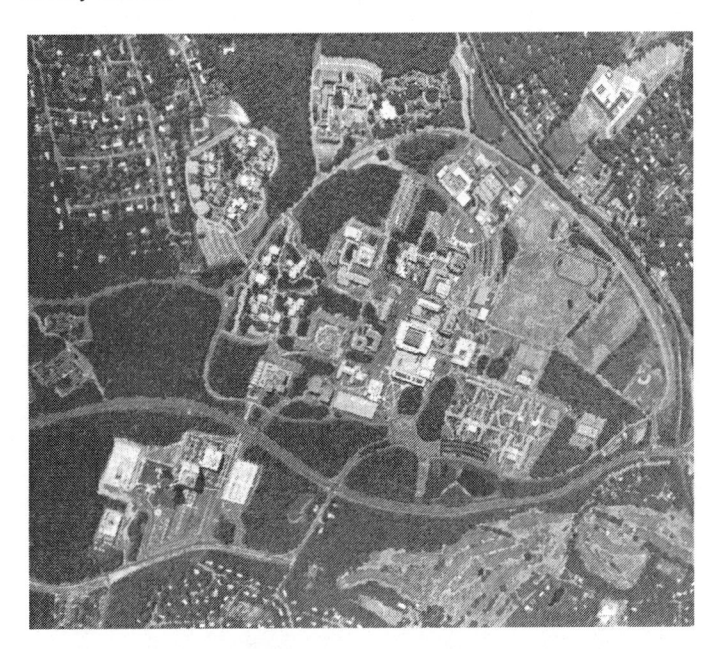

Aerial Photo, 1964-The original campus (i.e., that built for the original occupancy of 1962) was still a frontier settlement set in the wilderness of North Brookhaven. Photo 17 shows how this would change, especially as later buildings were apt to be taller buildings.

Moving in, 1963: If leaving home for college is always an exciting experience, coming to a new college and into barely-completed dorms was something out of the ordinary. We hope that those who survived the early years in G and H look back with fond memories.

Campus shot-Taken from the roof of the Ad Bldg in Autumn, 2001. The latest version of the central Mall shows to advantage on this sunny day.

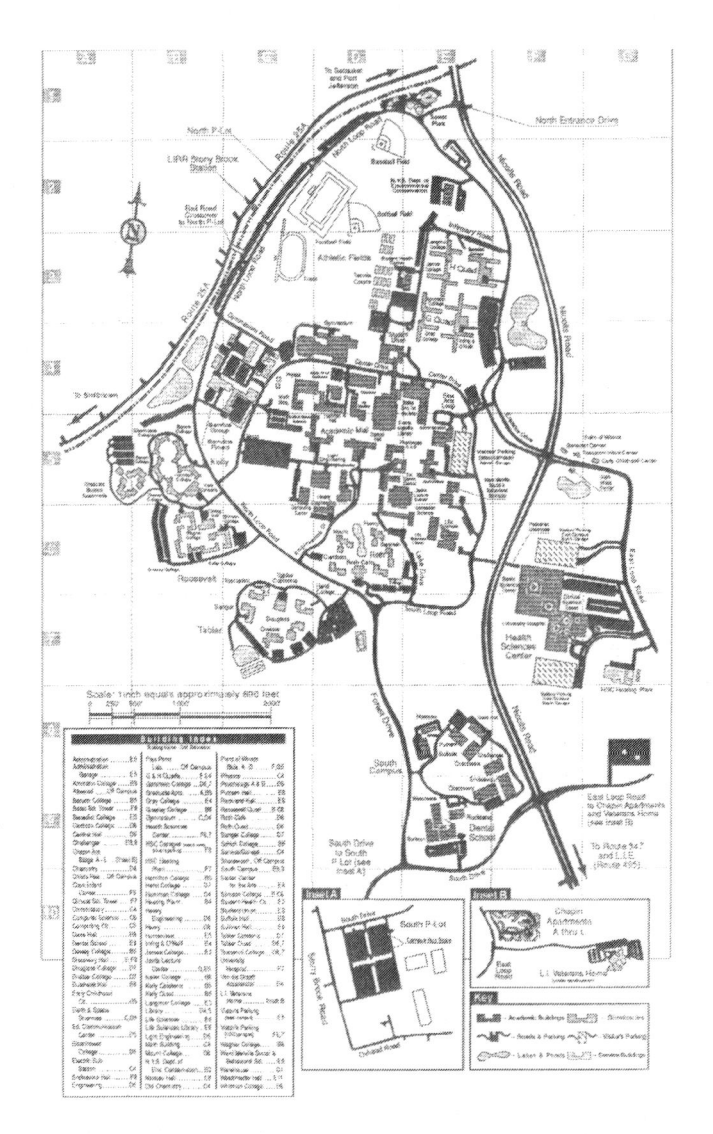

Map 1981-83-The campus is almost at full growth. It has spread to new space, compared to the map shown from 1965-66, and it has filled in much of the space that had been staked out but hardly covered over in the mid-60's. The overall size of the campus-running to its outermost edges-obscures the centrality of The Mall, the walkway that runs from the Administration Building and runs between the Library and Old Biology and leads toward ESS, with Harriman Hall and the Physics-Math tower eventually coming up on the right. The trees in front of Harriman provide the handsomest stretch of tree-lined walkway on the campus.

Map, 1965-66–The origianl campus in now in place;the next series of great waves of construction and expansion are yet to break. Stony Brook was still a small place, with trees and empty land pushing right up to the edges of buildings, and parking immediately outside buildings like Humanities still available for faculty and staff.

Map, 1990-91-More building since the early 1980's, and more going on at the present time. The maps do not show the relentless course of the rehabilitation of existing buildings, but as new structures go up old ones get converted to new uses or stripped to the walls to become a modernized version of their former usage (as is happening in 2002-03 to Humanities).

Tent City-The rallying point of the 1978 grad student protests against the deteriorating level of money, benefits, child care, and general treatment. From this encampment of the Union Army students were taken to jail, briefly, as President Marburger's customary calm temper gradually wore out and he called in the county police. The mall where the tents were set-up is now paved over, fenced off, and lavishly en-fountained. Thus any replication of this sort of protest would be too uncomfortable to be sustained.

Index

Adelphi University, 34, 45, 168
Air Force Academy, 92
Alloway, Lawrence, 128
Amherst College, 93
American Association of University Professors (AAUP), 140, 143,178-9, 231, 237
American Council of Learned Societies, 127
Ammann, Othamr, 76
Anit-Defamation League of the Bnai Brith, 233
Austil, Allen, 187-88
Awooner, Kofi, 195

Baraka, Amiri, (Leroy Jones), 112
Boyer, Ernest, 41, 241
Brookhaven National Laboratory, 102
Brooklyn Law School, 94
Brooklyn Polytechnic, 45, 111
Brown vs. the Board of Education, 37
Brown University, 93

California Institute of Technology, 5
Cardozo, Benjamin Nathan, 76
Carey, Hugh, 193
Caro, Robert, 42
Census data, 44-45
Cess, Robert, 128
CIA (Central Intelligence), 38, 118
Citadel, 92
City University of New York (CUNY), 37
    Brooklyn College, 34, 45
    City College, 33
    Hunter College, 34
Civil Rights Movement and Legislation, 8, 98. 241
    (see Race and Racism: SB, Affirmative Action)
Cleveland, Ohio, 44
Co-education, 91-2
Cold War, 14
    University Research as Part of, 31, 33, 38
College Histories, 4-5
College Age Population, 37
Columbia University (King's College), 33-34, 75, 111, 203, 216
Concordia College, 35
Cornell University, 34-6
    Cornell, Ezra, 5
Coser, Rose vs. Moore, 225, 239
Couey, Elizabeth, 186
Cuomo, Mario, 167, 227, 233
C. W. Post College, 42

Dartmouth College, 4
Democratic Party, 39
Department of Defense (DoD), 137-9
Dewey, Thomas, 39
Douglas, Ron, 238
Dillinger, Dave, 201
Dresden, Max, 130
Drug Bust (1/68), 136, 158-60, 232
Dube, Ernest, 139, 169, 224-32

Emerson Quartet, 222
Englebright, Steven, 78, 237
Evergreen College, Washington, 231
Feiffer, Jules, 201
Flanagan, Tom, 124, 145
Fordham University, 35
Fuentes, Carlos, 201
Fulbright Fellowships, 127

Gagnon, John, 125
Garcia, Joe, 243
Gelber, Sidney, 156-7, 167-8, 174, 213
Gershwin, George, 76
GI Bill, 32
Ginsburg, Alan, 201
Glass, Bentley, 11, 75, 155, 165, 176
Godfrey, Aaron W., 236
Goldstein, Stuart, 199
Gould, Samuel, 41
Graduate and Professional Education, 93
Grannis, Paul, 122
Great Depression, 37
Gregory, Dick, 201
Grumman Aircraft, 111
Gutmacher, Alan, 73

Hamilton, Alexander, 41
Harriman, Averill, 75, 154
Harrison, Beverley, 180
Hartzell, Karl, 15, 136, 159
Harvard University, 91, 93, 216
Heald Commission, 14, 91
Hendrix, Jimmy, 76
Henry, Joseph, 76
Hill, Patrick, 174
Hofstra University, 34, 42, 45
Hu, Shi Ming, 196

Institute of Advanced Study, Princeton, 102
Ivy League, 37

Javits, Jacob, 68, 75, 80
Jewish Community, 37, 228-9
Johns Hopkins University, 93
Johnson, Lyndon Baines, 8, 138, 161

Kahane, Maier, 201
Kaplan, E. Anne, 132-3
Kazin, Alfred, 103, 124
Keller, Helen, 76
Kenny, Shirely Strum
    Agenda as President, 7, 13
    Chosen President, 19-20, 173-4, 176
    Defends SB's Academic Freedom, 50
    Salary Equity, 243
Keuka Baptist College, 35
Kim, Chong Hee, Sculptor, 77
Kozol, Jonathan --------
Kunstler, William, 201

Labor Unions, 37
LaGuardia, Fiorello, 39
Larner, Jeremy, 124
Lauterbur, Paul, 78, 122
LaValle, Ken, 235
Lee, John, 14, 20, 153, 187
Lemay, Helen R., 133
Levin, Richard, 124
Levitt, Arthur, and Levittown, 42-3
    Strathmore, 52
Liberal Arts Education, 92-3, 95-6
Long Island
    Population Statistics, 51-2
    Private Universities of, 34, 45
    Suburbanization of, 42-3
Long Island University, 34, 45
Ludwig, Jack, 124

Marburger, John H.
    Agenda and Policies, 13, 19, 167-69, 179-80
    Chosen President, 18, 166-7
    Dube Affair, 229-30
    View of University History, 28
Marcus, Robert, 157
Marymount College, 35
Massachusetts Institute of Technology (MIT), 5
Mathabane, Mark, 201
McCarthy, Joseph, and McCarthyism, 38
McGrath, Robert, 243
McKinney, John, 233-4

Melville, Ward, 13, 17, 28, 45-6, 61-2, 217
      Frank and Melville Family, 66, 75, 81
Miller, Arthur, 38
Moore, Elizabeth (see Coser, Rose)
Morrill Act of 1862, 35-6
Moses, Robert, 42
Mount, William Sidney, 76

NAACP (National Association for the Advancement of Colored People), 37
National Endowment for the Humanities (NEH), 122, 127
National Institutes of Health (NIH), 122
National Science Foundation (NSF), 122, 127-8
Neal, Homer, 168, 180, 230
Neuberger, Egon, 238
Neville, Robert, 230-1
New York Public Interest Research Group (NYPIRG), 224
New York State, 5
      Governors of, 27-8, 40, 49
      Private Universities of, 33-4, 48
New York Times, 77, 123
New York University, 34
Newsday, 201, 227
Nixon, Richard, 8, 138, 158, 161, 172, 202, 223
Nobel Prize, 78, 102

Owens, Elsie,--------------
Owens, Leslie, 195

Pauling, Linus, 73
Pond, T. Alexander, 17, 165-6, 176-7
Port Jefferson and Port Jefferson Station, NY, 219
Pratt, George C., 242
Preston, Fred, 189

Race and Racism, Discrimination, and Apartheid, 37-39, 42-3, 94, 169-71, 173, 220-1, 226---
Rickover, Hyman, 201
Robeson, Paul, 38
Robinson, Jackie (Jack R.), 43
Rockefeller, Nelson, 16, 47, 78, 90, 153-4, 177
Rony, Vera, 180
Roosevelt, Eleanor, 76
      Franklin Delano, 39
Roosevelt University, 6
Ross, Stanley, 153-6

Saint Francis College, 35, 45
St John's University, Queens, 35, 42, 45
Schaeffer, Oliver, 109
Schiff, Ashley, 61, 73, 186

Schmidt, Richard, 17, 166
Schwartz, Michael, 131
Sexism in Academia, 239-40
Simpson, Louis, 103, 126
Slobodkin, Lawrence, 75
Small, Marsha, 203
Smith, Wayne, 203
Social Science Research Council (SSRC), 127
Sokal, Robert, 75, 126-7
South Africa, 225, 230
Spock, Benjamin, 201
Staller Family, 76
State University of New York (SUNY)
    Chancellor (and President), 51, 241
    Creation of SUNY, 33-39
    SUNY Central (in Albany) and the SUNY System, 14, 40-1, 50-1, 218
    Various (other) Branches of SUNY, 34, 48, 91, 114
Stony Brook, NY (and Setauket and Old Field), 215, 217-9
Stony Brook, State University of New York at (SUNY, SB)
    Academic Departments and Units: AFS, 225-6: Political Science, 226: History, 26, 99-100: Physics, 101-3, 118, 124-5: Psychology, 103-4, 118: Languages, 106-9, 125: Math, 107-8: Earth and Space, 109-10: College of Engineering, 110-11, 120: Education, 178, 225 (and see John Toll): English, 103, 118: Misc. Units and Institutes, 131-33, Humanities Institute, 132-3: Harriman College, 102-3: Staller Center, 222: Institute of Theoretical Physics, 103
  Administrative Structure, 151-7, 177, 184, 187-8
  Affirmative Action (and see Race & Racism), 169-71, 191, 240-2
  Campus Design, 58-9
  Costs and Fees, 100, 116-7, 185-7, 213
  Curriculum, 95-7, 174-5
  Degrees Granted, 99-100, 116
  Dormitories, 70-4, 85
  Employees and Economic Impact, 10, 220-22, 235
  Faculty Research & Governance, 18, 122-27, 134-5, 147, 180-1
    Unionization of, 142-4, 148-9
    Promotion & Tenure (Publish or Perish), 224
  Melville Library, 64-70, 83-4
  Naming of Buildings, 74-76, 86
  Naming of University, 24
  Oyster Bay Incarnation, 6, 12-13, 61-2. 97-9
  Research Foundation, 129-30
  Size (Physical and Demographic), 64, 101, 114-5, 117
  Stony Brook Council, 179
  Stony Brook Manhattan, 20
  Student Activities, Athletics, 24, 172-3, 198-200: Publications, 26, 191-8, 213: Speakers and Performances, 200-2, 206-8, 213-4: Dorms and Commuters, 184-5, 203: Student Government, 190-1, 203-4: Social Organizations, 205: Religious Organizations, 205-6: Graduate Students, 208-10: Alumni Association, 210-11, 214: Roth Pond Regatta, 204, 214

Student Body, 10, 18, 40-1, 171-2, 236
Strathmore Housing in Stony Brook, 43
Syracuse University, 34, 41

Tilley, Dave, 160, 189
Toll, John S.
        Agenda and Priorities, 9, 15-16, 63-4, 153-5, 162-3
        Chosen President, 12-13, 15
        Coser vs. Moore, 241, 244
        Drug Bust, 159, 232
        John Toll Society, 196
        Returns to Maryland, 17, 165
        Retrenchment of Education Department, 42. 155, 163-5, 244
        Vietnam Protest, 166
Troen, Selwyn, 238
Truman, Harry S., 33, 39-40

USSR and Sputnik, 14
Union Labor, 55-6
Unionization of Stony Brook, 134, 143-5
United University Professions (UUP), 143-4
University of California, 5, 36, 95, 203, 223
University of Chicago, 4, 5, 75, 92, 97, 216-7
University of Michigan, 5, 36-7
University of Rochester, 34
University of Wisconsin, 5, 37

Vassar College, 34
Vietnam War, 8, 56, 136-7, 154-5, 204
Vladeck, Judith, 241, 243
Voting, 223-4

Wadsworth, Elizabeth, 189
Weisinger, Herbert, 156
Wellesley College, 217
Wesleyan University, 4
Wharton, Clifton, 17, 166, 230-1
Whitman, Walt, 47
Williams College, 217
World War II, 37
Yale University, 210, 216
Yang, Chen Ning, 78, 102-3, 111, 124, 126, 128, 130, 146, 166, 172, 195-6
Yeshiva University, 35, 144
Young, Owen (and the TCNSU), 39

Zionism, 225-6
Zweig, Michael, 133, 160,193